Praise for **Hot Shots and Heavy Hits**

"Paul Doyle's book gives an amazingly accurate feel of what it was like to be a real narc as opposed to a TV narc during the early days of the drug wars. . . . I strongly recommend this book to anyone who wants a great crime drama that is real."

—Robert Stutman, Retired DEA Special Agent in Charge, Boston and New York City, and author of *Dead on Delivery*

"*Hot Shots and Heavy Hits* reflects the very real dangers and difficulties of drug law enforcement from a personal perspective. . . . This is not a standard cops and robbers tale. It is a story of dedication and friendships, of courage and compassion."

—Peter B. Bensinger, DEA Administrator, United States Department of Justice, 1976–1981

"Exciting reading . . . Many people write about the 'war on drugs,' but Doyle shows it to us in all its graphic detail. Students of American politics will also be fascinated by the author's chronicle of an agency in the making, as the DEA shifts from idealistic new enterprise to full-fledged bureaucracy."

—*Booklist*

"A riveting account of the day-to-day activities of an undercover drug agent . . . a gritty, action-packed glimpse into the criminal drug world and especially the golden age of Boston's 'combat zone,' told through a series of dicey anecdotes."

—*Library Journal*

HOT SHOTS AND HEAVY HITS

ADVISOR IN CRIMINAL JUSTICE TO NORTHEASTERN UNIVERSITY PRESS
GIL GEIS

HOT SHOTS AND HEAVY HITS

TALES OF AN UNDERCOVER DRUG AGENT

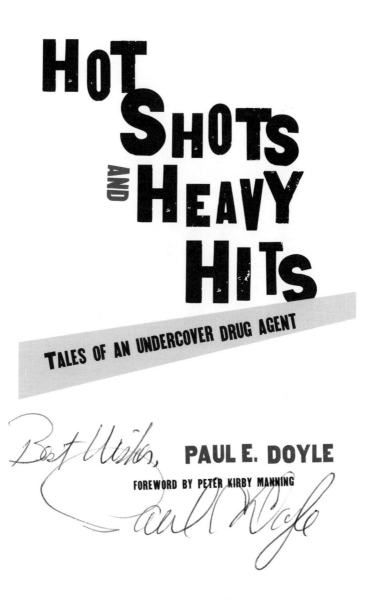

Best Wishes, **PAUL E. DOYLE**

FOREWORD BY PETER KIRBY MANNING

NORTHEASTERN UNIVERSITY PRESS · BOSTON
Published by University Press of New England
Hanover and London

NORTHEASTERN UNIVERSITY PRESS
Published by University Press of New England,
One Court Street, Lebanon, NH 03766
www.upne.com

© 2004 by Paul E. Doyle

First Northeastern University Press/UPNE paperback edition 2005

Printed in the United States of America   5   4   3   2   1

ISBNs for the paperback edition:
ISBN–13: 9781555536497
ISBN–10: 1–55553–649–2

Library of Congress Cataloging-in-Publication Data
Doyle, Paul E., 1946–
    Hot shots and heavy hits : tales of an undercover drug agent / Paul E.
Doyle ; foreword by Peter Kirby Manning.
        p.   cm.
Includes bibliographical references.
        ISBN 1–55553–603–4 (cloth : alk. paper)
    1. Narcotics, Control of—United States—Case studies. 2. Narcotic
enforcement agents—United States. 3. Doyle, Paul E., 1946–   I. Title.
HV8079.N3D68   2004
363.45'092—dc22   2003021867

FOR PAM

All the world's a stage,
And all the men and women merely players:
They have their exits and their entrances;
And one man in his time plays many parts.

—Shakespeare, **As You Like It**

CONTENTS

FOREWORD

Paul Doyle's memoir, based on his career in the Bureau of Narcotics and Dangerous Drugs (BNDD) and the Drug Enforcement Administration (DEA), is a candid and detailed description of a federal drug agent's work at the street level, primarily in Boston. The writing has a personal edge: Doyle captures better than any writer who has addressed this topic the emotions, exhaustion, fears, and epiphanies of drug work, and does so without self-aggrandizement. Although the book complements the handful of academic books on the interconnected worlds of drug use and drug law enforcement, its candid and revealing stories rival any that an academic might gather. Its rich descriptions of drug law enforcement convey its complexities and constraints, the nuances of the work, its pathos, and drama without moralizing or dramatizing.[1]

When Doyle joined, the federal agency most concerned with drugs was BNDD in the Justice Department. When DEA was created in 1973 within the Department of Justice, agents were transferred from BNDD, customs, and the FBI, and it was given a federal mandate to target major violators that became in time an international mandate. He then served in Boston and followed cases as far as New York and San Francisco.

Doyle puts powerful emotions at the center of the drama: his stories include chases, raids, arrests, fights and killing, love and affection, friendship and mutual respect, as well as failures and considerable self-doubt and questioning. After he shoots a man he goes to confession and then to Mass in a snowstorm and still cannot forgive himself. Doyle's encounters with priests, particularly his acquaintance Father DePaula, are revealing and candid, especially when he says on a walk they take together, that he can no longer "make sense of things."

In Doyle's narrative of good and evil, people and their emotions and actions seldom present themselves in a simple manner, but always seem blurred and ambiguous. He speaks of betrayal in harsh terms and describes informants as cynical, self-serving, and pragmatic, yet he sees drug law enforcement as requiring and rewarding precisely the same qualities. Doyle captures the moral complexity of the better espionage and policing novels of the past century. The players in the drama are neither fully compromised nor entirely virtuous. The scenes described are powerfully layered to include the overt and stated, as well as the covert and unstated.

The complexity of drug work, on either side of the law, is revealed in "Bad Acid" and "A Light in the Darkness." In "Bad Acid," for example, we first encounter Ted, a dealer, as a victim of an assault whom Doyle rescues, and then as an informant and middleman who unwittingly facilitates a buy-bust of an LSD-making lab crew in San Francisco. In "A Light in the Darkness" Doyle tries to help Joey, a friend of his brother's, with unforeseen consequences, including an attempted murder.

Because drug crimes (producing, manufacturing, dealing, and selling) are secret, conspiratorial, and consensual, drug laws cannot be enforced effectively by relying on the goodwill and help of citizens and random patrol. Drug agents "work forward" from information about a potential or known violator by making buys or through informants, rather than "backward" from the alleged or established facts of a committed crime. They select targets for investigation at their discretion, often as a result of the efforts of informants such as Emily, Serenity, and Ro, who appear in these stories. Drug officers—federal, state, or local—must create legally defensible circumstances in which evidence can be obtained. A variety of consequences flow from the fact that an officer, not a citizen, is the complainant in the typical case.

While the scope of a case is infinitely expandable up or down the dealing hierarchy (every buyer has a seller, each seller is in turn a buyer), the longer a case is continued the greater the chance of failure. Informants play a major role in these stories, and they are essential: the recruitment, interrogation, and protection of informants are key activities. Informants may come forward voluntarily, but usually they are previously arrested persons (for a drug-related or other offense) who agree to "work off the beef." They act in hopes of having their charges dropped or reduced, their bail waived, or conditions of probation altered. Agents such as Doyle rely on people like Emily (who does not actually make buys in these stories) to make buys of drugs, provide information on dealing and using activities, and make introductions (once introduced and trusted, an agent can try to make "hand-to-hand" buys). DEA usually does not like to use "controlled buys" by informants. They rarely testify because defense attorneys can easily discredit them in court by describing them as felons, drug addicts, and the like.

Strategies and techniques of drug enforcement, as Doyle tells us, are ingenious and often risky. In the stories, we see examples of a number of general strategies for allocating resources such as money, cars, officers, and equipment to produce the desired outcomes. Among the tactics used to implement these strategies[2] are some that create an appearance of crime under controlled circumstances: direct hand-to-hand buys from an illegal dealer to an agent with a warrant obtained later for the arrest, a buy followed by an immediate arrest ("buy and bust"), and buys and informant work aimed at establishing a pattern of conspiracy to sell drugs (evidence is gathered by assembling wire-intercept evidence, surveillance, photographs, videotapes, films, or the testimony of informants). The cases that involve establishing a conspiracy are the "big cases that cause big trouble" that Doyle mentions in his introduction. Stings, and reverse stings, in which agents set up dealing or manufacturing fronts to sell drugs in order to serve warrants and make arrests, were emerging as tactics in the late seventies, the period Doyle writes about. Street hassling, passing by and calling out to dealers, cruising (driving through drug dealing areas), and crackdowns on visible street dealing were also used, but these seldom lead to informants, arrests, or prosecutions.

Doyle discusses the importance of establishing the chain of evidence and keeping up the paperwork (disliked by agents). In fact, few cases ever go to court. While the aim of federal drug work is to target major violators, make large seizures of drugs and money, and prosecute major dealers, agents are not always successful in this. Many cases are thrown out by prosecutors' offices, withdrawn to protect informants or agents, flawed by violations of legal procedures, or simply never materialize in spite of investigative efforts, time, money, and personnel. These limits on drug crime enforcement, along with significant legal-procedural ones concerning control of property, informants' files, drugs, and money, are frustrating to agents. These constraints lead agents to develop elaborate means of penetrating and monitoring drug markets, such as getting people to inform on each other for money, favors, or leniency in prosecution.

All jobs contain a set of assumptions about what constitutes "good work." What is good, satisfying work to a drug cop? Activity and flair are perhaps apposite. In both patrol and drug enforcement, in varying degrees (depending on the level and quality of supervision), there are pressures to "produce" or show activity in terms of often tacit criteria. In a drug unit, activity with consequence is difficult to track. Although paperwork is required, it is often submitted after the fact and conceals as much as it reveals. There is no official record of clues or written evidence that would leave a paper trace—possible cases, tips, names, and alleged events that officers *did not* investigate. Agents make decisions about who and what to investigate largely on their own. Most cases are little cases. They are typically not assigned to drug officers but rather created, built by them with their partners or on their own and crafted from available, often scanty, information. Flair is important because so much goes wrong when one is dealing with marginal, often unreliable and frightened people in drug markets. Agents' activities are not reported if they do not lead to an arrest, buy, or long-term surveillance, and in general supervisors are ignorant of the number of cases (potential or otherwise), informants, and clues being worked by investigators.

There is a difference, in the rhetoric of drug enforcement, between an arrest, a good case, and the use of flair in carrying out a performance. Arrests *per se* are ambiguous because an arrest can result from a failed buy bust, a raid without a seizure, betrayal by a snitch, or a collapsed conspiracy case. An arrest in a marijuana case is of little value. Good cases can result without a seizure or arrest if good information or informants are obtained. Many cases lead to surprising outcomes—big seizures on a hot tip, or a raid that yields a lot of money, such as the one in the first chapter. Time, effort, patience, resources, and intelligence do not produce consistent outcomes. Hence, the importance of flair: how one handles oneself when things go badly, as demonstrated by the skill Doyle showed in the failed biker raid and throughout the San Francisco LSD investigation ("Bad Acid"). An agent who frames a case creatively and brings it to a conclusion also shows flair. Perhaps it is best to say that success in drug work is a highly contextual matter, relative to one's goals.

Doyle notes frequent tensions between agents and their supervisors. Consider as you read, the questioning of Doyle and his partner after the shooting by the internal inspection people from Washington, and when supervisors at first refuse to front money and raise questions about the course of the San Francisco investigation. Accustomed to an immense amount of freedom, an agent may resent a supervisor for questioning him or her about a legal shooting or a planned operation, case, or raid. While choice is essential to playing the game, however, it is also a source of concern to the supervisors who feel responsible. Supervision is usually nominal and it is agreed that an agent has to be a "self-starter," a "go-getter," and imaginative. In addition, as Doyle shows, organizational control over the drug officer's behavior and demeanor is always problematic because of variations in information (as to source, quality, and periodicity), low visibility of most of the decisions made, and the symbolism of a drug agent's role. The drug agent does not answer roll calls; has a flexible work schedule that is rarely questioned; can associate with known criminals, addicts, and dangerous felons at any time and place; can drink on duty (and have these expenses covered); and is typically out of radio contact with central dispatch or with supervisors outside the immediate street environment. The style of an undercover officer reflects that of the street. Names are chosen to mask real identities and responsibilities; Doyle was "Sully." An agent may have several street names over the course of a career.[3] These are used interchangeably with real names in and out of the department.

Street names deny the relevance of the ties between agent and organization outside of the agent's false or dissimulated identity. Ironically, the closer he or she is to the street world or the world of the dealer, the more effective the agent becomes. This effectiveness puts the officer at risk for becoming corrupt and adopting the lifestyle and morality of the targets or villains. Officers are tempted. Organizational pressures exist to show results, and officers may bend the rules to their personal or organizational advantage. Officers are fronted money for miscellaneous personal expenses and often keep hundreds of dollars in their pockets. They are in control of evidence of great value, namely drugs and money, which are easily concealed, resold in the case of drugs, or converted to personal use. While drug officers are distrustful of others, as well as of themselves, they are trusted widely in court by prosecuting attorneys and in local departments, by uniformed officers. When Doyle shoots out a street light in Boston, for example, he is protected by an old-fashioned Boston sergeant. The extent of drug agents' latitude and their patterns of corruption, if they exist, vary from agency to agency. Doyle and his partners are strikingly careful and concerned about their supervisors' approval, and apparently avoid the pitfalls of their chosen line of work.

Hot Shots and Heavy Hits provides a valuable picture of a configuration, a social form that shapes the mutually nuanced, interactionally attuned performance of people in the enforcement and the drug use/trade worlds. The two social worlds are tied together in many ways. While the inhabitants of each one are on different sides of the law, the exchanges, roles, and activities of users-dealers-producers and agents are interchangeable. They mirror each other. People in both worlds value violence, toughness, friendships (the loyalty of those to whom they feel close), and street-level cunning. The configuration is based on deception—actors in this drama must use duplicity to avoid detection, retaliation, and injury. Doyle captures this in describing his relationships to informants and criminals and the expedient ways in which solutions are brought to complex issues. As he shows, the line between good and evil is constantly blurred, in spite of the ostensibly adversarial roles played by cops and drug dealers. In many ways, the police are more like their counterparts than like other citizens; they share the social worlds shaped by the configuration.

The scenes in this book speak eloquently of violence and death. The work of a drug agent is episodic and unpredictable, and lengthy cases can be touched off by an unexpected phone call from an informant. It is violent work, and this violence punctuates a job that can be boring and frustrating and a mixture of failed arrangements, unmet promises, skittish informants, and mistakes. The confused and collapsed drama of Mr. Li and Tootie in "Chinatown" reveals these contingencies in a touching fashion. The uncertainty of the work takes its toll, as Doyle shows in his recollections about Warren Tabor's suicide and in his comments about his own existential concerns when he states that men who died in action "died with honor, whatever that means." Doyle's stories reveal the doubt around the edges of a drug agent's life and suggest a remarkable degree of introspection. About death, he writes fleetingly, but in many ways this book is about the shadow of death we all face.

Peter Kirby Manning
E. V. H. and E. M. Brooks Professor
College of Criminal Justice
Northeastern University
Boston, October 2003

Notes

1. While drug policing is sometimes called "narcotics policing," it is not. It focuses on eradicating the importing, production, or dealing of any illegal drug. Only opiate-based drugs are in fact narcotics. See the classic source, now in its tenth edition, *Gilman and Goodman's The Pharmacological Basis of Therapeutics*, ed. Joel G. Hardman and Lee E. Limbird, consulting ed., Alfred Goodman Gilman (New York: McGraw-Hill, 2001).

2. I draw here from my book, *The Narcs' Game: Organizational and Informational Limits on Drug Law Enforcement*, 2d ed. (Cambridge, Mass.: MIT, 1980); reprint (Prospect Hills, Ill.: Waveland Press, 2004).

3. During our observations of drug law enforcement, my colleagues and I chose fanciful street names—"Pepsi Wilcox," "Shorty," and "Pete Best."

HOT SHOTS AND HEAVY HITS

INTRODUCTION

This story began in 1971, when I returned stateside after thirteen months on the DMZ (demilitarized zone) in Korea. My wife, Pam, and I were just getting to know one another again, after being separated military style for most of our young marriage. We wanted to have a family, but we each wanted to commit to a cause that would make a difference. She already made an important contribution as a physical therapist. Pam taught people ways to help themselves overcome their disabilities.

I thought my future was probably in the military. I would extend my military commitment, be promoted to captain, head to Fort Bragg, North Carolina, for additional Special Forces training, then ship out for a thirteen-month tour in Vietnam. I was leaning in this direction because I loved the elite unit of the Green Berets that I was in and the guys I was with. Pam thought that law school was a better way to help people.

Then I heard that the U.S. Department of Justice was seeking experienced soldiers with top secret clearance for the position of drug agent. The thought intrigued me. The idea that I could help people and be a positive influence in the world by working with the Justice Department was attractive.

The strength, both mental and physical, that I developed through my highly disciplined military training in leadership, weapons, survival, hand-to-hand combat, intelligence, and ethics, along with the experience of serving with the Second Infantry Division and the Tenth Special Forces Detachment of Green Berets, were perfect prerequisites for my entrée into the life of a drug agent. I decided to try for the job.

As soon as I stepped into the windowless room in the bowels of the JFK Federal Building in Boston, I sensed that I was in for an experience. Six silent men, all very different in appearance, sat staring at me from around a conference table, weighing my every move. After a painfully long moment, a man sitting ramrod straight, an unmistakable reflection of his military background, smiled and addressed me from his seat in the center of the group.

"Good morning! Please be seated. I am Ed Cass, the regional director. These men are all agents, and we are going to ask you some questions."

"Yes, sir," I responded, taking a seat at the table opposite the men. The agents each nodded their heads as I scanned the room, my eyes meeting theirs. Each stare was fixed steadily on me.

"Why do you want the job, son?" the oldest-looking member of the panel asked. It was Matt Seifer, who, I later discovered, had worked with Harry Anslinger, the first federal commissioner of Narcotics. Seifer, a living legend, had interrogated some of the most notorious gangsters in history. His simple question gave me pause.

"I want to make a difference," I answered. Before I could catch my breath, I turned to face a hypothetical question from Special Agent Chris Regan on the other side of the table.

"Let's say you had a search warrant for a dope dealer's apartment; that means by law that you could only search the dealer's apartment. Now, it's hard to win with our hands tied by the law. You get to the dealer's apartment, execute the search warrant, and find nothing. The guy is laughing at you and threatening to sue for damages. As you leave the apartment, you notice a suitcase in the hallway, in plain view, with what appears to be white powder leaking out of the seam. What do you do?" It seemed like a trick question.

"The warrant specified the dealer's apartment only, right?" I asked, just to be sure.

"Only for the apartment and any drugs found inside," was the response, delivered with a wry smile.

"I would confiscate the suitcase, and I would tell the dealer I would be back another day," I answered. A wide smile swept across Regan's face. The other agents nodded their heads, and then they all laughed.

"The last guy we interviewed told us that he would nudge the suitcase in with his foot and pin it on the drug dealer. The guy before him said that he would leave it where it was and go get a warrant for the hallway!" a tough-looking guy said in a deep voice out of one side of his mouth, a cigar clamped in the other. The men all laughed at his remarks. The guy was Joe

Catale, who joined the feds after a brilliant career with the NYPD, fresh from working on the famed "French Connection" case. With a sparkle in his eye, he added in a distinctive New York accent, "I wonder which one of you is right!"

"Looks like you've had a little experience with firearms," an ominous-looking guy with an unreadable face commented somberly as he looked over my résumé. "Don't think you'll have a problem with the physical part. You may get a little bored at times," he added facetiously, while looking directly in my eyes. I caught the humor. He was Ed Drinan, a former U.S. Marine captain. He then asked one more question. "Why don't you join the FBI?"

"I want to work drugs. The FBI does after-the-fact investigations. After a bank is robbed, they interview witnesses; after a fraud is perpetrated, they interview victims and study the numbers. They are also preoccupied with Communists. None of that interests me. I think that drugs are a problem, and I want to be part of the solution," I explained.

The group seemed to like my answer. I looked around to see if there were any more questions and my eyes landed on Paul Maloney, a recently discharged Vietnam veteran. He winked.

"Well, I think that's about all we need to know. We'll be in touch." Ed Cass ended the interview, abruptly enough, with a poker face. Everyone around the table stood up and shook my hand. These men were serious, no-nonsense types. I knew that I wanted to be one of them.

In 1971 the Bureau of Narcotics and Dangerous Drugs, the elite enforcement arm of the U.S. Department of Justice charged with enforcing the narcotic laws worldwide, consisted of approximately fifteen hundred agents and had offices throughout the United States and in a number of foreign countries. The BNDD had the most extensive arrest powers of any agency in the free world. Today its successor agency, the Drug Enforcement Administration, has approximately four thousand agents, who struggle to hold off the relentless onslaught of drugs into our country.

The greed, violence, danger, and secrecy of the illegal drug business permeate an agent's life. An agent must pretend to be someone he (or she) is not. He assumes an untraceable criminal identity; his driver's license, passport, and social security cards are issued under false names. A successful undercover agent plays the part so well that he actually becomes the character he is portraying. He learns to "talk the talk" and "walk the walk." In time, an agent develops the thought process that enables him (or her) to infiltrate the drug world. The mission is to gather information and develop cases that lead to the highest levels of criminal organizations. He must purchase drugs and eventually arrest the major violators and seize large quantities of drugs.

The risks are great: informants have been killed for confiding information to agents, and agents have been murdered when their identities were compromised. On July 22, 1971, Special Agent Bobby Canales was ambushed by Mexican heroin dealers while working undercover in Los Angeles, California. Special Agent Canales survived, but he will never recover the use of his legs. On October 12, 1972, Special Agent Frank Tummillo was shot and killed in a hotel room in New York City by drug traffickers. The following spring, on April 1, 1973, Special Agent Richard Heath Jr. of the Bureau of Narcotics and Dangerous Drugs died from a gunshot wound while working undercover in Aruba, Netherlands Antilles. Four months later, on August 9, 1973, Special Agent Emir Benitez of the Drug Enforcement Administration was shot and killed during an undercover investigation in Fort Lauderdale, Florida. Agents must learn to overcome the fear of death.

This book is about one special agent. It is an account of my experiences while working undercover for the Drug Enforcement Administration. It is a worm's-eye view of a world only an undercover agent sees. My frustrations as a special agent are clearly explained as I deal with the seemingly senseless government bureaucracy and our sometimes noncompliant international partners, who complicate enforcement of the law.

I believe that the story of a DEA agent needs to be told. The common myth that experimental use of illegal drugs is a harmless rite of passage should not go unchallenged. Illegal drug use is mistakenly viewed by many as a victimless crime. The use of illegal drugs by celebrities is often glamorized by the media, leaving a false impression. My firsthand observations provide a different point of view. The tragedy is that people become disabled and even die as a result of using illegal drugs. People should consider both viewpoints.

I believe that I have found a way to tell my story without betraying the trust that every agent swears to uphold. In the following pages are some of my experiences as a special agent that took place during the 1970s. Many of the people I write about have retired or died. The names of the criminals have been changed to protect them and their families. Most have already paid their debt to society, but some are still in prison. My purpose is to share the work of an undercover agent with you so that you may understand the heart and soul of what we do.

NARCOTIC AGENT 1

The first three days that I spent at the John F. Kennedy Federal Office Building in downtown Boston were three of the longest days in my recent memory. I was fresh out of the agents academy of the Bureau of Narcotics and Dangerous Drugs. My group supervisor, Todd Downs, called me into his office a couple of minutes after eight o'clock on Monday morning, my first day.

I checked the knot on my tie to make sure that it was perfectly straight, then followed my fingers down to make certain that my shirt buttons lined up perfectly with my belt buckle, military style, as I hurried toward Downs's office. My white shirt was starched, my shoes were shined, and my pistol was holstered snugly on my hip. With eager anticipation, I stood in the doorway of the boss's office cubicle, ready for action.

"We got a big day ahead of us," Downs said from behind his desk. I looked at him earnestly.

Action scenes came to mind. I pictured myself crashing through a door, as I had been practicing at agent school, arresting a suspect at gunpoint, and putting the cuffs on him. That tingly feeling started in my stomach.

"There's a lot to do," Downs continued in a confidential tone, almost solemnly, with a pained expression on his face. Imagining the serious, difficult assignment he was about to give me, I nodded my head to assure him that I was ready to spring into action. Then, Downs squinted his eyes, as he fixed his stare at me and stood up. He was a big man physically and he seemed to fill the room with his bulk, his head almost touching the ceiling of his office.

"Let's go!" Downs ordered. He walked around the desk and ducked his head to get through the door as he marched out of the cubicle. I stepped aside to make way for him. When he passed by, I fell in behind him like a soldier. Downs stopped abruptly, maybe six feet from his office door. I would have walked into him if I had not reacted quickly and stopped. Downs turned, and almost like an afterthought, he motioned toward the secretary with his big hairy hand, which was almost in my face. He began to speak.

"We gotta purge the files," Downs announced. I stood obediently, listening politely to Downs's instructions to the secretary. I tried to appear as if I was interested, while he went on much longer than necessary about secretarial matters. Feeling self-conscious, I looked down at my shoes, then glanced at the secretary and smiled. The secretary was struggling to be patient with Downs's endless instructions while her eyes moved from Downs's to mine. Her eyes landed on me just as I was smiling at her feigned look of interest and she smiled slightly, rolling her eyes to convey her frustration. I could sense the eyes of the other agents in the group on my back, watching me standing helplessly next to Downs. Finally, the tone of Downs's voice signaled that he was coming to the end of his talk, so I straightened up and looked at him. He lifted his eyes from the manila file folder at which he had been staring during his entire talk, and he turned to me and said with an inappropriate smile:

"Mary's on vacation for the week, but I know that you and Jen can get the job done. Go get 'em."

My heart sank at the realization that he had been talking to me all along and that I was being relegated to a clerical assignment. I could feel my face drop as I looked at Downs in disbelief. I stood still momentarily in the wake of his departure, stunned at the put-down, and half listening to the sound of his shoes klunking down the hallway. I looked up at Jen and she returned a sympathetic look.

Feeling totally foolish with a Smith and Wesson strapped to my side as I combed through the file cabinets looking for outdated files, I decided to remove my pistol and lock it in my desk. It was not until the end of the day that Downs, after walking by Jen and me all day long, stopped and gave me an incredulous stare. Tucking his chin in, so that the skin bulged out over his shirt collar, he looked at me with a smirk and asked, "Where is your gun?"

Tired, humiliated, and fed up from looking at files, I almost lost it. I was ready to tell him to stick the gun and the job up his nose, but my military training kicked in and I did not.

"It's locked in my desk, sir," I answered. In my mind, I substituted the word "asshole," which I never used, for "sir."

"In your desk?" Downs repeated my answer in question form. I mentally underlined the word "asshole."

"Yes, sir, in my desk," I repeated.

"Agent's Manual, section so and so, page so and so," Downs shot back argumentatively. I then capitalized the word, with a big A. He continued, reciting from the manual, "an agent shall have his weapon in his possession at all times."

I did not reply.

"Do you understand?" Downs asked loudly, so as to capture the attention of every agent and secretary within earshot.

"Yes, sir," I managed. I went to my desk reluctantly and donned my weapon. Downs walked into his office shaking his head at what he thought was my disregard for the regulations. I boiled at his lack of discretion and rigid interpretation of the rules. Downs had the Agent's Manual memorized, but he had no common sense. My second and third days, also spent rummaging through the files, were no better.

When Pam asked about the job at dinner, I wriggled around in my seat, not knowing how to answer. Finally, I decided to tell her that I did not think the job was for me, and that I was considering leaving. There was no sense in being dishonest with myself or my wife. Pam was thrilled, especially when I agreed with her idea that I should attend law school. My mind was made up, and the following day I stood next to Jen, fingering through the files, waiting for the appropriate time to broach the subject with Downs.

Suddenly, the atmosphere changed. There was laughter in the hallway, and I could hear Chris Regan's voice. He was returning from New York City, where he had been testifying in a federal court.

"So, there I am in Foley Square," Chris begins, setting the stage for his tale. I could hear laughter.

"Fifteen years on count one! Fifteen years on count two, on and after count one! And, fifteen years on count three, to be served after count two," Chris raised his voice to mimic the voice of the sentencing judge. The laughter increased.

"Sweet Steve says to the judge, 'I don't understand!' The judge says, 'What part of the forty-five years do you not understand?' Sweet Steve looks at the judge like he is going to cry. 'Don't worry, Mr. Jones, you'll have plenty of time to figure it out,'" Chris added gravely, in the tone of the judge.

The agents walking with Chris laughed all the harder at his description of the events surrounding his testimony in New York City. I forgot my plight momentarily as I listened to Chris and his merry men blow into the office like a gust of fresh air. His eyes met mine as soon as he turned the corner into the office, and a wide smile spread across his face.

"Look at this!" Chris called out happily. The agents with him all looked at me.

"Ready to kick some ass?" Chris added. I had to smile, myself, at the invitation. Chris reached out and took my hand.

"Congratulations!" Chris spoke excitedly. I smiled back from my awkward position behind the secretary's desk. Chris gave me a puzzled look, then asked, "What are you doing?"

I felt foolish and did not know what to say. Sensing my predicament, Jen answered for me.

"Todd assigned Paul to work with me in place of Mary." She shot an apologetic look of exasperation at Chris. He bit his bottom lip and shook his head, then looked directly at me and spoke.

"Come on, kid, we got work to do."

The invitation sparked a sense of rebellion deep down inside of me. I hesitated, remembering my clerical assignment. Chris laughed knowingly and beckoned me with a wave of his hand.

"Come on, let's go. Duty calls. I need my partner with me on the street," Chris added convincingly, and I willingly walked away from my secretarial duties.

"Get into some street clothes and we're outta here," Chris ordered, and I joined him, gladly. Chris was full of enthusiasm, and his passion for working drug cases on the street was infectious. He shot a devilish look at the secretary as we were leaving the office area and said with a smile, "Jennifer, dear, when Todd comes in, tell him that Paulie and I are on the street. He may have a difficult time understanding that concept. We're gonna purge the city of drugs."

Chris laughed good-naturedly and everyone in the group laughed with him. The next thing I knew, I was out on the street and my world was about to change forever.

My partnership with Chris was a new beginning. I stole a glance at Chris as the door went up and we emerged from the underground garage and pulled onto the street. With his gangster lean behind the wheel of the late model Caddy and his Prince Valiant hairstyle blowing in the breeze, Chris looked like a cocky young criminal. He was wise guy personified.

"I gotta see a stool pigeon," Chris said, matter-of-factly. I nodded.

"What did you think of the academy?" he asked casually.

"It was good. They taught us well," I answered stiffly. I could feel Chris shooting a sly glance at me. I turned and met his eye. He smiled from ear to ear.

"It's a bunch a shit, ain't it?" Chris laughed. I laughed, too.

"They can try all they want, but they can't teach you shit!"

"Well, they gave us the law and the basics," I reasoned. Chris laughed again playfully.

"Our classroom's the street," he countered. Chris continued to drive until we got to the vicinity of Boston University, where he pulled over and parked in a space at the curb. Moments later, a tall, slender young lady wearing snakeskin cowboy boots, skintight brown corduroys, and an expensive-looking brown leather jacket came into sight. From under a Boston Red Sox cap, which she wore jauntily tipped slightly to one side, her long black hair flowed down her shoulders. As she came closer, I realized that she was smiling at us.

"Let her in," Chris said, catching me by surprise. I hesitated. "Let her in front between us," he added. I opened the door and got out so that she could get in.

"Hi," she said, as she brushed by me and slipped into the front seat next to Chris. Her freshly showered scent and the smell of leather and crisp, cold air filled the car as I got back in the car next to her.

Chris introduced us perfunctorily: "Serenity, this is my partner, Paulie. Paulie, this is Serenity." She smiled politely, and then they began talking together like old friends. I listened to the conversation as I sat quietly looking out the window at the people passing. It was a busy area, with hordes of students traveling back and forth from their apartments to classes. Chris and Serenity talked for almost an hour. Judging by the friendly tone of the conversation and the laughter, I would have thought that it was a date, if I didn't know better. When they were finished, Serenity gave Chris a peck on the cheek. She turned to me with a sexy smile and said, "Nice to meet you, Paulie."

"Me, too," I answered as I opened the door and stood on the sidewalk to let her out. My eyes followed momentarily, while she walked away with a swing and a bounce in her step, then I slid back into the front seat.

"Informant?" I asked, skeptically.

"The best!" Chris said. Ignoring my blank look, he continued, "She just gave us the source for all of the weed in Boston." With no further explanation, Chris smiled and winked. "Since we are parked in front of the world-famous Dugout bar, it would be sacrilegious not to make a visit. Don't you think?" I glanced out the window at the Dugout sign then back at Chris.

"I'm with you."

We got out of the car and walked toward the Dugout. Chris went in first, and I followed behind. He walked in with flair, like a gunfighter busting through the saloon's swinging doors. The Dugout was an old-fashioned bar, an anachronism. The smell of cigarette smoke and stale beer pervaded the atmosphere. The classic, old labels of the basic beers, Schlitz, Miller, and Bud, appeared on the tap handles that stuck up from the stainless-steel base in the middle of the bar. The fanciest drinks in the Dugout were a seven and seven and a gin and tonic.

The Dugout was an unusual college bar. In the daytime, old-timers, men in their seventies, took their medicine next to a steady stream of blue-collar guys—maintenance and janitorial workers from Boston University—along with an occasional college professor, a coach, off-duty cops, firemen, and people who lived in the neighborhood. At night, the students replaced the older working crowd. College guys with their hats on backwards and coeds in sweatshirts and jeans cheered for the Sox, the Bruins, or the Pats, if the BU Terriers weren't playing.

The thing that made the Dugout so special was the legendary owner, Jimmy O'Keefe, a true friend of governors, gangsters, and the common man for over a half century. Jimmy O'Keefe, wispy gray hair, wrinkled pale skin, sat sideways on a stool in the middle of the bar with his beloved old mutt, Blondie, at his feet. He grinned when he saw us. Chris shook his hand first, then introduced me as his new partner. A twinkle appeared in Jimmy's watery, red-lined eyes when he saw me.

"How ya doin' kid?" Jimmy asked, warmly. Chris was surprised that he knew me.

"You've already met?" he asked.

"Chrissake, I knew him as a baby," Jimmy said. He didn't volunteer that my father ran numbers for him in the old days. Those things were better left unsaid in mixed company. Jimmy and I both knew that. I stooped down to pat his dog and when I stood up, I noticed that Jimmy was still staring admiringly at me.

"You was quite a fighta kid. Your dad, too. Them were the days," old Jimmy remarked, nostalgically. I smiled self-consciously.

Chris and I sat at the bar on either side of Jimmy. I had a hamburger and a glass of orange juice, and Chris had a bag of chips and a bottle of Schlitz. While we were eating, a couple of off-duty firefighters walked in. They both had waist-length letterman's jackets on over their fireman's jeans and blue denim shirts.

"Hey, Jimmy, we got some team this year!" one of them said to Jimmy O'Keefe enthusiastically. Jimmy nodded.

"Tommy, this is Paul," Jimmy said.

"Nice ta know ya," Tommy replied. It turned out that Tommy O'Leary—they called him Bomber—lived in my new neighborhood. He recognized Chris because he had stopped in the firehouse on a number of occasions and borrowed battering rams and halligan tools to knock doors down. I had been filing records that morning, now I was relaxing with some great guys in a neighborhood bar. How lucky was I?

As we walked out of the Dugout, Chris informed me that we had a raid set up for later that afternoon, based on Serenity's information. He had called the information into the Boston Police Drug Control Unit from the pay phone in the bar while I was finishing my sandwich, and detectives from the unit were going to appear before a judge to secure a search warrant. They also had a search warrant for heroin at another location, and they wanted us to kick the door in with them later on. It was shaping up to be quite a night. My head was spinning at how Chris put all this together while we were having lunch.

We met the detectives from the drug control unit later that afternoon and went to an apartment building in Brighton to execute the search warrant. It was my first drug raid, so I got to knock the door down and go in first. We did what they call a no-knock search warrant, because if you knock and announce yourself as police, they run or destroy the evidence. I hit the lock with the sledgehammer and it popped right out. The door opened and everybody ran in. The apartment was empty. An inauspicious beginning for my career, I thought. While everyone was searching the inner rooms, I went to a chest in an anteroom and opened a drawer. The drawer was filled with stacks of money. I couldn't believe it. My first try and I find all this money. I had never seen so much money in my life. I called out to the rest of the search party, but no one answered. They were all busy searching the rest of the apartment. I closed the drawer and started to leave the room, when I decided to open the second drawer. It was filled with money, too. Every drawer had money packed in plastic, piled to the top.

I walked into the other room, where Chris and the detectives had a couple of kilos of marijuana sitting on a desk, but they did not look happy. When I told them I found some evidence, they all looked at me with doubt. I led them to the chest and opened the drawers. Everyone yelled. The dealers obviously sold the entire load and all that remained was the money, the profit. The kilos, the receipts, and the money made a great case. Everyone was happy on the way to police headquarters. We deposited the "grass," receipts, and money in the evidence locker in the drug control unit and went to the Victoria Diner on Mass Ave. for dinner. It was the first time that I had ever met any of these guys, and it was a very lively dinner because of the success of the raid. They toasted me with their glasses of water for knocking the door down and finding the cash. Someone joked that if the owner did not claim it in twenty-four hours, it would be mine to keep.

After dinner, we returned to our cars and headed to Seaver Street in the Roxbury section of Boston. When we arrived at the apartment building, I got out of the car with the sledgehammer again and rushed to the front of the squad. The detective sergeant opened the outer door with a passkey, a master key that opens most similar locks, and we all filed quickly inside.

There were two detectives running up the stairs in front of me. When they reached the top, they each stepped to opposite sides of a door and pointed at it with the barrels of their guns. They nodded and I planted my feet squarely and swung the sledge. The hammer went right through the door panel, but the New York lock remained intact. I could hear scurrying around inside, while I struggled to pull the head of the sledge back through the jagged hole in the door, and detectives took turns frantically trying to kick the door in. We stopped at the sound of two loud gunshots and a scream. Everything was quiet for a moment and the shuffling noises resumed. I finally managed to pull the hammer out from the broken door and slammed it solidly against the lock, but it didn't budge. With all the excitement, I swung again and missed the lock, but a large part of the door panel fell out. We could see the shirtless defendant running around in his underpants and knee-high black socks. A detective slid a halligan tool under the door and whacked the bottom of the lock while I hit the top of the door, which suddenly swung open. Big Billy Buckles, the most troublesome, arrogant pimp in Boston, wet himself as we rushed through the door with guns drawn. He told us that earlier, while we were banging on the front door, he had headed for the back. When he leaned over his veranda to see how far down it was to the street, one of our detectives fired a couple of warning shots in Billy's direction. That is when he lost his poise and wet his pants.

One of the detectives handcuffed Billy and sat him down in a straight-backed chair in the middle of the living room, and he watched us rummage through his belongings to find the heroin. He was not at all helpful. One detective turned to Billy and asked playfully if he was hot or cold in his search. Another detective came strutting out of the back room with one of Billy's hats on. It was a large-brimmed, plush purple fedora.

"Hey, Billy, can I borrow this to wear to church on Sunday?" The cop laughed, then disappeared back into the other room. Several minutes later the same cop reappeared. This time he strutted in, singing "When Irish Eyes Are Smilin'," with a Kelly green top hat cocked to the side of his head.

"Billy, I didn't know you were Irish," the cop joked. I couldn't help but laugh. Buckles, himself, even broke down at the cop's antics.

Finally, Detective Tabor called out from the back room, "Bingo! You won, Billy. An all-expense-paid trip for one." He came out of the back room with a large clear plastic bag of white powder.

"This amount should entitle you to about fifteen years," Detective Tabor teased.

At the end of the evening, after Billy Buckles was locked up in his jail cell, the heroin was locked up in the evidence locker, and we said good night to the drug detectives, Chris turned to me on the car ride home. "This calls for a nightcap."

14

I was a little tired, but still pumped from the excitement of the evening's events. It was not a suggestion. I smiled, not knowing what else to say. We cut across town, taking East Berkeley Street to Commonwealth Avenue, and turned left toward BU.

"Let's see what's goin' on tonight at Jimmy O'Keefe's," he said enthusiastically.

Before I knew it, we were parked and walking into Jimmy O'Keefe's. As soon as we cleared through the crowd and approached the bar, I spotted an old teammate, Roger Rozinski, our fullback, behind the bar. He moved quickly to keep up with the crowd, turning back and forth from the cash register to the bar, opening beer bottles, and handing them out to waiting hands. When Roger looked up and saw me, we both smiled. He obviously knew Chris, also.

"Hey, Chris," Roger said, as he opened a Schlitz and handed it to Chris without taking an order.

"Always a pleasure," Chris responded, raising his beer in a toast to Roger.

"Paulie, Hut! Hut! Hut! Ready! Ready!" Roger called loudly, perfectly imitating our old football coach's voice. I laughed.

"We know all the same people. We were destined to be partners!" Chris laughed. Roger hurried back to us whenever he had a momentary lull at the bar, and we talked about our old football days. I sipped orange juice while Chris had another couple of beers.

There was a young guy next to us in a hooded sweatshirt who seemed to be holding court with group of guys and girls, probably BU students. The guy kept watching Chris and me. When Chris passed the group on the way to the men's room, I noticed that he exchanged words with the guy. The guy smiled. It appeared that they knew each other. When Chris returned from his pit stop, the guy reached out over the heads of his group and handed him something.

"Paulie, that kid handed me the telephone number of his friend, who he claims is the source of all cocaine for BU." Chris wrinkled his forehead and gave me a wide tight-lipped grin.

"Let's go," Chris said as he finished his Schlitz and put the bottle on the bar. He handed Roger a five-dollar tip and we headed out of the bar. The guy in the hooded sweatshirt followed us with his eyes and waved when he caught Chris's eye.

"Tell him Bucky sent you," the guy called out to Chris.

"You bet," Chris answered.

When we got outside, Chris told me that he overheard the college kids talking about pot and acid. He said that he saw the guy staring at him, so he scoffed at them and mumbled "kiddie dope" as he went by. The guy obviously took it as an insult to his integrity and importance as a dealer and handed Chris the telephone number of his friend. I could not believe how Chris operated. He was so smooth and he made things happen effortlessly.

The excitement continued on the following day, as my real training continued.

"What do you think?" I asked, with anticipation.

"I don't know. . . ."

The snow was falling lightly as we drove out of the federal building's underground garage. This would be my first actual undercover experience. Neither one of us said anything for a long time. I wondered what Chris was thinking about.

"What should I say when I meet him, Chris?"

"We'll just make our story up as we go along. . . . He'll dig the Caddy right away. We'll tell him we have some broads, hookers, working the street, and you're the protection, my leg breaker. Hippies are the easiest, Paulie, they believe anything you tell 'em."

That sounds good enough to me, I thought. As a matter of fact, it sounds perfect. Talk comes so easy to Chris. I guess that is why he is such a good undercover guy. I know in my heart that someday I can become as good undercover as he is, and I am glad I am working with him. Chris has me out in the street where the action is and that is just the way I want it. It is a well-known fact that you have to crank it up a notch to work with Chris and you have to pay attention or you will be history. I like it that way.

Everything I ever liked to do seemed to involve a little tension and more than a little danger. Every time I jumped out of an airplane in the army, every time I climbed through the ropes of a boxing ring, I always got the butterflies going. I never got completely used to these things, but I needed to do them. It was just part of my makeup. I must be drawn to the challenge, I concluded.

"Is it before or after the Cadillac-Olds dealership?"

"What?"

"Is the Ski Mart before or after Cadillac-Olds?"

"I think it's before," I answered as we moved off of Storrow Drive and headed toward Kenmore Square.

"What does he look like?" I asked.

"He's a hippie kid, probably looks like the rest of 'em. I haven't seen him myself. I told him we would be driving the Cadillac, so he'll be lookin' for us. His name is Steve. That's all I know. There's the Ski Mart now, on the left. We'll have to go by it and turn around."

"Do you see our man?" I asked, anxiously.

I scanned the sidewalk in front of the Ski Mart to see if I could see any possibilities on the other side of the trolley tracks, as we whizzed down Commonwealth Avenue.

"No, I don't see him yet," Chris answered. "We're early."

There was a lot of foot traffic in front of the Ski Mart, but none of the passersby matched the description of the dope dealer I envisioned in my mind. Chris pulled the Caddy into a space next to a mailbox, directly in front of the Ski Mart, and he shut off the engine. We made small talk while we waited.

"Is this him?" I pestered Chris, repeatedly.

"No," he answered patiently.

Ten minutes passed as we sat and waited. Customers went in and out of the Ski Mart carrying skis, ice skates, boxes, and bags. They mingled with BU students hurrying along the sidewalk, coming and going to classes.

Suddenly, Chris said in a hushed tone, "That's our man."

"Where?" I asked.

"Right there. Call him over."

As I fumbled for the button to open the window, the kid turned away.

"Chris, are you sure it's him?"

"That's him," Chris assured me.

I watched as the young-looking kid in the olive green army field jacket and blue jeans paced nervously back and forth in front of the Ski Mart, looking up and down the street. As I was watching, a postman walked up to the mailbox next to our car and blocked my view. The kid walked toward us as though he were coming to our car, but suddenly stopped short to talk with the mailman. I tried to listen to what they were saying, but all I could hear the kid say was "have a nice day" before they both started to walk away. I looked at Chris again, and he nodded anxiously.

Finally, I called out, "Steve!"

The kid in the army jacket spun around and answered immediately, "Yeah!"

Smiling apprehensively, he walked over to our car and looked at Chris, then at me, then back at Chris.

"Chickie?" he asked with an inquiring expression. Chickie was the undercover name Chris was using at the time.

"Yeah, man, get in," we answered simultaneously.

I watched the kid as he got into the backseat of the car, and I wondered why he had stood around for so long, looking up and down Commonwealth Avenue, like he was waiting for someone else. We were right in front of him! I was anxious to know what he was thinking, and I soon found out.

"I can get you anything you want. I can get you anything. My man is capable of weight," Steve began bragging, as all dealers do, to impress us.

Chris immediately took charge of the negotiations.

"Now wait a minute, Steve, we've heard that tune before. Paulie and I meet them all, guys that can do the world. Calm down, tiger. Let's start off easy with an ounce and see how that goes."

"Okay, that's fine, Chickie. You can get an ounce and as soon as you get it, you'll want more. It's dynamite stuff, believe me. My man is supplying BU with cocaine, and everyone loves it."

"How much for an ounce?" Chris asked.

"Eleven hundred," Steve shot back without hesitation.

"Eleven hundred? Are you crazy? Paulie, did I hear this kid right?"

"Stevie, you're not dealin' with college kids anymore, you unastand? You're dealing with us, now. Chickie and I are businessmen. We like you, Stevie, so let's keep it that way. We wanna do business, so smarten up."

"He comes down, or we don't do no deal," Chris interjected.

"Okay, okay, I'll talk to my man and see what he says, okay guys?" Steve answered obediently, folding under Chris's ultimatum.

It was obvious to me that Steve was quite impressed with our presentation. Like taking candy from a baby, as Chris explained it earlier.

"Okay, Stevie, we have to move on. Tell your man that we wanna do a steady thing if we can agree on a price, and give us a call after you talk with him. By the way, Stevie, is your man black or white?"

"He's white," Steve answered with a baffled expression.

"Oh, good; more dependable. Can't trust the spades," Chris smiled, devilishly. "That's our market. We sell to them. We give 'em their poison. But, we get our money up front . . . always up front."

"Yeah? Oh, yeah, okay," Steve replied, seeming not to know quite what to say. "Bye, Chickie. See ya, Paulie."

Steve crawled out of the big backseat and walked away. It was an incongruous scene. A young hippie college student getting out of a long, blue Cadillac pimpmobile with a chrome figure of an ample-breasted naked lady mounted on the front of the hood. It seemed to underline the fact that Steve was in over his head. A feeling of exhilaration came over me. Stevie was the first dope dealer I had ever met. You have to start somewhere.

Chris smiled at me as we drove away.

"What did I tell you, Paulie? Is he easy or what? Did you see his eyes open up when we told him we were unloading our dope on blacks in Roxbury? This kid is lovin' it. He's gonna make a good informant when we bust him."

"Do you think he can do what he says?" I asked.

"We'll give it a shot. He said he would call us tonight around seven, so let's go back and run it down to Todd Downs."

I kept thinking about our meeting. I wondered what the chances were that the deal would develop. Was Chris being overly optimistic? Did this kid really have a big connection? He was only a college kid to me. Was he playing games? Was I going to make my first undercover buy from this kid with the long, shaggy hair and dirty jeans? I couldn't stop thinking about our conversation with Steve. Was this the real thing? Before I knew it, we were back in the office.

"Todd, this kid says he can get any amount we want, and he can do it on a regular basis. He said he wants eleven hundred an ounce, but I know we can jew him down." Chris explained the details in the best light possible so that Downs would approve the deal.

Todd Downs was about thirty years old, the same age as Chris, but he looked and acted much older. He was a big hulk of a guy. Chris said that Todd's ass was wider than his shoulders because he sat at his desk all day. He dressed conservatively in white shirts, striped ties, and wing-tip shoes. He wore his pants up high so that his belt looked like the equator, dividing the top and bottom half of his body as it stretched around the expanse of his waist. He was a group supervisor, but he supervised from his office. He seemed preoccupied with the paperwork he held in his hand as Chris and I followed him around the office. Todd was decidedly less than enthusiastic about our proposed drug deal.

"We're tight for money right now, Chris. I can't go and approve a buy for eleven hundred dollars," Todd whined.

"Why not?" Chris demanded. "If the kid is talking shit, we return the money tomorrow. If the kid's got it, we buy it. I thought our job was to buy dope. It is, isn't it?" Chris added, sarcastically.

Their personalities clashed. Chris liked to steam straight ahead, while Todd preferred not to rock the boat. The tension between them was high. It was a classic confrontation between the street guy and the bureaucrat. Physically, Chris was the more impressive of the two by far. At six foot three, his longish hair hanging rakishly over the turned-up collar of his black leather coat, Chris posed a formidable figure. It was clearly the case of the pencil pusher versus the street guy. Tempers flared, shouting ensued, but Chris prevailed. After considerable argument, Downs finally handed over eleven hundred dollars grudgingly, so that we could make the buy. Downs was the group supervisor, but Chris was "the man." Our job as agents was to buy dope, and Chris made sure that we did. It was known throughout the region that Chris bought more dope and locked up more dope dealers than any other agent by far.

It was a little after seven o'clock that night when the undercover telephone rang. It was Steve, and he was ready to introduce us to "his man." Chris and I saddled up, and headed back to the Ski Mart.

When we arrived, Steve and a little guy wearing a floppy hat, rumpled old jeans, and cowboy boots were standing in front of the sporting goods store. After we parked at the curb, they both walked over to the Caddy and got into the backseat.

Steve was full of enthusiasm as he made the introductions.

"Paulie and Chickie, this is my man."

I could see that "his man" was as nervous as I was. This gave me some consolation and a slight edge.

"You got the stuff?" I asked.

"No," he answered apologetically, "you have to follow me."

"What?" I questioned sarcastically. "What is this, a circus?"

"You have to follow me," the guy in the floppy hat repeated, looking down at his lap. "I don't have it with me."

I was all pumped up, but I was slightly confused by the change of plans. I didn't realize that dope deals never went as arranged.

"Don't play games with us!" I yelled in his face, as he continued looking down to avoid eye contact. I could see that he was scared.

He answered timidly as he exited the back of the Cadillac, "We won't . . . won't play games. Trust me."

"You stay with us," Chris ordered, as he turned around in the seat and poked Steve in the chest with his finger, "that way there's no funny business."

The two young dope dealers looked at each other nervously and nodded. They had no choice but to comply. I could see that they were trying desperately to look cool. We were not their typical customers. The dealer in the floppy hat got into his beat-up old car, and we followed him as he drove off.

"This is the most screwed-up deal I have ever seen, Stevie. You and your man in that silly hat are a couple of losers. If you think we have time to follow that wanna-be hippie all over the city to cop an ounce of coke, you must be nuts! If this ever happens again, I will personally bang both your heads together." Chris continued to lambaste Steve while we followed his sidekick's jalopy outbound on the Jamaicaway, through Brookline to Jamaica Plain.

The jalopy suddenly turned off the Jamaicaway onto Green Street, and Chris followed it down several side streets before it pulled over and stopped. Chris pulled in behind the old car, bumper to bumper, and stopped. Quickly, before I could begin to process what was happening, Chris counted out nine one-hundred-dollar bills, which he handed to me. Meanwhile, the sidekick was walking back toward our car.

"Go with the man, Paulie, and get the stuff. Stevie and I will wait here," Chris ordered.

Talk about baptism by fire, I thought to myself, as I got out of the car and closed the door. Without any conversation between us, I followed the dealer into a dark hallway of a triple-decker and up several flights of stairs. It didn't take long for me to learn that a drug deal allowed little time to gather your thoughts. Once it got going, it generally went full speed ahead.

"The man" knocked lightly on the solid mahogany door, which opened slightly. The squeaky sound of the door hinge broke the silence in the dark hallway. A skinny, bushy-haired young hippie wearing gold wire-rimmed glasses peered out at us. He was barefoot and shirtless, clad only in jeans. He stared at me momentarily, and I stared back.

"Hello, Dave," he said softly, revealing to me the first name of the man in the floppy hat.

"Tom, this is Paulie, the guy I told you about," Dave responded.

"Hello, Paulie," Tom answered, uneasily.

This was not only my first drug deal but also my first real encounter with hippies. They were a strange phenomenon to me that materialized in the sixties. There were no hippies from my neighborhood. They were from someplace else. Hippies were the ones who picketed against the administration at Rutgers University. They held "sit-ins" and smoked pot while I was working full-time and trying to study at the Rutgers University library. They protested the war in Vietnam and practiced free love in their communes while I walked through the rice paddies and minefields in Southeast Asia. Many people praised them for their opposition to the war, but I could not relate. Hippies were the unknown enemy to me. I was too naive to realize that people in our government were talking out of both sides of their mouth on Vietnam. They got us into a war and never let us win. The issue divided our population as never before. Our secretary of defense, Robert McNamara, kept referring to himself and the rest of the cabinet as "the best and the brightest." I was sick of the whole mess and wanted to forget about it, but it would not go away. In my mind, "the best and the brightest" were the young people who were being sent across the sea, many of whom never came back alive.

Tom extended his hand and we exchanged the peace handshake. My gut tightened; I found it difficult to suppress my feelings.

"What's happenin' man?" I managed, trying to break the ice.

"Cocaine," Tom replied with a weak smile. "You got the money?"

My mind shifted into high gear, racing like an automobile engine stuck in neutral. I was confronted by my philosophical archenemy, and I wanted to knock him out cold. My emotions were so high that I had a difficult time reasoning with myself. My thoughts seemed so loud inside my head that I was afraid Tom might hear them. I was stuck in attack mode, but I was undercover, and I knew that I had to get control of my thoughts and make the buy.

"Yeah, I got the money," I answered, and then challenged him. "But first, show me the coke."

I relaxed a little. I could see that Dave and Tom were both nervous now. Tom went into another room. I hoped he wouldn't go out the back door and was relieved when he returned with the coke wrapped in a small, plastic baggie and a set of pharmaceutical scales. After an elaborate but awkward ceremonial weighing, Tom handed me the ounce of coke. I squeezed the coke tightly in my fist and I asked the price. Tom looked over at Dave, and Dave stared back, blankly.

Dave said nervously, "Steve told you a thousand, didn't he, Paulie?"

I tucked the baggie of coke in my front pant's pocket. I then counted out nine one-hundred-dollar bills, snapping the crisp bills deliberately for effect, and held them out toward Dave in my right hand. I felt as though I had total control of the situation, and I sensed that Dave and Tom thought the same.

Then, with the discussion of price concluded by me, Tom asked if I was going to taste the coke before I left the apartment. Suddenly, I felt as though I was losing control again. This was becoming an emotional roller-coaster of a negotiation. I didn't know what to do in this situation, so I pretended not to hear him. I ignored the question, but Tom persisted. I was stumped. I didn't remember this scenario from the training academy or from my discussions with Chris, but I know that federal narcotic agents do not use drugs, ever. I was on the spot, and he was challenging me.

"You gonna taste it?" he repeated.

As I scrambled to think of a response, a way to get out of the predicament, my mind froze. I got angry with my inability to solve the problem. This little hippie is trying to intimidate me, I thought.

"You better taste it," he continued, "so there won't be any argument about quality. I want to know that you are satisfied before you go."

"Listen, you little asshole, if I get burned, I know where you live! Don't worry about me. Worry about yourself. If this stuff is bogus, I'll be back in the middle of the night. You'll wake up with me in your face! You understand, hippie man?" I responded, heatedly.

Tom and Dave were shaken at my angry outburst. I could tell by their expressions that I reacted a little too violently. I overdid it. They both looked like they were going to cry. I could see in Tom's eyes that he was still nerved up after I finally handed him the money, so I tried to ease the tension. I told Tom that I trusted him for the ounce, and that I was sure that we would continue to do business. I told them that I get a little tense when I'm doing a deal. I reached out and shook hands with Tom, then I walked away triumphantly, with Dave following on my heels. We descended the creaky stairs, walked through the pitch-black hallway, and out to the car. Man, I just bought dope! Two days with Chris, and I had done everything I was hired to do, I thought to myself as I got into the car.

"How did it go?" Chris asked calmly.

"Huh?" I responded.

"How did it go?" Chris asked again, more urgently this time. "Did you score?"

"Yeah, I scored," I answered, absently, lost in thought.

Meanwhile, I could hear Dave asking Chris if he could "cop a few spoons" from our package. I was still in a trance from the excitement, thinking about my first undercover drug buy.

Chris brushed off Dave's request. "No way, kid. This little package already has someone's name on it, and it ain't yours. We'll get in touch with you when we're ready to do it again. Later guys."

I watched Tom's dumbfounded expression through the glass as Chris shut the car window in his face. I grinned and proudly displayed my trophy, the small plastic baggie full of cocaine, to Chris as he pulled away from the curb.

"That's Mexican cocaine," Chris pointed out in a teachable moment. "See the brown crystals? That's the new stuff we've been hearing about."

Chris knows it all, I thought to myself. I heard about Mexican cocaine in the Academy, but Chris already knows by experience. I have a long way to go before I catch up.

"You got a field test?" Chris asked.

"What?" I was still reeling from the excitement of being undercover.

"A field test?" Chris repeated, impatiently.

"Oh, shit, I forgot." I panicked as I fumbled through my pockets.

"Here, I have one," Chris said, handing me a small test tube.

I opened the plastic baggie clumsily and scooped a small amount of the cocaine into the test tube. I could feel my face getting flushed with excitement as I watched the test tube turn cobalt blue as the cocaine reacted positively to the chemicals.

"It's coke," I announced proudly. "It's a good turn, it's coke, Chris."

"Turn the radio on, Paulie."

I could hear Todd Downs calling out the names of the side streets to the surveillance team as soon as I turned the two-way radio on.

"Undercover to surveillance," I broke into the radio transmission excitedly. "It's a score. I got a positive test. It's Mexican cocaine."

"201 to 212, what number did you go into?" Downs droned.

Downs's question baffled me. Man, I thought to myself, I don't even know what door I went into, never mind what number. I am in a real mental fog.

"212 to 201, I'm not quite sure," I finally answered, after a prolonged delay.

"201 to 212, was it the brown house or the green house?" Downs questioned.

I hesitated again, trying desperately to remember, but I had no idea. I could not recall the house no matter how hard I tried. The details of the deal were so clear to me, so vivid, but I couldn't think straight when the supervisor asked me. I was unable to respond.

"It was the green house, Paulie," Chris volunteered sympathetically. He knew what I was going through. He understood.

"212 to 201," I answered, my confidence bolstered. "It was the green one."

"10-4," Downs responded, much to my relief.

"What's that asshole, Downs, doing out in the street anyway?" Chris shouted angrily as he reached over and turned off the radio and Todd Downs. "He does it all the time, Paulie. Whenever he comes out on surveillance, he never sees a goddam thing. Why doesn't he just shut up, instead of asking all those stupid questions?" Chris continued. He was fuming!

It was clear that Chris and Todd did not get along. It was the gap between the street agent and the administrative agent that would never be bridged. Guys like Todd Downs complicated the war on drugs and frustrated guys like Chris. A long silence followed Chris's outburst. Then I noticed Chris looking at me with his mischievous grin, and I wondered what he was thinking about. He had a twinkle in his eye.

"What color was the guy you bought from?" he asked.

I returned a look of confusion. For a brief moment, I struggled to remember what color the guy was. I realized that Chris was teasing me, because he could relate to the experience. It was a common reaction, like being stagestruck, on the first buy. Chris laughed that devilish laugh of his and held out his right hand, palm up. I burst into laughter myself as I thought how ridiculous my sudden memory losses seemed, and I slapped him five. It was really a funny scene. The old veteran and the new recruit. At that moment, I knew that Chris and I were a team. We clicked.

I didn't sleep very much that night. The excitement of making my first undercover buy would not subside, and I lay awake into the early morning hours, reflecting on the evening's events. I thought to myself, should I have said this or should I have said that? I went over and over the deal in my mind, wondering what I could have said or done to improve my performance. After all, undercover work is a performance, isn't it? "All the world's a stage," Shakespeare's famous words from *As You Like It*, crossed my mind, and I finally drifted off to sleep.

I awoke slowly from my dreamy reverie to the fresh scent of a woman. I struggled to open my eyes when I felt a soft kiss, and saw through my squinted eyes that it was Pam.

"Good morning," Pam said cheerfully as she moved around the bedroom briskly, taking her car keys from the dresser, and slinging her pocketbook over her shoulder. "I'm leaving for the hospital."

I propped myself up on my elbows and focused my eyes on my wife. She was so beautiful, especially in her white uniform, and she seemed to grow more beautiful every day. She hurried out of the bedroom, and I could hear her opening the latch on the door.

"See you tonight," she promised. Then the door closed behind her and like a beautiful, fleeting dream, she was gone.

I glanced at the small round clock on the night table; it was six o'clock in the morning. I rolled over and went back to sleep.

The next few days were spent on administrative matters. In order to process the cocaine evidence, I had to weigh the drug, seal it in an evidence envelope, and send it to the BNDD (Bureau of Narcotics and Dangerous Drugs) laboratory for a complete chemical analysis. I had to complete all the necessary reports, and I did this all very carefully and deliberately, under Chris Regan's watchful supervision. It was time-consuming. This was my first buy, and I wanted everything to be right. I wanted to complement my undercover activities with perfect paperwork. I wanted to be the best narcotic agent who ever hit the street.

I diligently followed the basic investigative procedure to identify our subjects. United States Postal Service and utility company checks revealed that Steve's last name was Cominsky and Tom's was Hoffman. Criminal records checks were negative for both.

About a week later the undercover telephone rang. The undercover phone was an unusually important means of communication for drug agents. It was in an old-fashioned telephone booth with folding glass-paneled doors, and was centrally located off of a hallway that connected the office cubicles of the enforcement groups. Undercover agents gave the numbers out sparingly to people they were dealing with. The special numbers were all unlisted and virtually impossible to trace. Whenever the telephone rang, it would be answered in a noncommittal voice. When the caller asked for Wolfman, Dante, or Sully, the person answering would look on the chart to determine that "Wolfman" was Tom Batten, "Dante" was Dan Santarpio, "Sully" or "Paulie" was Paul Sullivan, and so on. This time when it rang, I picked it up and it was for me.

"Hello," I answered.

The voice on the other end was Steve, and he was excited. "Paulie, are you ready for this?"

"Yeah man, what's up?" I pretended boredom.

"I did it, Paulie! For you and Chickie! I got a key of coke all set up! It's all set up!" Steve boasted, as if he wanted to make me really proud of him.

"Is this another circus ride, Steve?"

"No, Paulie, I'm telling you the truth. It's all set up. Twenty-five thou for the coke, and it's pure," Steve asserted. "Do you want it?"

"Do I want it? You bet your ass I want it!" I laughed.

"Okay, Paulie, I'll call the people and have them get it together. When it's ready, I'll call you back and we'll go pick it up!"

"You sure it's pure?" I demanded.

"Yup," Steve replied confidently.

"Who's the man? Where's his crib? Is he dark?" I questioned, trying to get as much background information and intelligence as possible.

"I don't know. I don't know who he is. It's Tom's supplier. I don't know him myself, but I know he's not black," Steve tried to explain.

"Steve, make arrangements for us to pick up the coke. Meanwhile, I'll get the dust together," I said.

"I told you I could do it, Paulie!" Steve exclaimed.

"That's right, Steve, I shoulda had more faith in you," I answered. "Now, hurry up and put the deal together."

"Okay, Paulie. I'll call you back when the stuff is there," Steve promised.

I hung up the telephone and stared into space momentarily, until Chris opened the door to the undercover booth and asked, "Who was that?"

"It was Steve," I answered.

"He got something for us?" Chris queried slyly.

"Yeah," I answered as I looked up at him, "a kilo of coke."

I sensed that Chris felt the same excitement I did, but he had reservations. He was anxious, and he wanted to believe it, but he was finding it difficult to comprehend that they could go from an ounce to a kilo.

"How much they want?"

"Twenty-five. He says it's pure," I answered.

"That's what they always say. How did it sound to you?" Chris asked.

"I think it's right," I answered thoughtfully.

Chris was getting psyched. He put his arm over my shoulder and said, "C'mon, let's run it by Todd."

We walked down the hallway together and turned into Group Two. Todd Downs was in deep concentration, poring over paperwork as usual, when we barged into his office. He looked up from his desk at us, and it was clear that he wished we were any place but in his office.

"Todd, Steve Cominsky just called Paulie and asked him if he wanted to buy a key of coke."

Todd peered at us over his half glasses and said, "I've heard that before."

I did not acknowledge his sarcasm, but quickly added, "He wants twenty-five for the key, Todd. It's coming from Tom Hoffman's source, a white guy." I wanted to get in as much information as I could before Todd dismissed our request. I wanted to make it sound as good as I could.

"Do we know the guy's name?" Todd quizzed me, his lips twisted in a derisive grin.

"No, Todd, not yet. Steve doesn't know him personally," I explained.

"I don't know," Todd replied with exaggerated hesitancy, in a most discouraging way. "Twenty-five thousand dollars for a John Doe defendant? I don't know if we can get approval from Washington for something like that."

I couldn't believe it. Our deal for a kilo of cocaine was evaporating in front of us because our group supervisor was unable, or unwilling, to make a decision. I was reaching my boiling point when suddenly Chris tore into Todd.

"Shit, Todd, we're not even going to spend the twenty-five thousand. It's only a flash roll. What's the problem? We've got three defendants already, and they are all identified. What is wrong with that?"

"Well, uh, let me check the manual on this. I'll have to call Washington." Todd was stalling. He thought some more and added cynically, "This guy has never come up with more than an ounce, and all of a sudden he has a kilo! I'll believe it when I see it."

Chris stormed out of the supervisor's office, and I followed, bewildered by an example of the constant agent-supervisor conflicts that arose when things didn't happen according to the manual. And they seldom did.

Chris grabbed his jacket and said, "Let's go."

As soon as we got into the car, Chris mimicked the supervisor. "I have to call Washington." He added bitterly, "He has to call Washington every time he wipes his ass!"

As we drove down North Washington Street and turned right on Commercial Street toward the waterfront, Chris explained to me that there was a saying in the DEA that went, "Big cases, big trouble, little cases, little trouble, and no cases, no trouble." I would hear it over and over again, because it was the philosophy of the bureaucrat. It was the best way to stay out of trouble and make the grade. Guys like Chris, undercover agents, were anathema to guys like Downs. Undercover agents made cases, and cases led to trouble. Chris made a sweeping U-turn and stopped next to the curb in front of a small Dunkin' Donuts.

"Did you ever wonder why some guys in the group are happy to do surveillance and follow us around?" Chris asked.

"Yeah, as a matter of fact I did. There can't be anything more boring than watching the front door to a nightclub or an apartment while the undercover guys are inside for two or three hours at a time. I wouldn't want to do it," I answered.

"Of course not, because you're like me. You want to be where the action is. You want to beat the dopers at their own game, outsmart them. That's what this job is all about, Paulie, putting drug dealers behind bars and taking dope off the street. It's easier to sit around and wait until a stool pigeon walks into the office and tells us when and where a shipment of drugs is coming in. You write it up in the reports, you get a search warrant, and bingo. But if we sit around on our asses all day waiting for that to happen, the streets get flooded with coke, heroin, acid, and people die. We can't let that happen," Chris explained.

Chris handed me a twenty and told me to get a dozen coffees. We were greeted with good-natured teasing when we got back to the office, variations on "the delivery boys are here with our coffee." The agents and detectives who had arrived to listen to the briefing for our arrest plan were happy to see us and the coffees, which disappeared before I had a chance to put them down.

At three a.m. we were all still standing by. The deal was delayed several times and everyone involved was pretty tired. Boston Police Detective John Sheffield and I were swapping favorite hand-to-hand combat techniques and trying them out on each other in a basement office. John Sheffield was approaching sixty years old, but he knew every way possible to bring a man to his knees. In his thirty years as a cop, he learned by experience how to make the most reluctant defendant "come along." I was always interested in learning the secrets that could make my job a little easier and even save my life. I was learning from the expert, in these early morning hours, techniques that I would use over and over in my career to make arrests and disarm attackers.

The office was full of cops and agents. They were huddled in different groups, talking to pass the time and to stay awake. An unlikely-looking group of guys of all ages in varied dress—sports jackets, jeans—talking about the Boston Bruins, their kids, court time, and drugs while most people were in the middle of a good night's sleep. The stark office, lighted by fluorescent ceiling lights and cluttered with empty coffee cups and sandwich wrappers, accentuated the improbable gathering of tired-eyed men. I felt increasingly uneasy as the night crept on because Chris and I were the reasons they were there.

Earlier in the night, the group of agents and detectives had covered the surveillance for Chris and me during our meetings with Steve at various locations in and around Boston, BU, the Ski Mart, and Kenmore Square. In a Kenmore Square restaurant, I had almost lost my cover when a young lady whom I had not seen since high school recognized me. The woman, a plain Jane eight years ago in high school, was now a long-legged beauty. I could hardly believe my eyes when I saw her staring at me. Parting her long, dark hair from in front of her face with her fingers, she winked, and struck a come-hither pose. I smiled, and she took off like a shot. She brazenly barged in between the two drug guys, threw her arms around my shoulders, and kissed me like a movie ending. Fortunately for me, she was so drunk that she was not able to talk clearly. Her words came out garbled, in mumbles. I quickly put my arm around her waist and led her to a booth in the corner of the restaurant. I told her that I wanted to buy her a sandwich, and promised to call her the next day. She sat straight in her seat while I propped her up with my hands on her shoulders. I carefully removed my hands while watching her heavy eyelids open and close slowly, worried that she would fall face forward onto the table. I called the waitress over, gave her ten dollars, and told her to give my girlfriend the special and keep the change. I gave her a fake hug and peck on the cheek while I adjusted her more suitably in an upright position, and then I left her.

When I returned to Steve and Tom, I realized that the chance encounter worked to my advantage. They were both impressed with the chance encounter with my sexy lady friend. I told them that it happened to me all the time! Our conversations with Tom and Dave had resulted in an impasse, though. We could not reach an agreement acceptable to both sides. Chris and I would not front the twenty-five thousand dollars, and Tom would not front the kilo of cocaine. We went round and round in our negotiations.

Now lack of sleep was getting to me, and I was beginning to wish that we had never met Steve. Finally, at 3:15 a.m., the undercover telephone rang, and Chris and I sprinted to it.

"Ya?" I answered.

"Paulie, it's all set," Steve said, doggedly.

"Whaddaya mean, it's all set?" I asked.

"My man will do it your way," Steve answered.

"You mean a hundred percent our way?" I questioned.

"Yup," Steve replied proudly.

"You mean, we go with the money to meet the man? Cash on delivery? I give him the money, and he gives me the dope?" I drilled him, in order to clarify everything.

"Exactly, but he only wants to meet one of you," Steve added.

"That's okay, Stevie. That's fine. Now let's do it," I said, trying to hide my excitement, because the adrenaline was pumping.

"Meet us at the 700 dormitory at BU right away," Steve instructed me.

"Okay, see you there," I said. But I wasn't quite finished. "Steve?"

"Ya?" he answered.

"This better not be a rip-off," I warned.

"Paulie, believe me," Steve pledged.

"Okay, we'll be there in five," I said and hung up. I looked at Chris to see his response. His eyes were tired-looking and bloodshot. It had been a long day, but the moment of truth was at hand.

"What do you think, Chris?" I asked.

"I think we do it," Chris answered positively. "There's always a chance of a rip-off with this much money involved, but we'll be loaded for bear. Let's fill the troops in."

Everyone was standing around, waiting as we came out of the undercover booth. As tired as they were, they came to life when we related the telephone conversation to them.

Chris stood in front of the group and detailed the plan. "Now we have twenty-five thousand dollars of Uncle Sam's money, and needless to say, uncle be pissed if we get ripped. So be ready for anything! Paulie and I feel that Steve Cominsky and Tom Hoffman are harmless, but we don't know who their man is or what he is capable of. Wolfman, you come with us in the undercover car as our protection for the money."

Tom Batten, "the Wolfman," nodded. He was perfect for the role. Batten was so far into his undercover role that even the other agents wondered about him! He was average height, about five feet, nine inches tall, stocky build, with an unmistakably wild Irish look. His bushy red hair and full red goatee accentuated the vacant, unreadable look in his eyes. Batten was dressed in a black motorcycle jacket, peg-legged dungarees, and black motorcycle boots. He presented a very sinister appearance. Batten worked undercover, almost exclusively, with motorcycle gangs like the Hell's Angels and the Devil's Disciples; his job was extremely demanding, stressful, and dangerous. Chris had made the right choice. Wolfman was an expert shot. We would have ample protection for the money tonight.

Back when I had first reported to the office the day after graduation from agent training school, I saw Tommy Batten at the water fountain in the hallway. He was an odd-looking sight in his well-worn black leather motorcycle jacket, boots, and rumpled jeans. There was a faraway look in his eyes that was completely unreadable. Most troubling, however, was the smell of marijuana and motor oil that came from his clothes. My instincts were alerted immediately. Is he an informant? I wondered. What was he doing in the office without an agent escort? Should I challenge him? I really did not know what to do. I attempted to appear nonchalant and said hello to him. He mumbled something that I could not decipher and walked back in the same direction from which he came. I hustled into Todd Downs's office and told him what I saw. Todd laughed and knew right away that it was Tommy Batten. And now, here was the Wolfman, a part of my first drug deal.

We left the office like a stampeding herd. Everyone was carrying some tools of our trade—walkie-talkies, binoculars, shotguns. We were going after a big one. Chris and I got into the undercover car, a sky-blue Cadillac Eldorado with wide whitewall tires and custom chrome grill, which we had seized from a drug-dealing pimp. Wolfman got into the backseat, and Chris gave him a quick, hurried overview of the deal as we headed toward the meeting place. Wolfman didn't say anything; he just nodded that he understood. It was fascinating to see a drug deal unfolding before my eyes, like playing a part in a story that was not yet written.

As we rolled up to the BU dormitory at 700 Commonwealth Avenue, I advised the surveillance agents that we were going off the air, and I placed the hand-held radio in the glove compartment. Steve Cominsky was already there when we arrived. He was sitting in Dave's Toyota. Dave was in the driver's seat, and I noticed Tom Hoffman seated in the rear when I walked up to them.

"Paulie, we're all set. Get in and we'll go meet the man and," Steve began excitedly.

"Stevie, don't rush me now," I cut him off. "Explain what's going on."

"He's got the kilo, and he wants to do the deal," Steve answered, almost out of breath from the excitement. "Do you have the money?"

"Do I have the money?" I repeated sarcastically. "No, I don't have no money, you asshole! Whaddaya think I'm doing here at four a.m.? Sightseeing?"

"Okay, okay, let's go then. You can get in the front," he said.

"No, Stevie, you come with us, and we'll follow them. That way, if we get ambushed, you'll die too," I countered. I wanted to make it clear that it would not be a good idea for anyone to try to rob us.

"Oh, uh, okay, Paulie, I'll go with you," Steve answered. Quickly he turned and shouted to Dave, "Go ahead, I'm going with Paulie and Chickie." Steve slid into the backseat of our car, next to the Wolfman.

Chris quickly introduced Steve to Tommy Batten. "Stevie, this is Wolfman, he's with the Devil's Disciples. He's here to protect our interest, you know what I mean."

"Oh, hi, Wolfman. Don't worry. There's nothing to worry about, really, I mean," Steve muttered, glancing cautiously at the Wolfman.

"You can call me Wolf," Batten replied. Steve was taken aback by the odd-sounding proposition.

"Oh ya, Wolf, sure," Steve responded uneasily.

We followed the Toyota in silence for a very long time. Steve talked constantly, assuring us that the cocaine would be delivered smoothly. Every so often Chris would ask a question to try to piece together the puzzle. Wolfman, sporadically punching his fist into his palm for no reason, sat silently in the backseat, which must have been unnerving to Steve and added to the drama. My stomach was tied in knots. My nervous anxiety was probably heightened by the amount of coffee that I had consumed during the back-and-forth exchanges of the evening's negotiations. I glanced out the rear window, and saw a string of headlights from the surveillance vehicles in our wake, looking like an evening funeral procession. It's pretty difficult to follow someone on dark roads with no traffic at four a.m. and still remain inconspicuous. I wondered if the dope dealers planned it this way, and it made me more nervous.

Finally, approximately forty-five minutes after we began following Dave, he signaled for a right-hand turn, and pulled into a parking lot. The sign said Driftwood Motor Lodge. Chris followed Dave's car into the lot between some buildings and parked our Caddy next to the Toyota. Tom got out of the Toyota alone and walked over to our car. I rolled down my window and Tom said, "Okay, Paul, follow me."

The time had come, and I couldn't believe it. The procession ended so abruptly, and the headlights lighting up our trail suddenly vanished. There were no surveillance cars in sight, now. Everything suddenly seemed to focus on Tom Hoffman and me. I faltered for a moment and then swallowed. My mouth was completely dry. I really didn't know what to do next. You know how it is when you do something for the first time, the uncertainty. I searched for the right words, but they wouldn't come. So, I said, "Oh, we're all set, Tom, huh? Uh, what are we doing?" trying to get some directions for Chris as to where I was going. I knew what I wanted to say, but inexperience kept me from finding the right words. It didn't matter, though, because Tom explained everything.

"The source is in a room with the coke, and I'm taking you to meet him," Tom volunteered.

"What room is he in?" Chris asked, matter-of-factly.

"Room 212," Tom replied, immediately divulging the crucial information. As Chris said, it was as easy as taking candy from a baby.

Chris swung his right arm across the top of the seat and turned his head to face the Wolfman, in the backseat.

"Go with him, Wolf. When you see the stuff, Paulie, and you're satisfied, send Wolfman down to get the money." With that, Wolfman and I followed Tom to room 212 and waited in the hall as he knocked.

"It's T. Open up," Tom called.

I imagined someone eyeing us mysteriously through the peephole as I listened to the sound of the lock turning and someone unfastening the security chain. Then the door opened up, and I came face to face with the source. For a moment I thought that we had the wrong room, and I wanted to laugh. The man in the doorway looked like a guy you would see selling peanuts at Fenway Park, or tomatoes from a pushcart in the North End, not a dope dealer. He was short and dumpy, around five feet, six inches tall and well over two hundred pounds. He wore badly wrinkled chino pants and worn construction boots. Thin, straggly hair stuck out from under the scally-cap perched on the back of his oversized head. Our eyes met as he fumbled awkwardly with his fat fingers to adjust his ill-fitting black-rimmed glasses, which had slipped down toward the end of his sausagelike nose.

The guy extended his right hand and said, "I'm Joe da big man."

"Good to meet you," I responded as I entered the room and shook his hand.

"Relax, don worry 'bout a ting. We do bizniz like dis every day. Right, men?" Joe said, directing the question to the two other unlikely-looking people inside the room who were manipulating a pharmaceutical scale. They were very studious-looking guys wearing chinos and blue cotton dress shirts. One had long blonde hair, down to his shoulders. The other had shorter brown, wavy hair. They both wore gold wire-rimmed glasses. They laughed nervously under their breath and answered, "Right, Joe." There was no doubt from Joe's demeanor and the manner in which he took control of the situation that he was the boss.

"Now, where's da money? Da twenny-five thou?" Joe asked.

"It's downstairs in the car," I answered. "Steve already saw it," I assured him. "After we see the coke, Wolf'll go down and get the money."

"Yah, bee-u-ti-ful. Dats good. Steve seen it, anyway," Joe reasoned out loud, preoccupied with removing a plastic bag, bulging with cocaine, from a briefcase and handing it to me. "A hundred percent coke. Da best."

I broke the seal on the clear plastic bag and examined the white crystalline powder, not really knowing what to look for, but pretending just the same. I held the powder up to a lamp and studied it. I showed the bag to Wolfman and offered him a taste. Wolfman put his hand in the bag, stuck his index finger deep into the white powder, then pulled his hand out of the bag. He then put his middle finger into his mouth and ran it along his gums. No one noticed that he had switched fingers. All eyes were on the Wolfman as he conducted his unorthodox test. He broke the tension with his bug-eyed remark. "Feels good to me, Paulie. I got a freeze."

"Right on, Wolf," I smiled. "It's time to go down and get the money."

"Yeah, Paulie, sounds good," Wolfman answered and walked, flat-footed, out of the room. Joe saw him to the door and locked it. The butterflies began again inside my stomach. I was standing in the hotel room, looking nervously between Joe and the two "chemists," trying with much difficulty to appear relaxed. Joe looked over at me and then looked away. It seemed as though time had stopped when Wolfman walked out the door and left me alone with the subjects, suspects, or drug dealers. I wanted desperately for time to begin again, and then I felt the vibrations in the floor. The arresting agents were hurrying up the stairs and stepping lightly down the hallway toward us, trying to be silent, but their commotion was like a racket to my ears. I panicked inside, wondering if Joe and the chemists could hear. I looked over at Joe. He seemed to be unfazed, in a world of his own with the cocaine.

Suddenly, I could hear footsteps shuffling noisily outside our door. It was like standing under a high kickoff, waiting for the football to come down, so that you can catch it and run. You have to keep your eye on the ball, but your ears can detect the sound of the tacklers charging downfield to tackle you. It sounds like thunder, like a thundering herd. My eyes met Joe's. There was no doubt now that he knew his time had come. I fumbled under my coat, and somehow came out with my service revolver in my hand and pointed it at Joe.

"Don't move, Joe," I said firmly as we stared at each other. He looked at me with a telling expression that comes at the moment of truth. Almost simultaneously, the hotel room door came down with a crash and federal agents poured into the room.

"Federal agents! Everybody freeze!" they yelled as they placed everyone under arrest.

It was certainly a nice way to begin my career. The delivery of a kilo of pure cocaine was a record seizure for the Boston office in 1971. The development of the case illustrated how undercover agents could begin at the street level and work their way up the ladder through the drug hierarchy. In addition, special agents of the Bureau of Narcotics and Dangerous Drugs and detectives of the Boston Police demonstrated that they could work together.

Joe, the source of the cocaine, turned out to be Joe Colangelo, a midlevel organized crime figure, a made man with a criminal record spanning forty years for violations that included stolen cars, assaults, weapons violations, arson, and murder. He became known far and wide as "the man who got away with murder" after a government witness, waiting to testify against Colangelo in a murder case, was found dead by police in the trunk of his car. A copper penny was placed in each eye, and the witness's private parts were found in his mouth. It was a Mafia farewell to a turncoat and a reminder to others that "omertà," the underworld code of silence, should not be taken lightly. With no witness to corroborate the evidence, Colangelo was found innocent of murder in court. Subsequently, the police were unable to find enough evidence to charge Colangelo with the murder of the witness. Needless to say, no one volunteered to come forward to testify against him.

As I walked into the John F. Kennedy Federal Office Building on the morning of the arrest, leading Joe in handcuffs to be fingerprinted and photographed, I naively suggested that he could help himself by providing information to the government. The other subjects flipped, or began cooperating, as soon as they were handcuffed. Agents in the backseat, sitting next to informants, took notes and statements as they transported them to the federal building. It did not take much to convince these guys that it would be the wise thing to do, to save themselves from the dreadful prospect of jail. I told Joe that I would ask the judge for leniency in exchange for his cooperation. In other words, if Joe told me where he got the cocaine and who his partners were, I would suggest that the U.S. attorney ask the judge for a lesser sentence. After I made my offer, Joe Colangelo turned slightly to look at me out of the corner of his eye.

"Agen Sullivan, please don ask me no questions. I can't tell ya nuttin' about nuttin'. I did da wrong ting, and you got me. I'm in enough trouble now."

"Joe, you are facing twenty years in prison," I replied.

Joe said, "Pleeze, I opened Walpole Prison."

"Joe, you won't be going to Walpole, you'll be going to a federal penitentiary."

I knew that my attempt to recruit Joe as an informant was futile when he replied, "Dat's even bedda."

Joe Colangelo spoke without anger or defiance. In fact, his personality and manner were almost likeable. I didn't see Joe again until the day of his trial. He was standing outside of Room 4 in the federal district court in Boston with his hands folded behind his back, twirling his thumbs, looking around at the people, more like an observer than a Mafia member and the subject of the upcoming trial. I had to pinch myself to make sure that it was really Joe Colangelo standing there. He looked so casual. He also looked odd in the ill-fitting suit. Mafiosi are always portrayed in expensive custom suits!

"Joe?" I asked incredulously, as I approached him.

"Howya doin'?" Joe answered enthusiastically, sticking out his right hand.

"I'm doing alright," I replied as I automatically shook his hand.

"You done a great job, kid. I tawt you was a college football player or sumptin'," Joe laughed as we stood there shaking hands for a long time.

"Well, I guess this is it?" I said, uncomfortably.

"Yah, I guess," Joe answered.

"I see you have your toothbrush," I commented when I noticed a toothbrush sticking out of the breast pocket of Joe's baggy black suit, in place of the fancy silk handkerchief that I would have imagined a Mafia soldier would wear in his tailored suit.

"Yah," Joe repeated as he held up a silly-looking shaving case. "I'll need it and a couple a udda tings."

"You think it's going to be a long trial?" I asked.

"Nah," Joe laughed. "They ain't gonna be no trial. I'm pleadin'."

I didn't know quite what to say. I was glad that I didn't have to testify and go through a long trial, but I was surprised at the unexpected ending of the case. Is this what it's all about? I wondered.

"Good luck, Joe," I said, realizing immediately after I said it how foolish I must have sounded.

"Tanks, kid," Joe replied, apparently sincere as he looked me in the eye. "An good luck ta you, too."

I never saw Joe Colangelo again. He pleaded guilty and was sentenced to twenty years in prison. Since that time, I have thought of him many times. You could be fooled by Joe's likeable personality and seemingly principled refusal to rat on his friends, but Joe was an absolute contradiction. He was not what he seemed to be. He was a psychopath, a cold-blooded killer. Joe and guys like him have no principles. Their lives are driven by profit and greed. Mobsters like those in La Cosa Nostra are romanticized in movies, but movies are make-believe. Real-life mobsters are ruthless, treacherous, and deadly. There is no doubt in my mind that Joe would have killed me if he ever got the chance, but he didn't. As a criminal, Joe was good, but he wasn't that good, because he got caught. There is a degree of satisfaction in knowing that I played a part in catching him and taking him off the street. In spite of all this, however, I guess I still have a certain respect for him. He was a criminal, but he was a stand-up guy. There aren't many stand-up guys anymore.

CHINATOWN

I n the early 1970s, some of the purest white heroin in the country was pouring out of Boston's Chinatown. In an elaborate smuggling operation, Chinese merchant seamen jumped ship in Boston harbor and swam ashore to deliver heroin directly from Hong Kong to local Chinese distributors. As a reward for their crimes, the seamen received asylum in Boston working as kitchen help in Chinese restaurants. The local Chinese heroin distributors would then supply the midlevel Chinese dealers in Boston and other major cities across the United States. Only Chinese were involved at the time, and it was impossible for any American to break into the chain of distribution. The Tong, the powerful, unforgiving Chinese underworld, controlled all drug smuggling, and they did not tolerate informants. The U.S. government tried several wiretaps, but the taped conversations in Chinese, with its many dialects, were undecipherable. Telephone toll records only revealed that the calls were made to and from pay phones in Chinese restaurants from Bangor, Maine, to San Francisco, California.

The midlevel dealers utilized prostitutes to distribute the heroin, thus creating a protective buffer between themselves and the police. To interrupt the flow of heroin at any point higher than the street level seemed virtually impossible, but then again, with perseverance and a little luck, almost anything is achievable. The break for the U.S. government came via a telephone call from Detective John Sheffield, a wily thirty-year veteran of the Boston Police Department, to Chris Regan, my partner at the Boston office of the

BNDD. The Bureau of Narcotics and Dangerous Drugs later became the DEA, the Drug Enforcement Administration.

"Chris, I got a stoolie that is willing to introduce an agent to a pretty good heroin dealer," John Sheffield offered.

"We accept all offers!" Chris joked.

"It's a Chinaman," John added.

"He's Chinese?" Chris repeated.

"Yeah, they call him Kyung Fung," John mused.

"We'll be right there." Chris ended the conversation and hung up the phone. "Paulie, let's go," he said excitedly, as he got up and put on his jacket. "You're not gonna believe this," he continued talking, as we headed out of the office. Chris filled me in on his conversation with Detective Sheffield as we walked to the underground garage. The stoolie that Detective Sheffield spoke of would turn out to be our entrée into the Chinese drug mob.

When Chris and I arrived at the Boston Police Drug Control Unit, I was introduced to a young woman who would become the best criminal informant that I had known up to that point. She was Mary Elizabeth McNulty, also known as Tootie, a young prostitute with a notorious reputation. Tootie's area of operation was Boston's nefarious Combat Zone, which borders Chinatown and the theater district. Tootie would teach me more about narcotics, firsthand, than any other source or experience in my entire career as a narcotic agent. There are informants, and then there are informants. Tootie was a diamond in the rough. Detective Sheffield had taken this tough young streetwalker under his wing following her arrest in a drug raid several months before. Since that time, John treated Tootie with the respect and compassion that she had never encountered before in her short, unfortunate life. Tootie came of age in South Boston's tough D Street Housing Project, where she was abused and put out on the street by two alcoholic parents. She was first arrested for prostitution at fourteen, a classic example of the kid who never had a chance in life.

When I met Tootie, she was only twenty-four years old but had already lived a lifetime. All of her teeth were either missing, rotten, or broken, and she was infected with second-degree syphilis. Yet I could still see traces in her features of the beauty that never was, and I could detect a certain girlish innocence that was invisible to most people who crossed paths with Tootie. Violence robbed Tootie of her childhood. There was no place for joy in her life because she was too busy trying to survive. That is why Tootie was so tough, and her toughness was legendary.

Tootie was a bad junkie. She was so badly strung out that she needed to shoot three to five bags of heroin into her arm every two hours, day and night, to stave off the horrors of withdrawal. She was so addicted that she could not sleep through the night without her usual dose. Tootie was that addicted, or as they say in the street, she had a "bad jones."

Detective Sheffield became, for Tootie, a caring father figure. The fact that he allowed Chris and me to work with her was a sign of the hard-earned, mutual professional respect that existed among us as drug cops. Informants are closely held, prized possessions within the law enforcement community, and they are not usually revealed to others. John Sheffield, however, knew that the only way to arrest and jail major heroin dealers was to continue making drug buys at progressively higher levels in the chain of distribution. John knew that the U.S. government had the money to reach beyond the street junkie, and he knew that Chris and I could be trusted.

It did not take long for me to understand why Detective Sheffield developed such a deep personal attachment for Tootie, because I soon did so myself. It was like rooting for the underdog. Tootie was the first real junkie informant I had ever worked with, and to actually witness the humiliation and degradation that she endured was an education in itself. It made me more committed than ever to fighting drugs. I learned of the agony and hopeless desperation of the junkie at the end of the heroin distribution chain created by the greedy international drug kingpins. Tootie was a "stone junkie," which is as bad as it gets. I lived with Tootie, and I laughed and cried with her. I watched Tootie nod off to sleep in the middle of a conversation after taking a heroin fix. Her speech would begin to slur, as if someone switched her brain off, and she would mumble and then stop talking altogether. She would then lose consciousness and collapse, like she was dead. For all intents and purposes, she was dead. That is when, Tootie told me, she experienced the ultimate rush of the heroin high. More than once, I thought that Tootie had died when I saw this happen.

The symptoms of withdrawal were painfully obvious. Tootie's nose would run, and she would rub it nervously, as all junkies do when the effects of the heroin started to wear off. Then she would break out in cold sweats and suffer the dry heaves. Tootie told me that her body hurt all over, and she said the pain was indescribable. She was not the crying type, but her eyes would fill up, and the tears would fall uncontrollably. She would cry, shake, and tremble until she could get that needle in her arm again. Watching her go through this hell was painfully sad, and the worst part of all was my own helplessness. I couldn't help her a bit. No one but the "candy man" could ease her pain. I will never forget scenes like this. They are etched in my mind forever, everyday scenes in the drug-ravaged life of the heroin addict. I developed a feeling for every last junkie because, as an undercover agent, I witnessed their helpless condition. I came to see them as the ultimate victims. They were victims of their addiction and dependence on heroin, and they were preyed upon by the drug pushers and sought after by the police. The junkies were society's real losers.

Information provided by Tootie corroborated intelligence reports indicating that two Chinamen, Kyung Fung and Hu Kai Wong (also known as Who Wrong Wong), were the biggest heroin dealers in Boston. The problem was that it was virtually impossible to get near them because they operated in the shadows. The sly old men ran whorehouses in Chinatown. Each house had five or six young women between the ages of seventeen and twenty-three working for them. Their modus operandi was the same. All of the girls were junkies, and in exchange for sexual favors and all of the money they earned on the street as prostitutes, the old Chinese drug peddlers provided them with enough heroin to supply their habits. Various girls told me that the sexual appetites of Kyung Fung and Who Wrong Wong belied their age. The girls were captives in this web of addiction and perversion. There was no escaping because of their insatiable desire for heroin.

The old men benefited further from these young addicts by using them to distribute the heroin. The women effectively protected the dealers from prosecution because the men never made direct sales of the drugs to anyone. In fact, no one ever saw the men. This made it almost impossible to apprehend Fung and Wong. Tootie, however, changed all that.

On May 19, 1972, I made my first heroin buy from Hu Kai Wong in Boston's Chinatown. Tootie and I went to the South Seas Restaurant on Harrison Avenue, where Tootie made a brief call from a public telephone. Chris Regan stood across the street and watched us from the doorway of a bar. After the telephone call, Tootie and I went around the corner, through an entrance door, and up a long set of squeaky stairs in a dark, dingy hallway. A small, slightly built Chinese man stood on the landing at the top of the stairs. There were no introductions. Who Wrong began speaking in broken English.

"You got money?"

I tried to engage him in conversation, in order to find out more about him, but Who Wrong refused to answer my questions. "Hurry up! Give me money! Get out before police come!" Who Wrong said, and I did just that. With this curt, demanding, tight-lipped approach to a heroin sale, "Operation Seaboard," the government's code name for the Chinese caper, began. As Operation Seaboard unfolded, Tootie introduced me to a number of other midlevel heroin dealers and then finally to Kyung Fung, one of the alleged kingpins.

Chinatown became our new area of operation, and we worked there for the next several months. Every night I would drive downtown, let Chris out of my powder blue Cadillac convertible in the dark, then make the turn slowly onto Tyler Street, park my pimpmobile in an obvious place by the curb, and wait. I would sit with the windows down and the radio blasting loudly, until Tootie showed up. She would pretend to give me her earnings from the street, and we would hold hands and strut around Chinatown and the Combat Zone. To the casual observer, I was a pimp and Tootie was my whore. I would pretend to get fresh with her some nights, and I would pretend to get rough with her on others. Sometimes I would hug and kiss her and call her baby, and other times I would slap her around and call her bitch. We were the perfect criminal couple in the warped, perverted world in which we were operating. In her high heels, jacked-up miniskirt, and slightly overdone makeup, Tootie was the stereotypical hooker. With Tootie on my arm, at three a.m., in Chinatown, I was the typical pimp.

In reality, each time Tootie got close enough for me to kiss, she would whisper bits and pieces of intelligence information in my ear. It was intelligence that was vital for developing our case, obtaining search warrants for locations, and getting arrest warrants for individual drug dealers. After Tootie reported information to me, she would disappear for a time, and I would make a call from a pay phone to let Chris know what was going on. We did this night after night throughout a long, hot summer. We bought heroin from different Chinese dealers, located stash pads, and identified distribution patterns. I worked undercover, alone, but I never worried. No matter where I was, I knew that Chris was always nearby. If I glanced out of the corner of my eye, there Chris would be, across the street, walking in the same direction. When I made a buy, Chris would stand in a barroom window, looking out at me as he drank a beer. If I were sitting in the pimpmobile, Chris would be watching me from a doorway down the street. I always trusted and knew that Chris would be there in an instant if I ever needed him. You don't get any closer to a guy than trusting him with your life.

Chinatown came alive after hours, when the rest of the city shut down. After the strip clubs, pornography shops, and peep shows in the Combat Zone closed down for the night, the players emptied into the streets and alleys of Chinatown. Pimps, whores, strippers, and bartenders were ready to play. Two o'clock in the morning was the witching hour. Drunks from all the other bars in the city found their way to Chinatown. The action was fast. As the revelers were arriving, a steady stream of vans loaded with workers from suburban restaurants all over the state pulled into the center of Chinatown. They filled the illegal after-hours gambling clubs to play mahjong and other games before returning to their tiny rooms, where they slept, packed in stacked beds like sardines.

After a while the days and nights became a blur because we never took time off. Monday through Sunday we slipped into Chinatown and did our thing. Tootie and I played our roles, and Chris watched and took notes. It was monotonous and tedious at times, and at other times it was very dangerous. We had some close calls: physical encounters with other drug dealers and pimps, which go hand in hand with undercover work. We also had some very funny moments. Several times, people from my past suddenly appeared from nowhere to find me engaged in nefarious, criminal activities. Once, a high school classmate walked by as I was standing in an alley, with my arm around Tootie, and a coke spoon around my neck. I read his mind as he passed. Is it him? he must have wondered as he passed by, hesitating for a moment before glancing back. No, it can't possibly be, he must have concluded, because he never acknowledged me, thank God. Whenever an incident like that happened, I held my breath and said a little prayer. I guess God heard me.

Another potentially dangerous problem was the ever-present Vice Squad. I was hanging around the seedy section of Chinatown that bordered the Combat Zone so much, that the Vice Squad detectives were curious to find out who I was. One detective, John McMahon, put his face about two inches from mine one night and said, "I don't know what you are doing down here, but you don't belong. If I see you spit on the street, I'm gonna lock you up. Do you understand, son?" I understood! Tall and ruggedly handsome, John McMahon was the typical, no-nonsense Irish cop. He had the demeanor of John Wayne. The fear of being arrested by McMahon scared the shit out of me because it could jeopardize our investigation. I was constantly ducking him. (Years later, McMahon and I met through a mutual acquaintance and we became fast friends.)

I developed surprising, though grudging friendships with some of the other pimps in the neighborhood. They would walk by, with their signature walks, and nod or mumble "Mmm" or "Alright" as they walked by. I got to know "Punky," "Green-Eyed Jack," "Butchie Banks," and their ladies from a distance, and they got to know Tootie and me. I was an enigma to them, a white pimp from Southie, and they couldn't figure me out. Pimps are loners, and they are very territorial. The term that the pimps use is "doin' a hard single." We strolled the same streets, and shaped up when we passed one another, each of us affecting the air of the baddest pimp of all. The situation almost came to a head early one morning, when one of the girls got into my car and snuggled up next to me. The girl had one arm around my neck and the other on my knee, when I noticed Butchie Banks, her pimp, loping toward us. She was telling me that she could make more money for me than I could ever spend, when Butchie interrupted her proposal with a tap on the windshield. Butchie was fuming.

"Out, bitch!"

The girl jumped out of the car, and I did too. It had the makings of the showdown at the OK Corral in Chinatown. Butchie caught his lady in a compromising situation. That was a crime in the street, punishable by a severe beating, but I couldn't let that happen. It was not my nature to stand by and watch a pimp beat a woman, but even more important, I could not allow it because it would be an insult to me in my role as a pimp. In street lingo, he would "dis," or "disrespect" me, and I would be history. I did the only thing that I could think of to derail his anger. I warned him, "Butchie, don't you ever put your hands on my wagon again."

Butchie looked at the girl, then back at me.

"What?'

"I said, Butchie, don't ever put your hands on my wagon again."

He looked at the girl again and then back at me. He directed his attention to his girl.

"Mmm, we gots bizniz to take care of."

Butchie and his "lady" walked away arm in arm, and I breathed a sigh of relief. Things worked out that time. I gave Butchie the chance to bow out gracefully, and he did. Pimps don't want to fight, anyway; they're lovers. Plus, he could accept my warning about my car. As a pimp, he understood my attachment to my pimpmobile! I looked across the street at Chris, and I could see him smile as he lit up another cigarette.

Another quiet night in Chinatown, I thought to myself, as I leaned against the façade next to the entrance of a tavern frequented by a diverse mix of Combat Zone regulars, Chinese shop workers, maintenance men from the local university hospital, and assorted losers. It was almost two a.m. and the tavern was about to close, when a panel truck pulled up and parked in front of the entrance. The van obscured the view that Chris and I had of each other. There was a great deal of noise, loud Chinese voices that became louder as the doors opened and six young martial arts types danced out of the van in combative poses and sprang toward me. I stood up straight to prepare myself for the attack, but they whirled past me and entered the bar. Chris followed behind in their path with his hand inside his shirt, ready to remove his nickel-plated 45-caliber pistol and start blasting. When he realized that I was not the group's target, he raised his eyebrows, removed his empty hand from inside his open shirt, and walked past me. I resumed my position nonchalantly, with my back against the façade, one foot on the sidewalk, and the other on the wall. I could hear muffled noises from inside the bar, like a sound track from a Bruce Lee martial arts film. Suddenly, the tavern door opened violently. The six men who had gone in moments earlier came crashing out onto the street. Carrying a badly beaten Chinese youth, they stuffed him, shouting and hollering, into the van. Although I had been startled, I resumed my leaning and tried to appear as disinterested as possible. The van full of Chinese warriors pulled quickly away from the curb and disappeared around the corner onto Harrison Avenue. Chris stood hidden across the street, shaking his head. The dazed barroom patrons flowed out onto the sidewalk, under the streetlights, and stared at one another in disbelief.

One of the regulars looked at me and asked, "What happened, man?"

"I didn't see nothin', man," I answered. "I don't know what you're talkin' about."

He nodded, looked back at the others, and said, "He didn't see nothin'."

The others nodded at the regular, then nodded at me, and stumbled away into the night. That's how it is in the early morning hours in Chinatown.

Although we were working deep undercover long into the night, our bosses required that we continue to report to work in the daytime. Monday through Friday we went into the office around ten a.m. to do paperwork and process the evidence. Chris and I were constantly justifying our case to supervisors and answering their questions, like Why are you spending so much time in Chinatown? Why are you down there so late at night? Why are you spending so much money?

We knew why we were spending so much time in Chinatown, because that was where the dope was! We were down there late at night and early in the morning, because that was when the action was! And it seemed obvious to us that we spent so much money because heroin, and the pursuit of heroin, cost money! We were developing the case on our own, with only the help of the Boston Police. We were no burden on our office because we never requested manpower. What were they complaining about? It was so frustrating to listen to this harassment, but we had to put up with it because we were zeroing in on some of the biggest names in Chinatown. Our intelligence all pointed to Benny Yang, the owner of the China Dream Restaurant and the unofficial mayor of Chinatown. Chris and I were very excited. After months of undercover work, the pieces of the puzzle were falling into place. Just before we completed it, though, someone mixed them all up.

On a warm summer night, Chris and I and several Boston Police detectives were sitting around a desk in a corner of the drug control unit of the Boston Police headquarters. The night got hotter as we sat there, trying to convince John Sheffield to do something that we didn't want to do ourselves.

"For chrissakes, you goddam feds say one thing and do another!" Detective Sheffield vented his displeasure at the prospect of bringing in an unknown agent.

"John, you know that's not true," Chris pleaded. "Downs told us that Washington was taking over the case, and we were ordered to support them."

"Support them, my arse! Tootie's mine. They ain't gonna tell me what to do. Those big feelin' arseholes," Sheffield continued bitterly.

"We agree with you, John. You initiated the case. We owe it to you, you know that. Now the bigwigs want to step in and take over. They want to tell us what to do, and they want all the credit. We're bullshit!" Chris screamed.

"If we don't do it their way, then the case is over. They take their ball and bat and go home," I added.

"Well, what is it that they want?" Sheffield offered.

"They have a Chinese agent who speaks the same dialect as Kyung Fung and Who Wrong Wong, and they want Tootie to bring him around. They figure he can do a better job than Paulie and me."

"A Chinese BNDD agent?" Sheffield inquired.

"No, he is actually an IRS agent; Washington is borrowing him for his language capabilities."

"He any good undercover?" Sheffield seemed to bend a little.

"We'll soon find out!" Chris smiled.

"I don't like it, Chris, but for you, I'll do it. Have the Chinese guy here at eleven tomorrow night. And tell those arseholes you work for, I'm doin' it for you and Paulie. If the Chinaman comes here with anyone else, it's no go."

"John, you're a good man," I said, as we all shook hands and ended our meeting.

When Chris and I left headquarters, we both felt lousy and for a good reason. As usual, we had initiated another good case, and Washington was throwing a monkey wrench into the works. The next day we met our new undercover replacement, and from the beginning we could see that he was a square peg in a round hole. Mr. Li was Chinese, and he spoke a dialect similar to that spoken by Kyung Fung and Who Wrong Wong, but that is the only thing that he had going for him. He was a bookish-looking fellow with Coke-bottle, horn-rimmed glasses and a personality to match. The extent of Mr. Li's undercover work experience consisted of examining the books of an illegal Chinese gambling operation in San Francisco after it was raided. When we told him that he was going to be introduced by a hooker to a Chinese heroin dealer so that he could buy heroin, his face dropped. Whoever sent him up from Washington failed to mention this minor point; Li thought that he was going to listen to wiretaps and interpret the dialogue! Chris and I informed our supervisors of Mr. Li's misconceptions, but they told us to disregard his wishes and immediately put him to work undercover. After convincing the Boston detectives and Tootie to attempt the impossible, we staged Mr. Li's undercover entry into the Chinese underworld of drug trafficking on a moonlit Friday night.

At approximately ten o'clock, we let Mr. Li and Tootie out of the van at the corner of Tyler and Pearl Street, a few blocks away from Kyung Fung's building. Chris and I proceeded in the van to a location on Harrison Avenue, between Essex and Tyler, where we parked. Boston Police Detectives

Sheffield and Moore remained in the back of the undercover van while Chris and I got out and went into the bar directly across the street from Kyung Fung's residence. We stood at the bar near the front window and watched as Mr. Li and Tootie walked into view, alongside the South Seas Restaurant. From our vantage point in the bar we observed that there appeared to be some confusion, along with some animated conversation. Mr. Li handed Tootie some cash and then stood waiting on the sidewalk while she went to Kyung Fung's doorway and promptly disappeared inside.

Chris and I looked at each other and rolled our eyes. We stood at the window in disbelief as we sipped our beers and watched nerdy Mr. Li standing alone in front of the restaurant. It was obvious that our plan went awry on the very first try. We had gone over the plan with Tootie and Mr. Li again and again for hours the night before. "You both go to the door," we instructed. "You both enter, and Tootie introduces Mr. Li to Kyung Fung. Mr. Li then buys an ounce of heroin from Kyung Fung for twelve hundred dollars." What went wrong? Chris and I knew. Tootie was a junkie. She conned Mr. Li into giving her the buy money! One hour and forty-five minutes later Tootie emerged from Kyung Fung's doorway, and we watched lamely as she and Mr. Li headed back to the prearranged meeting spot. Chris and I went back to the van, and as soon as we opened the door, the detectives started razzing us.

When we picked up Tootie and Mr. Li at the corner of Harrison Avenue and Hayward Place, John Sheffield tore into Tootie. "You son of a bitch! You had us out there for two hours while you shot up! You're a no-good, ungrateful son of a bitch! You're just like the rest of them!"

"I'm sorry, John." Tootie slurred a pathetic apology.

I looked at Mr. Li, and he looked back with embarrassment. He was bewildered, way out of his league.

"What the hell happened to our plan?" Chris yelled.

"Tootie say change plan," Mr. Li answered sheepishly.

"Tootie say change plan?" Chris repeated, mimicking Mr. Li's voice. "Well, I got news for you, you asshole! Tootie ain't runnin' this show, Mr. Li. She can't change shit. What the hell's wrong with you?" Chris yelled in Li's face.

We all got into the van and drove back to police headquarters in silence. Together with the detectives, Chris and I went over the plan for the next buy with Tootie and Mr. Li. We made them rehearse it over and over, so that there was no misunderstanding. Then we took Mr. Li to his hotel room and went over the plan again. We called our group supervisor, Todd Downs, at home and told him what happened. He laughed and said that it was all right because it was Mr. Li's first time! If Chris and I had ever given a similar performance, we would have been fired. To make matters worse, when the heroin was tested at the laboratory, it contained only traces of heroin. Chinese heroin was the purest in the country, and Mr. Li's bag was less than 1 percent heroin. Tootie took most of the heroin that she bought with government money and gave Mr. Li the leftovers. We had been taken.

Several days later we tried again. This time, Chris and I set up in the observation van, while Detectives Moore and Sheffield went into the bar and watched from the window. From inside the van, we peered through the one-way glass windows as Tootie and Mr. Li walked into view. They stopped in front of the South Seas so Tootie could make a telephone call, and Mr. Li stood nearby, nervously looking around. Tootie hung up the phone and walked with Mr. Li to Kyung Fung's doorway. Chris and I gave each other a high five as Tootie and Mr. Li entered the hallway and disappeared up the stairs together. We were excited to think that the case was back on track again. Detective Sheffield called us from inside the bar and congratulated us on our Chinese agent's fine beginning.

As the hours slowly passed, our happiness began to fade. At midnight Detective Sheffield called us from inside the bar again. "Where the hell are they?" he asked.

"God only knows," I answered.

"Here she comes!" Chris interrupted urgently. "She's alone."

"She's out. She's alone," I repeated over the telephone to Sheffield.

"Son of a bitch! Something's wrong," Sheffield replied. "I'm gonna see what's goin' on."

Chris and I watched through the window as Tootie stumbled away from the doorway, struggling to stand up. Disoriented, she sat down on the step of the South Seas Restaurant, her knees spread apart, with her miniskirt hiked up around her hips, and her head drooping forward. John Sheffield, dressed in street clothes, walked up to her and leaned over. He cupped her face in his hands and said something to her. Then he helped Tootie up, walked her to Kyung Fung's doorway, and left her. He continued walking down Harrison Avenue toward Beech Street. We watched as Tootie stumbled back inside the entrance to Kyung Fung's apartment building, and Detective Sheffield walked out of sight. Moments later, the phone rang.

"Tootie's high. Mr. Li waited in another room while Tootie bought the dope from Kyung Fung. She shot up, and she's starting to come out of it. Now she doesn't know where Mr. Li is. I told her to go back inside and get Mr. Li's ass out of there. I got the dope. I took what's left of it from her," Detective Sheffield reported to us.

I could sense the anger and frustration in Detective Sheffield's voice. I had the same feeling, and I didn't know what to say. As we were talking, Tootie and Mr. Li emerged from the doorway. Tootie was walking back toward the rendezvous spot with her elbows out to the side, brushing her hair back with one hand and holding her purse in the other, swinging her hips garishly from side to side. Mr. Li followed her like Mr. Magoo. When we pulled up, an angry Sheffield got out of the van and lectured Tootie as if she were a naughty schoolgirl.

"Don't you ever pull that shit on me again! I'll have your ass in jail so fast, your head will spin! Do you hear me?" Sheffield admonished Tootie with the rigor of an army drill sergeant.

"I'm shorry," Tootie slurred.

"It's not her!" Chris yelled as he glared at Mr. Li. "It's the asshole with her! We tell him to do one thing, and he does another!"

Mr. Li looked down at the ground. He was not used to such a verbal assault. Mr. Li was scared to death. I could see that the situation was deteriorating.

"Let's call it a night," I said, as I winked a high sign to Steve Moore, the other Boston detective who was working with us.

"Enough's enough," Steve responded on cue. "Let's adjourn for the night and get some rest."

Our plan was perfect, but our people were not. We found out that as soon as they had gone inside, Tootie told Mr. Li that Kyung Fung would not sell directly to him. She convinced Mr. Li to wait for her in an empty apartment while she went into Fung's apartment to buy the heroin. Tootie bought the heroin and shot some of it into her arm. Mr. Li, with a Stanford graduate degree, could not match wits with Tootie, an eighth grade dropout! Junkies are pathetic, hopeless people in many ways, but they are ingenious when it comes to getting a fix. Mr. Li was a smart man and a linguist, but he was not an undercover guy. He was putty in Tootie's hands.

We dropped Tootie and Mr. Li off, then drove back to the federal building and put the heroin in our evidence locker. We needed to unwind after another frustrating night, so Chris and I went to J. J. Foley's Bar on Berkeley Street in the South End, where we listened to Irish jukebox music and complained to each other till four a.m.

The next day, with two strikes against Mr. Li, Chris and I went to Todd Downs to plead with him to take Mr. Li off our case. When we finished explaining, Todd Downs smiled and told us to do our job. Our job, Downs reminded us, was to do what Washington wanted us to do. He told us to make it work with Mr. Li because Washington thought very highly of him. We fretted and fumed, but we had no choice. It was back to the street with Mr. Li.

On this particular night, the Red Sox were playing, so the Combat Zone was busier than usual with out-of-town baseball fans. There was action in the air. It's an odd phenomenon, but business in the bars, strip clubs, and on the street increases noticeably whenever there is a game at Fenway Park, in another part of town. Buses from New Hampshire, Maine, Vermont, Connecticut, and Rhode Island drop the fans off at Park Square, and that is as close to the park as some of them ever get. Since Mr. Li had two strikes on him already, it was an appropriate night for him to take another swing.

Chris and I had another strategy session with Tootie and Mr. Li at Boston Police headquarters. We mapped out their evening very clearly for them, leaving no room for failure. At approximately midnight, Detectives Sheffield and Moore dropped Tootie and Mr. Li off at the intersection of the Southeast Expressway and Tyler Street. Then they drove the undercover surveillance van to Harrison Avenue and parked across from the South Seas. Detectives Sheffield and Moore got out of the van and went into the bar. Chris and I took up our surveillance position in the rear of the van. At approximately 12:20 a.m. we could see Tootie and Mr. Li walk into sight and proceed to Kyung Fung's doorway. Both Tootie and Mr. Li entered, and Chris and I simultaneously whispered, "Alright!"

After the first hour, with no sign of Tootie or Mr. Li, our confidence level dropped and our patience began to wear thin. We watched that door for two hours, while a steady stream of Chinese, junkies, hookers, and tricks went in and out. Detectives Sheffield and Moore called us periodically from the pay phone in the bar and we speculated about Tootie and Mr. Li, and what they were doing. At three a.m. Tootie came marching out of the building with Mr. Li in tow. They walked on the sidewalk in front of the South Seas toward our predesignated meeting spot. Tootie was dragging Mr. Li like a reluctant puppy on a leash. Sheffield and Moore got back into the van. We all agreed that something was wrong, but we didn't know what. Sheffield drove as fast as he could to the meeting place, and we all practically jumped out when he stopped the van next to Tootie and Mr. Li.

"What happened?" Chris asked quickly in a demanding tone.

"We bought the dope," Tootie answered.

"*We* bought the dope?" Chris repeated.

"Yeah," Tootie answered with her eyelids opening and closing sluggishly as she swayed lazily from side to side.

"How did *we* buy the dope?" Chris demanded impatiently.

"He, he did. Mr. Li made the buy," Tootie answered tentatively, her eyes glancing back and forth between Chris and Mr. Li.

"I did the buy," Mr. Li stated unequivocally.

As Chris looked around at the detectives and me to see our reaction, Tootie clumsily withdrew a package from inside her halter top and handed it to Mr. Li. Chris snatched the package out of his hand.

"What's this?" Chris demanded.

"What you think it is?" Mr. Li retorted sarcastically.

Chris grabbed Mr. Li by the throat and pulled him up on his tiptoes as he shouted, "Listen, you little sawed-off Mr. Peepers, I'm askin' the questions around here. You understand? I've had about as much of you as I can take! Now, who bought the dope? Why does Tootie have the dope if you bought it?"

"I buy. I buy, Chris," Mr. Li answered desperately in beginner English.

We knew that something was wrong, but we were not going to find the answer from Tootie and Mr. Li.

"He bought the dope from Kyung Fung. That's what you wanted," Tootie interjected with slurred speech.

"Yeah, so what was it doing in your bra?" Chris snapped. "What the hell were you doing in there for two and a half hours?"

Tootie stopped talking, copped an attitude, and clammed up. She stared right back at Chris through glassy eyes. We decided to end the staring contest at that point. We were at an impasse. After we left Tootie, the detectives drove the rest of us back to headquarters. Chris and I took Mr. Li back to his hotel, went to the federal building, and locked the heroin in the evidence locker. Then we went to J. J. Foley's for a hot dog and a couple of beers.

"This Mr. Li is a problem," Chris began, after a sip of Miller.

"He's a little difficult to work with," I agreed.

As I looked in the mirror, I could see John Sheffield enter the bar through the side door, followed by Steve Moore.

"Hey, John, you found us," I turned around and said with a laugh.

"Your Mr. Li bought the heroin from Kyung Fung alright, but he handed it over to Tootie to hold after she fixed him up with Suzie Q," Sheffield started somberly and sarcastically, as he picked up the Miller that I ordered for him.

"He what?" Chris asked.

"Tootie needed a fix, so she set Mr. Li up for a quickie with Suzie Q, and Mr. Li gave the dope to her to mind, so he wouldn't get ripped off while he and Suzie were getting to know each other," Sheffield explained. "Meanwhile Tootie goes into the other room and shoots up with the rest of Kyung Fung's girls. Suzie Q made fast work of Mr. Li, then joined Tootie. Mr. Li waited alone in the room by himself for two hours until Tootie finally returned. That package that Tootie handed Mr. Li was what was left of the dope after she and the rest of the girls shot up."

"I dare say, our evidence will prove to be a little lighter and more diluted than anticipated," Steve Moore joked dryly.

"What did you say about three strikes and you're out, Paulie?" Chris asked, as he looked at me.

The next morning we went to Downs with Mr. Li's undercover exploits. That afternoon, Mr. Li was on an airplane back to Washington, where he belonged. Operation Seaboard was immediately put on hold. Downs's simple analysis of the fiasco was summed up in his response, "You two really screwed this case up."

Downs's words hit me like a kick in the stomach. Chris and I began this investigation, thoroughly convinced that it would lead us to the heroin source in Hong Kong. We worked day and night, without respite, neglecting our families and ourselves, as we "chased the dragon" with an enthusiasm known only to men on a mission, but we were stopped in our tracks by another bureaucratic wall.

Chris and I spent the next couple of days typing reports and writing affidavits for search and arrest warrants. The long hours of undercover work and surveillance were all falling away to nothing in a flurry of paperwork. My final trip to the federal court to secure signatures of approval on the search warrants added to my frustration. I walked into the office of U.S. Magistrate Rafael Roncari and stood at the counter waiting, while his receptionist looked at me and smiled, then answered the telephone.

"Hello, Mr. Yang. Yes, sir," the receptionist answered, as she continued to look at me and smile. She then punched a button on her telephone and said loudly, "Magistrate Roncari, Mr. Yang is on the line for you."

"Is that Mr. Yang, from the Chinese Civic Association?" I asked matter-of-factly.

"Yes. He is so nice," the receptionist replied.

"You know him?" I asked in disbelief.

"Oh, very well. He and Magistrate Roncari are longtime friends. He always brings me fortune cookies whenever he drops by the office. They are having lunch together this afternoon," she added.

Magistrate Roncari and Benny Yang are longtime friends? A sudden nauseous feeling came over me. Benny Yang was the main man in Chinatown. He was behind all of the heroin. Benny Yang was the mastermind. All of our intelligence pointed to him. Were Chris and I the only ones who thought that this heroin ring was for real? Magistrate Roncari signed each and every one of our warrants from the beginning of Operation Seaboard. It was beginning to sound more like Operation Stonewall to me.

When I returned to the office, I told Chris about the secretary's unwitting disclosure. He was stunned. We were both so angry and disappointed to see our case go up in smoke that we decided to call it a day. We had to get out of the office before Todd Downs said something to frustrate us. He was sitting on a keg of dynamite, and we didn't need much to set us off.

"Paulie, whaddaya say we drop into Brandy Pete's for a sandwich and a beer?" Chris proposed. It was almost three o'clock in the afternoon, and neither of us had eaten anything all day long.

"Sounds good to me."

Brandy Pete's was a gin mill on Broad Street, in the financial district, that catered to corporate lawyers and investment people. It was a place where we could slip in anonymously and unwind without bumping into any government types. Several of the suits at the bar stared at us momentarily. We were not average customers, obviously. Our hair, muscle shirts, and jeans set us apart immediately. Chris and I met their stares, then looked at each other and chuckled as we found our way to a corner booth. Chris sat with his back to the wall, and I sat facing him, watching the entire bar in the mirror behind him. I could see the waitress as she approached us.

"Two Millers and two cheeseburger specials," Chris ordered.

"Sounds like you guys know what you want. I like that," the waitress answered as she scribbled in her pad. She smiled seductively and quickly brought us two Millers from the bar, then turned around and disappeared into the kitchen.

Chris smiled as he spoke of the waitress in the short, tight-fitting skirt and sipped his bottle of beer. "She doesn't waste any time."

By the time our cheeseburgers were delivered to the table, Chris was finished with his beer.

"Two more," Chris requested.

"No, I'm all set for now," I said, as the waitress looked at me, and then at Chris.

"Two more," Chris demanded as he stared coldly at the waitress, then added with a smile, "for me."

We sat and talked about Operation Seaboard. We had worked without rest all summer, and now it was going nowhere. Washington pretty boys stole our case, and then they ruined it. The more we talked, the more frustrated we became, and I could see Chris glancing toward the bar. The suits reminded us both of the pretty boys in Washington and the alcohol was fuel to the fire. I looked at my watch and it was almost nine o'clock. We had been sitting there for more than a few hours, and I realized that it was time to go.

"Chris, whaddaya say we make a move?" I said.

"I'm ready, Paulie," Chris answered with a smile. "The fat boy's mine!"

I laughed as I looked at the two heavy guys in suits sipping cocktails at the bar. "No, Chris, I mean, home. Let's get outta here and go home."

"You never want to have any fun," Chris laughed good-naturedly as we got up to leave.

"That wouldn't be fun. Besides, we don't need to get into any more trouble. Isn't there a law against hitting guys with glasses?" I joked.

I led the way out of the bar, carefully staying as far away from the guys in suits as I possibly could. I knew that one wrong look could lead to a double knockout, and I did not want that to happen.

"Let's go back, Paulie," Chris said, shadowboxing as we left the bar.

"Hey, what do we need them for? We got each other!" I laughed, as I threw a few left jabs into the air myself, trying to distract him.

"I don't mean them. I mean the waitress!" Chris laughed, good-naturedly.

We stepped off the curb and walked along Broad Street. I could smell the ocean a few blocks away, and it made the night seem cooler. High overhead the streetlights shined with halos around them. The financial district was almost empty at this time of night.

"Paulie, you think I can shoot that streetlight out?" Chris teased.

"What?"

"You think I can shoot the light out?" Chris repeated.

"That one?" I asked quickly, as I drew my nickel-plated forty-five and fired a shot at the streetlight in front of us. The noise of the gun blast reverberated like thunder between the buildings, and glass fell to the vacant street like snowflakes.

"No, that one!" Chris laughed, spinning around and shooting out the streetlight behind us. "I need the rest of my ammo in case I see Todd Downs, or else I would shoot them all out!" He laughed again and blew the smoke from his pistol for effect, before he stuck it back into his waistband.

We continued walking in silence toward the waterfront. I felt relaxed for the first time in months. I felt like we had control. The frustration was gone. In the distance, I could hear sirens.

"Oops!" Chris giggled and glanced over at me.

The sirens got louder, and I could see a Boston Police cruiser out of the corner of my eye. The siren fell silent and the cruiser inched up slowly next to us. We ignored it and continued walking.

"Chris?" a voice called out from the cruiser.

"How'd you guess?" Chris quipped, without looking.

"Well, I wasn't sure, seein' only two lights were gone, an not the entire street," the voice with the Irish brogue answered, then added facetiously, "You must be followin' the guys that shot the lights out, I would imagine."

"That's exactly the case," Chris chuckled.

The old-time sergeant put the microphone to his mouth and announced, as he shook his head, "These are not the subjects! I repeat. These men are not the subjects. All units back off." As the cruiser drove away, the sergeant stuck his right arm out the window, without looking back, and waved good-bye to us.

"They don't make 'em like that anymore," Chris mused.

"You know everyone, Chris," I marvelled.

"You don't need to know everyone, Paulie, you just need to know the right one," Chris answered.

We were finally ready to call it a night, knowing we had a long day ahead of us. We would officially conclude Operation Seaboard with a series of early-morning raids, beginning at six a.m., designed to catch the subjects unaware and, preferably, still sleeping.

The next morning, Chris and I went over the plan together, then briefed the raiding parties. Numerous arrest and search warrants would be carried out simultaneously at the designated hour to prevent leaks. Once a raid or arrest is effected, the word travels fast. As soon as the word gets out that "the law" is coming, evidence is destroyed and subjects flee. We wanted to confiscate as much heroin as possible and prevent flight. When subjects become fugitives, they are extremely difficult to find and the process is very time-consuming. Chris and I wanted to personally execute the search and arrest warrant on Kyung Fung. He was the first, and seemingly most diabolical of all the subjects. We all left the John F. Kennedy Federal Office Building shortly after five a.m.

I was stepping slowly and softly on the squeaky wooden floor of the dimly lit hallway approaching Kyung Fung's apartment. Sweat dropped off of my forehead as I looked at my watch. It was 5:55 a.m. At exactly six o'clock, Chris would jump through the rear window and I would crash the front door down to surprise Kyung Fung. I could picture Chris standing on the fire escape, five stories high, waiting to spring through the window. As I glanced at my watch, the time seemed to tick by ever so slowly. At six, I hit the wooden door as hard as I could with my shoulder, but it did not open. At that same moment, I heard a loud crash and the sound of shattered glass. The adrenaline was pumping as I backed up as far as I could and charged the door again. This time it popped open and I stood there with my government-issue Smith and Wesson 38-caliber pistol pointed straight ahead, sweeping the apartment with my eyes. I could hear loud screams coming from a back room, and as I moved quickly in that direction, I could hear Chris's voice. The screaming subsided.

"Stay right where you are, ladies, until the rest of the party arrives," Chris ordered.

"Good morning, Paulie, glad you could make it," he added, as I opened the bedroom door.

"Glad to be here," I wisecracked, looking around the room. Three hookers, in varying states of undress, were standing or slouching in front of Chris, and they were not happy to be there.

"Mr. Kyung Fung is not here, unfortunately, for his own party. So there will not be any telephone calls allowed, if you know what I mean. It's a surprise party, and we wouldn't want to ruin everything for him," Chris said to the girls.

"We have rights, you know. You just can't come bargin' in on us. We're ladies. We get a right to make a call," the hookers complained.

"You are right, ladies, you are entitled to a complete set of rights according to U.S. government policy and procedure. So, let's make sure that you receive everything that you have coming," Chris assured them, and they smiled.

"Paulie," Chris continued, "would you kindly place a set of handcuffs on each of the ladies as provided by U.S. government policy. And be sure to place their hands behind their backs."

"You bastard! You can't do that to us," the hookers yelled, as I began cuffing them one at a time.

"Oh, yes I can!" Chris assured them.

The hookers looked at us sadly as I recited the Miranda warnings, and it began to sink in that they were under arrest for violation of the federal narcotics law. Detecting a moment of weakness, Chris began, "Of course, you beautiful ladies don't deserve to be thrown in jail with the dregs of society, and we, as special agents, know that. Therefore, we would like to offer you a chance to redeem yourselves. We are interested in Kyung Fung, not you. If you would like to tell us where we can find him, we have the power to release you. Now, which one of you is going to be the first on your block to give the correct answer?"

The young but hard-bitten hookers looked at each other, and we could see that none of them wanted to go to jail. Before long they each gave up as much information as they could about Kyung Fung and where we could find him. We dispatched a team of surveillance agents to "put the peek" on Kyung Fung at his other address, while we went back to court and obtained a search warrant. It was late morning before Chris and I arrived with the warrant.

"It's that doorway on the corner, Chris. The oak door with the leaded glass," Jack Fender, one of the agents, pointed out.

"Any activity?" Chris asked.

"Not much. A white female in jeans and a red T-shirt, looked like a hooker, went in about two hours ago. Another white female in a white blouse, black skirt, black stockings, and suede shoes went in about fifteen minutes ago. The second one looked clean-cut," Jack answered.

"Have you seen Kyung Fung?" Chris asked next.

"It's hard to tell. An old Chinese guy answered the door the first time. I think it was him. The description fit, but I didn't get a good look," Jack explained.

"That's him," Chris assured us.

"I'm pretty sure," Jack nodded.

"You and Paulie take the front door. I'll go around the back. Give me about five minutes to get set up. Let's go," Chris instructed, as we got out of the car and closed the doors quietly. We all walked to the corner. Jack and I stopped, and Chris continued to the rear of the building. I leaned up against the bricks and peeked around the corner so that I could see the sidewalk in front of Kyung Fung's.

"Paulie, you all set?" Chris's muffled voice came out of the walkie-talkie.

"All set," I answered quietly as the adrenaline started pumping.

"Let's do it!" Chris commanded.

Jack and I hurried around the corner and up the stairs to the entrance. I jumped in the air and delivered a solid kick just above the doorknob. The door flew open and we rushed inside.

"Everybody freeze! Federal agents!" I shouted, as I pointed my service revolver straight in front of me. I could hear Chris and the other agents as they knocked down the rear door. Over the sights of my revolver I looked into the eyes of a terrified young girl. She was startled by our entry and attempted to button up her blouse while standing awkwardly alone in front of us.

"Put your hands on the dresser, and don't move," I said.

The terrified girl, with her blouse still hanging open, carefully placed her trembling hands on the dresser. Tears began to flow from her eyes as she stood there looking sad and lost in the middle of the drug world.

I walked closer and cuffed her wrists behind her back. I saw that she had no weapons as I guided her away from the dresser and stood her in the middle of the room. I could hear Chris and the other agents in the other room. They apparently had Kyung Fung and someone else under arrest. I noticed that the girl with the open blouse had fresh blood on the inside of her arm.

"What's that from?" I asked.

"It's from the needle," she answered quietly, almost repentantly.

Her answer confirmed my thoughts, and it made my stomach turn.

"I was clean for six months. I went back to school. I was doing so good, and my parents were so proud of me," she wondered out loud. "I came to Boston today to go shopping and I thought about that feeling. I went right to a pay phone and called Kyung Fung. He told me to come over, and I did. I couldn't say no. I couldn't stay away."

After Kyung Fung and Hu Kai Wong were arrested, they were released on bail and became fugitives. Months later, we located Wong living in a Boston suburb and arrested him without incident. Almost a year after his initial arrest, we found Fung living in New York City. He attempted to escape, but was captured and arrested on a fire escape in New York's Chinatown. Fung and Wong were sentenced to ten years in federal prison. Both men were released before their sentences were completed.

The arrests and seizures that resulted from Operation Seaboard temporarily interrupted the flow of Hong Kong heroin into the country. Within several months, however, new players replaced Hu Kai Wong, Kyung Fung, and the others. Unknown smuggling methods were implemented, new patterns of distribution were set up, and before long, the heroin supply was flowing once again.

Benny Yang managed to avoid prosecution in Operation Seaboard, but was later convicted for racketeering. After serving time in federal prison, Yang was released and returned to Boston's Chinatown.

In a candid discussion, Magistrate Roncari, a wonderful man of unquestionable character, told me that he felt shock and disbelief when he first learned of Benny Yang's double life and his involvement in the criminal underworld. The honesty in his eye convinced me that the magistrate was not capable of duplicity. The magistrate could not hide the embarrassment that he felt by his naiveté.

Tootie disappeared shortly after the culmination of Operation Seaboard and was never seen again.

INFORMANT

Lucifer, a Boston hot spot, stood in the shadow of the famous neon Citgo sign at Kenmore Square. Danny Santarpio, Jason Germano, and I were regular customers there during our undercover investigation of the nightclub scene. Lucifer, appropriately named, attracted a young, upscale crowd. It was a disco. Many of the patrons came from local colleges; Boston University, Northeastern University, and Simmons were right in the neighborhood. Boston College was only a trolley ride away. Students from everywhere flocked to Lucifer to dance and mix with young Bostonians. Lucifer was also a drug dealer's paradise. My usual routine was to go to the bar, get my messages from the bartender, then get a beer and stand off to the side to watch the action. One night, as I was straining my eyes to read my scribbled messages in the dim light, a pretty young woman approached me cautiously and smiled. She was an advertisement for beatnik chic. Dressed entirely in black, she wore a sweater over a turtleneck jersey, a short skirt, tights, and clogs. A French beret added to her bohemian look.

"Hi, Sully," she greeted me, seductively.

"Hi." I crumpled up the piece of paper, quickly stuffing it in my jacket pocket, so I could direct my attention to the young Garbo before me. She glowed with the luster of youth. Her almost childlike look of innocence belied her studied attempt to appear cosmopolitan and worldly. She was about nineteen.

"I'm with Bobby," she volunteered.

Bobby was a young, part-time bar back (an apprentice bartender), a Boston University dropout. He had started working at the club when the fall semester began, then his grades dropped, and he flunked out of school. I knew him slightly, and he seemed to be a pretty good kid. Lately, though, I suspected that he was starting to experiment with drugs. He was probably twenty-one, just old enough to work legally in a licensed drinking establishment. That explained the young woman's underage presence at the nightclub.

"He's a nice kid," I acknowledged.

"Thanks. I'm Martha," she added, in a curiously friendly way.

"I gotta be goin'. I'll catch you later," I said, coolly.

"I hope so," she responded quickly, with a flirtatious smile. I hustled through the crowd and left the bar.

Wow. Martha, what a beautiful girl, I kept thinking long afterwards. I wonder what she wants? The suspicions I had as an undercover guy led me to wonder if she somehow knew that I was a cop.

As time went on, I realized that was not the case. During my many trips to Lucifer, I got to know more about her. I was a good listener and after many extended conversations, we developed a certain trust. Eventually, she began to confide in me, as if I were her older brother. She told me about her professors and her classes at Boston University and how she missed her little brother and sisters and her parents in her sleepy hometown in rural New Hampshire.

One night, after finishing my conversation with a dope dealer, I handed the telephone to the bartender to hang up. When I turned around, I caught Derek Sanderson, the Boston Bruins star center and infamous bad boy, looking at me. I seized the moment to step closer and extend my hand, and he willingly obliged. I leaned closer and spoke into his ear to congratulate him on the win over the Montreal Canadians earlier in the evening. Sanderson, his eyes glancing down at the diamond-studded coke spoon dangling from a thick gold chain I wore around my neck, thanked me for the compliment in a very Canadian accent. I noticed Martha in the distance on her tiptoes, craning her neck, and I told Sanderson that I wanted to introduce him to a good fan. I signaled Martha to join us. She made a gesture with the tips of her fingers of both hands to her chest. I nodded my head emphatically, yes. Reluctantly, she came to us, and Sanderson autographed a napkin for her little brother. She blushed when he kissed her on the cheek.

After a while, I began looking forward to seeing her. The drug dealers would approach, and I would excuse myself to make deals. She became an unwitting prop. Many of the dealers assumed she was my girlfriend. She even told me details about her relationship with her boyfriend and the problems that they were having. She seemed to ignore my advice to leave him, though. She must have felt that she could save him from a life of sin.

Martha thought that it was laughable when I began to lecture her one night on the evils of illicit drugs. "Sully, you expect me to listen to that baloney? I am not that young, you know. I know what you do," she teased, coyly.

"You bet I expect you to listen," I responded heatedly. "And you don't know what I do!" Martha smiled nervously at my unexpectedly aggressive response.

"Everyone knows what you do," she assured me. "You are the main guy around here. You're the go-to guy. Every drug dealer in the city comes to see you."

"Don't believe everything you hear, Martha. Have you ever seen me use drugs?" I argued. Martha did not answer the question; she only rolled her eyes in stubborn disbelief.

Martha's fresh wholesomeness and naiveté stood in stark contrast to the shadowy drug culture that was slowly enveloping her boyfriend and threatening her. As the weeks and months went by, I watched as her girlish innocence disappeared. More and more, she seemed to be drifting away from the newness and excitement of college life and sinking deeper and deeper into the netherworld. Her beautiful dark eyes became dull and tired. Her laughing face turned sad. The nervous, worried look of someone burdened with too much on her mind replaced her simple smile. That pretty little country girl was losing her sparkle, and her brightness was fading fast. I could see that the rush and allure of the drug scene was beguiling her. It was something that I had witnessed many times before in my travels in the drug world. I could tell what was happening, but I couldn't stop it.

Driving to work in my dark green Porsche on a sunny December morning, I heard on the eleven o'clock news that a Boston University student had died of an overdose of heroin. The news of the overdose didn't really sink in; it blended in with the hockey scores and the traffic reports. I enjoyed the feeling of the cold, dry air hitting my face as it rushed in through my open window. The sky was blue, the newly fallen snow shone brightly in the glare of the late morning sun, as students and hospital workers rushed about on Longwood Avenue, all bundled up in their woolen scarves and hats. Boston seemed to be bustling and alive in these last days before Christmas, and I loved it. The excitement of the holiday season was in the air. I put on my sunglasses to view the scene.

It wasn't until twelve o'clock that night that I realized the significance of the news flash I had heard earlier in the day. When I stepped inside the door at Lucifer, one of the waitresses rushed over and told me that my friend Martha and her boyfriend had overdosed on heroin the previous night. Both of them died.

As the waitress's words hit me, my mind froze. I was unable to comprehend the magnitude of what she was saying. The words did not register. My mind would not accept the reality of what she was telling me. If I refused to hear the news, then maybe it didn't happen. I wanted to see Martha again. I convinced myself that she would be there tonight. I would just wait around. I was going to tell her about my friend's younger brother, a Boston University hockey player, to get her away from her boyfriend. It's a perfect match. I drifted off in thought.

"Sully, Martha's dead. She's dead," a soft female voice whispered. I felt the waitress, squeezing my hand. She was looking at me with tears running down her cheeks. She was trying to comfort me, but she needed someone to comfort her. There was desolation and despair in her crying eyes.

"What happened?" I asked.

"Her boyfriend, you know how he always wanted her to try heroin. He talked her into it. She did it for him, to prove that she loved him. It was her first time mainlining. She shot up, then he shot up, and they nodded off. They never woke up. It was a hot shot, poison junk," she explained, squeezing my hand tightly in her warm, moist grip. Anger rose up inside of me and tension strained every muscle in my body. Then, the waitress put her face on my chest, her arms around my shoulders, and held onto me like her life depended on it, while she sobbed uncontrollably. I had never spoken to this waitress before in all my visits to the bar, and now she was hanging on to me like a lifeline. It is strange the way things happen in life. My instinct told me to push her away, but I did not. I let her cling to me. That beautiful little girl is dead, I thought to myself, while the waitress cried herself out. Then I picked up her chin and looked into her eyes.

"Baby, it happens," I said, fighting my feelings and trying to look unfazed. She tried to regain her composure, and looked at me for assurance. I couldn't assure her of anything. I was overcome with conflicting emotions. Anger exploded in my gut, while grief tore at my heart.

"I have to go, baby, I have business to take care of," I added, trying to fight back my own tears. I did not feel like working any more that night. I was sick to my stomach.

"Have a drink?" she asked in an effort to keep me from leaving the bar. "It's on me tonight."

"Thanks, baby, but I gotta go," I answered.

"Take me with you," she replied. Her eyes pleaded. She wanted to get away, too. She wanted someone to take care of her and make things right again.

"I would, but I can't take you where I'm going." I didn't know where I was going myself, at this point.

"Please, take me. I can't stand being here any longer," she begged. The dim blinking lights threaded through the silver tinsel of the Christmas decorations encircling the disco underlined the despair in her voice. She was a college kid herself, just like Martha, and the devastation of Martha's overdose was too much for her to bear.

"Here, take a cab. Get outta here and go home." I handed her a ten-dollar bill. I knew that she was hurting, but there was nothing that I could do. She gave me another hug and I could feel her tears on my cheek as she pressed against me, then I pulled away and looked at her.

How many other young people are going to die from drugs, I wondered. I pulled the lapels of my woolen coat together, and nodded one last time. Then I moved quickly through the crowd and left the bar. I took a long deep breath when I got out on the sidewalk. The sadness was overwhelming. As I walked to my car, I noticed the Christmas lights in the windows along Bay State Road. I had all I could do to keep myself from crying. I took a left off Bay State Road onto Granby Street and stopped at the red light where it intersected with Commonwealth Avenue. Waiting in the cold car for the traffic light to change, I watched the cars moving across in front of me when I realized that I was facing 700 Commonwealth Avenue, the dormitory where Martha lived. The finality of it all was too much for me to think about. My mind was numb. Nothing seemed real. I had to get away from Kenmore Square and get out of the drug world. I had to go home.

I passed overloaded trolley cars filled with students on my outbound drive down Commonwealth Avenue through Brighton and Brookline, past Saint Ignatius Church at Boston College, and it struck me that they were all alive. The passengers were all alive. I wanted to look into the window of one of those trolleys and see Martha sitting there with some of her friends.

As I approached the VFW Parkway, I passed Saint Joseph's Cemetery, where my brother Hank was buried. I pictured Hank's headstone inscription, Died March 16, 1968, Vietnam, and I asked him in a prayer to help me make sense out of things. I realized that I still had not been able to comprehend Hank's death. He was only nineteen years old when he was killed in Vietnam, the same age as Martha. My mind went blank again at the thought. It was almost two o'clock in the morning when I pulled into my driveway. I was physically drained. The last thing I did before putting my head on my pillow was to look over at Pam sleeping peacefully. I asked God to protect her always.

The next morning, Pam awakened me with a fresh kiss on the lips. Her nearness enlivened me.

"See you tonight," she said, brightly.

"Tonight? Where are you going?" I asked, sleepily.

"To work," she answered, laughing.

"Go late," I tried.

"I am already late. I will see you tonight. I begin my vacation tonight," she answered again with a laugh. I could hear the door close behind her as she went out. I thought about how much I loved her and how good she was. She was always helping people and she never stopped smiling. She loved life, she loved her work, and she even loved me. I wished that I could be like that. There was no use trying to sleep. The thought of Pam lingered in my mind. I decided to get up and go to work.

I would go into the office and pretend to be busy so that the boss could see me, then I would slip out and go to the gym to work out. Working out always made me feel better. The sky was a gloomy dark gray and the air was damp and cold. My mind drifted back to Martha again. She was standing next to me at Lucifer and we were talking. She was laughing and smiling, and then suddenly everything stopped. Like a snapshot, her laughing face was frozen in time. She was gone forever. She was dead. There was nothing that I could do to change that fact. I needed to think about something else. After I reported to my supervisor at the Bureau of Narcotics and Dangerous Drugs, Fred Borne, I spread out some papers on my desk, hung an old sport jacket on the back of my chair, and then left the office.

As soon as the brick building at the end of L Street came into view, I began to relax. An old fight trainer once told me that 90 percent of fighting was psychological. If you are not mentally convinced you can win, you probably won't. Much of life depends on your outlook. He may have been more of a philosopher than I gave him credit for. Once I parked and went inside, I felt even better. The familiar faces of the regulars changed my perception of things as I returned to reality as I knew it.

Johnny Pretzie, an old prizefighter who bragged to everyone that he was the model for the Shawmut Bank's Indian logo, tightened his face into a mock-threatening scowl when I walked into the lockerroom. Pretzie, who lost a decision to Rocky Marciano and took a dive in a fight with Jake La Motta, greeted me with the usual gibberish, shadowboxing and bouncing on the balls of his feet as he said, "Hey, PD, police department, punch drunk, blah, blah, Paulie. Keep those no-good dope pushers on their toes, knock 'em on their ass! Take me with you, I'll give 'em the old one two."

Gerry Mitchell, another fighter, a prosperous businessman and local success story from my old Roxbury neighborhood, smiled at Pretzie's remarks and added glibly, "Take him with you and give the rest of us some peace and quiet around here!"

I was aware of how the simple act of getting into my workout gear eased my mind. The familiar feeling of preparing to fight or train was oddly cathartic. I stretched, shadowboxed, and then did a series of dumbbell exercises. When I was finished with the weights, I put on sixteen-ounce boxing gloves and began punching the heavy bag. My usual routine was to throw punches in quick, hard combinations for about fifteen minutes without taking a break. After a few seconds, I became so focused on my punching power and mesmerized at the steady, loud thumping of the leather gloves as they landed on the old canvas bag that I was unaware of anything or anyone around me. I was in another world. Fifteen minutes later, at the bell, I threw a final left hook with all the power that I could manage, then I stood up straight and took a deep breath to fuel my exhaustion. I realized then that several guys had stopped working out and gathered around to watch me annihilate the bag. I looked in their direction and smiled self-consciously.

"I'm glad that bag's not me!" one of the guys remarked so that I could hear him. He was a firefighter from Ladder 19 on K and Fourth.

The workout was exactly what I needed. I felt energized and empowered. Throwing punches was something that I have been doing since I was a small boy. The physically exhausting feeling of my lungs straining for every drop of oxygen as my heart worked to pump the blood faster and faster tested my cardiovascular system to the maximum, and I enjoyed it. I liked the sensation of the blood flowing through the veins in my arms. More than anything else, though, I liked the feeling of confidence that I experienced when I battered the bag. I knew that if the bag were another man, I would have knocked him out. The feeling was important to me. It was survival.

When I left the gym, the sky was even darker than it was before, but it didn't bother me now. Driving dreamily along Day Boulevard, by the edge of the bay, a swatch of black caught my eye. I pulled to the side of the road and stepped on the brakes when I recognized him.

"Hey, Fatha!" I called through the open passenger-side window. He stopped in his tracks.

Father D was the kind of guy who came around once in a lifetime. The tough North End neighborhood where he grew up was the Italian equivalent of Southie. Father D's family lineage was checkered with full-blooded Mafiosi. North Enders still talked about how much of a scrapper he was as a kid. By some strange occurrence, I believe it was divine intervention, Buster DePaula went into the priesthood. He was the only priest I would ever level with.

"Paul! It's good to see you!" Father DePaula said warmly in his always welcoming voice, leaning over to see me more clearly.

"Too bad about Danny McGinty," I remarked. McGinty was a troubled seventeen-year-old kid from the D Street project. I spent some time with him at the gym teaching him to box. The kid had been making a lot of progress lately with the help of Father D.

"It was too much for him," Father answered with empathy.

"I know."

Young McGinty woke up in the middle of the night to find a strange man, a sailor from nearby Boston Navy Yard, taking liberties with his all-too-willing mother. McGinty went into a rage and killed the sailor.

"She was the only person in the world Danny loved," Father reasoned. "You and I would have done the same thing," he added. We were silent for a moment, just shaking our heads, and then Father DePaula perked up. "What are you doing?" Without waiting for an answer, he continued, "C'mon for a walk around the island."

He was perceptive enough to know that I had something I wanted to talk about. I cut across the boulevard and parked. Then I ran back across to meet Father DePaula. We shook hands and began walking together along Day Boulevard toward Castle Island.

"Fatha, can we talk?" I struggled to begin. Father D laughed.

"Of course. What's up?" he asked, more like an invitation than a question, while we continued to walk. Once I opened my mouth, the words rushed out like a river through a floodgate.

"Fatha, I can't seem to make sense out of anything any more. Nothing seems to matter, nothing seems to work. Sometimes I feel like I'm going backwards, like I'm fighting a losing battle. I feel like I'm running as fast as I can and it's not fast enough. You know what I mean?

"Things were always so clear to me before. Everything was in black and white. I knew who my opponent was. I had to beat the guy in the other corner, in the different-colored trunks. In football, you were either with me or against me. That was understood. Everyone else understood that too, because our teams had different uniforms. There was no doubt.

"I always knew what I was doing. I knew right from wrong. I just knew. I treated other people the way that I wanted to be treated. I didn't need anybody to tell me what was right; I just knew.

"I joined the army for my buddies and my country. I couldn't let other people fight for me. I joined the bureau for the same reason. The paradox is that a lot of people do not see it that way. It's just not war and peace or legal and illegal. There are degrees of each and there are shaded areas. There are different interpretations of the truth. Not everyone agrees on anything. Meanwhile, the young guys are still being drafted, trained for a couple of months as soldiers, then sent to the other side of the world to fight for something that nobody understands. In addition to that, they don't even know who they are fighting. Uniforms don't mean anything anymore. Some of the enemies wear pajamas, but so do some of the friendlies. Slanted eyes don't mean anything, either. Everyone looks the same; enemy and friend! The north and the south, Vietnam and Korea. How do you tell the difference? How do you do it? They're ordering nineteen-year-old kids to do it!

"What about drugs? Some people want them. Other people don't. There are laws, but they don't mean anything. Pushers get arrested, and they are out on the street before we finish our paperwork. I feel like I am wasting my time. Shoveling shit against the tide. I'm emptying the ocean a bucket at a time and a tidal wave of drugs is rolling in. People are dying every day. Doesn't anyone know what's goin' on? People with more degrees than I'll ever have want to legalize drugs. What the hell is going on? Excuse me, Fatha." I looked in Father D's direction and he was nodding his head slowly, listening intently. I still had more to get off my mind.

"Fatha, two young kids died last night with needles in their arms. I knew them both. The girl was only nineteen; she was a beautiful kid. I was so close. I mean, I was so close to what was going on. I should have been able to do something to prevent it. I . . ." My rambling about the frustrations that were weighing me down ended in midsentence. We continued past Kelly's Landing in silence. Finally, Father D spoke.

"Paul, you're a good kid yourself. You always have been. Everybody gets confused, especially today. Who wouldn't be confused with drugs, busing, Vietnam, race riots?

"There's no accountability, no leadership, no direction from our government. Nobody wants to step up to the plate and call strikes. Nobody wants to admit that there is a strike zone, but there is. The truth never changes. Socrates, Plato, all the great philosophers have searched throughout the centuries for the truth. The important thing is to keep searching, to keep looking for it.

"Right and wrong, good and evil have not changed. The trouble is that no one wants to listen. Everyone wants to talk. Everybody wants to do their own thing. If it feels good, do it is today's philosophy. It doesn't work that way. Life was not meant to be an endless party. There is suffering and persecution. Remember Job? Then, Jesus. You can't forget Jesus! He told the people 'like it was,' and you know what they did to him!

"Popular culture wants us to do our own thing. Are we our brother's keeper? That is a question that people have trouble with. I'll tell you what the answer is, but you already know it. The answer is, yes! 'Whenever you do this for the least of my brothers, you do it for me.' That's right from the scriptures. It's clear as a bell.

"That's what you do. Ever since you were a kid, you stuck up for other kids who got picked on. You kept the bullies at bay. That's what you are doing now. You made a decision to make a difference in the world, you took a stand. You put yourself in harm's way. Most people are content to look from afar and make judgments. You are not that way. You never were!

"You have a very important job to do now. Someone has to get down in the mud and mix it up. You got the nod. The problem is that when you are in the middle of the fray, you can get hurt. Drugs is a dirty business, you know that. It's evil. You cannot do it all by yourself, but remember that you are not alone. God is always with you.

"There is a prayer, a Jesuit favorite, that I say every morning and I think it's perfect for you. It goes like this: 'Father, you created me and put me on earth for a purpose. Jesus, you died for me and called me to complete your work. Holy Spirit, you help me to carry out the work for which I was created and called. In your presence and name—Father, Son, and the Holy Spirit—I begin my reflection. May all my thoughts and inspirations have their origin in you and be directed to your glory.' I say that prayer as soon as I wake up, and it stays with me all day." When he ended the prayer, a calm that I had never felt before came over me. It was as if the prayer were written for me.

We were back at the beach where we started. Our walk took us out around the sugar bowl and back, over two miles, but our talk was so absorbing that I hardly noticed the distance. I never considered myself a particularly religious guy, but there was surely something spiritual about our chance encounter.

It was the Friday before Christmas. I got back to the office and hurriedly completed the reports that were due. When Borne returned from his extended lunch, I smiled and wished him a Merry Christmas. I even thought that I saw a faint semblance of a smile as he wished me the same. He looked puzzled, though, when I walked into his office and placed a vacation request on his hand. As soon as I stepped out of his office, before I could return to my desk, I heard his dispirited voice, full of misgivings.

"What about the files?" Borne recited the case numbers of files that were due by the end of the month.

"Done," I answered before he was able to finish reading the numbers. There was a long stretch of silence. I could hear the noise while Borne flipped through the pages in the files. Unable to find a fly in the ointment, he did not respond immediately. Then warily, permission was granted. I heard his mistrusting voice come from the confines of his office.

"Well, if you think you can keep up with your paperwork," Borne warned.

I had more vacation time than I could use, because I never took a day off. I never called in sick, either. None of the street agents did. We loved our work. Why would he begrudge me a few days off? The spirit of Scrooge was not lost on Fred Borne.

"Thanks, Fred, you're the best!" I replied in the spirit of Tiny Tim.

Pam and I had a great Christmas. No matter what I gave her for a present, she always loved it. This year, though, I picked a particularly nice necklace out for her. She was thrilled. She was happiest of all that I was taking some vacation days to spend with her. We had a little Christmas party with my partner, Danny Santarpio, and his wife, Helen, at their house in Medford. It was really fun to see the holiday anticipation in their little daughter Dina's eyes before she went to bed. We spent Christmas Eve with my parents and Christmas Day with Pam's, but we had the best time alone.

Several days after Christmas, we drove to Sugarloaf in Maine. We found a rustic lodge where they served delicious meals. Early on the last morning of our stay we were on the first chairlift to the summit. At the top of the mountain, Pam and I skied away from the lift and stopped briefly to adjust our equipment. Standing next to each other, we paused to look down from the top of Sugarloaf at the breathtaking 360-degree view of the magnificent, snow-covered mountains surrounding us.

We nudged each other, a silent signal, by touching shoulders and hips, then began sliding slowly downward through the snow. We picked up speed quickly as we went over the precipice, and only moments later, we were racing down the steep incline. Pam led the way, leaving tracks on the newly fallen snow. I skied as fast as I could to keep up with her along the black-diamond trails. We were surprised by ever more glorious winter scenes at every turn.

It was a treat just to watch Pam ski. Whether pounding her skis into the snow as she maneuvered through the rugged moguls or swishing gracefully from side to side through the narrow trails, she was a wonder to see. The subdued rattling of her skis as she flew down the mountain was a symphony in the snow. For the first time ever, I thought to myself that it would be nice to give up everything and ski like this every day.

We skied against time to discover every trail before the day ended. I could not remember ever having had more fun. By the last run of the day, my body was tired all over; a wholesome, healthy exhaustion. We skied more slowly then, almost gliding down the slope, as if to prolong the pleasure. We were the very last ones to come off of the mountain. After balancing our skis on our shoulders, I reached out and put my arm around Pam's shoulder, and we walked awkwardly in our oversized boots, like spacemen, to the lodge.

That evening, in celebration of New Year's Eve, Pam and I joined the other guests for an after-ski wine and cheese social before dinner. We found a wooden bench near the hearth, sat down next to each other, and leaned back. A few sips of wine, after our exhausting day of skiing, almost put us both to sleep. We relaxed by the heat of the fire and dreamily watched the others. The bejeweled snow bunnies, in full makeup and stylized hairdos, posed in their latest fashion skiwear, as they sipped their wine and socialized with their male counterparts. The thought suddenly occurred to me that I was the luckiest guy in the world. Pam and I did not have very much materially. Compared with the stylish jetsetters we were with, we had nothing. When I looked at Pam, though, I realized there was no comparison. She stood alone. We had nothing but each other and yet we had everything.

We talked every minute of our four-hour trip home on New Year's Day and resolved to support each other in our work so that we could make a difference in the world. We made a commitment to work as hard as we could, because we believed in what we were doing, and most of all we believed in each other.

Ever since Judas Iscariot turned Jesus Christ over to Pontius Pilate for thirty pieces of silver, informants have been squealing on people for their own personal gain. Informants get favors or money in return for their betrayal. It's a sordid, but necessary paradox. Law enforcement would be powerless without the cooperation of informants.

The informant is the essential ingredient in the law enforcement recipe to solve crimes, but he or she is also the ingredient that sometimes taints the entire recipe and leads to scandal and corruption. Law enforcement agencies take many precautions to ensure that their officers and agents handle informants properly, but it is a very complicated and difficult process.

Informants are debriefed, documented, and utilized according to strict guidelines, but the unpredictable human element is usually the most troublesome. The law enforcement officer who is handling the informant has to make split-second decisions in very difficult situations. In drug enforcement, and undercover work in particular, the situations are often precarious. The undercover man is governed by certain guidelines, but he operates with a great deal of discretion. Every drug deal is different.

Drug agents have occasion to meet and work with many informants. They are ubiquitous in the illegal drug business. I met numerous informants, and I came to despise most of them. For the most part, they are selfish, amoral people who set up anyone they can to benefit themselves. They do it in exchange for money or a lighter prison sentence, and they do not care whom they hurt. Informants set up fathers, mothers, sisters, brothers, sons, daughters, uncles, aunts, and friends. You get the picture. Treachery and deceit is the name of the game. That is what it is all about. Save your own ass.

Informants are hated by other criminals and scorned by police. They are the lowest of the low. Nobody likes a rat. It goes against all of society's moral standards. Today there seems to be more of a tendency to inform than in years gone by. Criminals used to say, "If you can't do the time, don't do the crime." A more appropriate saying today would be "If you can't do the time, drop a dime."

Despite all this, cops and agents sometimes become attached to the informants they are handling. Although the informant's business and motives are despicable, they are often personable and even charming people. That's the nature of the business. It's smoke and mirrors, treachery, and deceit.

Romeo ("call me Ro") Fragone was such a character. He was an informant whom I worked with and actually grew to like in some ways. When I first interviewed Ro, I was sitting in the back seat of his Cadillac with my partner, Danny. Ro was leaning on the steering wheel with his left arm and taking noisy bites from an apple that he held in his right hand. He twisted his big body around in the front seat to look at us. He had a round baby face and a light brown moustache and goatee. He wore a cashmere coat and a matching cashmere scally cap. The hat was pulled down on his head in such a way that it created a shadow that extended below his cobalt blue eyes and across the bridge of his nose like a robber's mask.

"I can give you every niggah in the South End, every niggah in Boston. All I want is money. I gotta pay my rent, pay my car. They're gonna repo my car, I'm six months behind. I'll give you all these shitbums and move away, out of state, and start all ovah," Ro offered in quick staccato style, as his black and tan Doberman pinscher moved around menacingly on the seat next to him. He hesitated momentarily to look at me and to get my reaction.

"Ro, do you know anyone in the Shanty Lounge?" I asked, in an effort to gain control of the interview and get him on track.

"Do I know anyone in the Shanty?" Ro repeated. "The Shanty? I know every one of those niggahs. You want to go down there and cop right now? You want methadone, heroin, what?"

"Wait a minute, slow down. You're willing to introduce me to dealers in the Shanty Lounge so that I can make buys?" I asked in an attempt to pin him down and to clarify his rambling.

"Yeah, that's what I'm willin' ta do," Ro answered, looking straight into my eyes. He never flinched. I studied his response, and I believed him. He was no shrinking violet. All the major black drug dealers in the Boston area operated out of the Shanty Lounge on Washington Street, so Ro's information was very welcome. It was ironic that a white guy from East Boston, an Italian, would be the one to bring me to the black heroin dealers, though. The Shanty Lounge was a dangerous place, but it didn't seem to bother Ro.

"Ro, what are the crutches for?" I asked, curiously.

"Oh, I got shot," he answered nonchalantly. "See, this guy I know got robbed by this other guy I know, and he kind of knew that I set him up for the robbery. I was standin' on the corner one day up on Blue Hill Ave. and Seaver, near the park, and I see this guy that got stuck up coming up to me real slow with another guy in the car. The last thing I remember, after seeing him pull a 44 magnum, was a burning sensation, and I woke up in the hospital."

"So, what are you going to do about it?" I asked.

"Ah, what the fuck, I set him up," Ro answered casually.

"You think they tried to kill you?"

"Maybe," Ro answered, indifferently.

"You been carryin' a piece since the shooting?"

"Sometimes," he admitted.

"You got a piece on you now?" I asked.

"What are you gonna do, bust me or somethin'?" Ro tested me.

"What do you think?" I asked, to feel him out. Ro remained outwardly calm as he thought about my rhetorical question.

"Ro, I want dope. I want heroin. That's my business. Whether or not you like to play with guns is none of my business, you know what I mean? I just want to know what's goin' on. You got a piece or what?" I explained, emphasizing my lack of interest to ease the tension and to test his truthfulness. After evaluating my response, he reached into his camel hair coat, and very slowly pulled a 38 Smith and Wesson revolver out of his waistband.

"Yeah," he said, displaying the pistol carefully to me as a jeweler would display his finest diamonds. The way that he handled the gun told me a lot about him. It was not his first time. Ro had a fascination and a respect for guns. He knew what a handgun did to him, and he knew what it could do to someone else. Most important in his line of work, he knew how to use it. And, most important in my line of work, he showed that he was being honest with me. I looked down at the pistol long enough to see that it was loaded, and then I raised my eyes, indifferently, and looked out the window.

"It's against government regulations and it's against the law to carry a firearm. That is why you don't have a firearm, and that is why you are not allowed to carry a firearm while you are working with a federal agent." I recited the official rules to him as if I had never seen the gun.

"Gotcha," Ro answered as he slipped the pistol adeptly into his belt.

"If I see a crime committed in my presence, like unauthorized possession of a firearm, I am obligated to make an arrest," I continued, indifferently, while gazing through the windshield of the car at the people on the other side of Albany Street, walking in and out of the Boston City Hospital.

"Uh huh," Ro answered.

"If I know that an informant is carrying a weapon, I cannot work with that informant. In fact, I am obligated to arrest him."

"Uh huh." Ro looked at me out of the corner of his eye and winked. I knew, then, that we had an understanding.

It was officially against the rules for informants to carry guns, but the people who write the rules weren't roaming the streets with Ro, like I was going to be. Sometimes you have to make exceptions. Ro and his friends were not playing games, and I wasn't, either. I was not going to take any chances with his life or mine. Every time that I worked with Ro, I asked him if he was carrying a handgun, and he always answered no. I gave him a light frisk before each case to comply with the regulations, and I never felt a gun. That way, we were both covered if anything went wrong. In the event that Ro was set up again while I was with him, I figured that two guns were better than one. I could obey all the rules, or I could protect my life. It was a survivor's choice, a calculated risk.

My first try with Ro was a successful one. Chris Regan, Danny Santarpio, and I drove onto the Massachusetts Avenue exit ramp off of the Southeast Expressway, and we pulled in behind Ro's Cadillac, which was parked at the curb in front of the Boston City Morgue. Ro got out when he spotted us in his rearview mirror and hobbled back with his crutches to meet us. He was a hulk of a fellow, approximately six foot two, 240 pounds, and he appeared even bigger with the crutches. Chris told him, through his partially opened window, to get into the backseat.

When Ro finally settled in, with his crutches and all, he looked at each one of us and nodded approvingly. Chris introduced himself and shook hands, then Danny and I shook his hand. I debriefed him while Chris scribbled notes on a legal pad. Chris, Danny, and I took turns asking him questions, and Ro looked back and forth between us as he answered. After about ten minutes of steady questioning, we decided to make a drug buy.

"You ready, Ro?" Chris asked.

"Ready as I'll ever be," Ro answered. "Let's go."

"One more thing, Paulie," Chris added. "Search him."

"You don't have any firearms or illegal drugs in your possession, do you, Ro?" I prompted him. Ro looked at me skeptically before answering.

"Nah, I got nuthin'," Ro answered cautiously. I leaned over and patted him down, over the outside of his topcoat, and I didn't feel a gun. But in fact, it would have been impossible to feel much of anything through that heavy coat.

"He's clean as far as I can tell," I answered. Ro looked at me skeptically.

"Okay, go do it!" Chris said, enthusiastically. Ro and I got out of the car. I got into his Cadillac on the passenger side and waited while Ro slid in and leaned his crutches upright against the seat between us. He glanced across the seat at me with a questioning look on his face.

"I thought you were gonna 'do me' when your boss told you to search me. I thought I was gone. I thought it was a setup—good guy, bad guy routine," Ro said.

"You gotta believe, brother. Do unto others, as you would have them do unto you. Like I said before, treat me right, and I'll treat you right. Now, let's buy some dope," I reassured him.

"I'm ready. You got money, Sully?"

"Yeah, I got money," I answered.

"We're all set then. All we need is money. Money talks and bullshit walks. I can introduce you to a dude named Jasper. You can cop a few biscuits of methadone and make arrangements to do your own thing with him from now on. I'll tell him that you're from East Boston, 'cuz that's where I'm from, and we'll tell 'em you're interested in doin' a big thing," Ro said.

"That's cool, Ro. Just give me the right introduction," I said while Ro drove inbound on Mass Ave.

"There's Jasper," Ro said excitedly, looking toward the sidewalk where a middle-aged black guy was standing in front of a dilapidated pawnshop. Ro pulled the Caddy over and slowed down to a roll. Jasper, wearing an old U.S. Air Force jacket and chino pants, recognized Ro and walked toward us. Ro lowered my window, and Jasper looked right past me to talk to him.

"Happenin' Ro? Drive roun this buildin' an wait," Jasper said, nervously.

"Jasper, this is my man. He wants to score," Ro said.

"Dig it, Ro. Go roun back," Jasper instructed in a smooth, melodic voice with a trace of a southern drawl. Then he turned around and disappeared into an alley next to the pawnshop.

When we drove around to the back and parked, we found ourselves across from a relatively new low-income, high-rise red brick apartment building. We watched as a heavy steel door, the entrance to a basement apartment, swung open, and Jasper emerged. He turned to lock the door behind him and stopped momentarily to look around. Then he shuffled across the street to meet us. He bent down and peered into the open driver's window to get a look at me.

"Get in, Jasper. Jasper, this here is my man from East Boston. We was partners when I was doin' my own thing. Now, he's gonna do his own thing, and I want you to take care of him." Ro introduced me in quick, rapid-fire style. His spontaneity seemed to put Jasper at ease. Jasper looked from Ro's eyes to mine and put his outstretched hand in the open window. I leaned across the front seat and reached past Ro's face to shake hands with Jasper.

"Nice ta meet ya, man," he said to me while we shook. When he smiled, I noticed that Jasper was missing several of his front teeth.

He switched his attention back to Ro. "You got any more credit cards, man? I need more cards. Them cards is beautiful, man. Specially on the shuttle. Ain't no way they gonna check, when you whip 'em on 'em twenty thousand feet in the air, when you gonna land in five minutes!"

"Use this one. It's no good to me no more. I used it a month already around East Boston. I'll keep my eyes open for some more for you, Jasper,"

Ro said as he produced a credit card from the visor of the car and handed it to Jasper.

"Thanks, man."

"Get in," Ro said, and Jasper shuffled to the rear door and let himself in behind Ro. Jasper moved his head back and forth from Ro to me as he began to talk.

"Down to bizniz, now. How many biscuits you want, man?" Jasper asked to no one in particular. I took my cue and began my rap.

"Well, what kind of price we talkin', man? I'm lookin' to score a good load like clockwork, my man. I'm gonna be here with my money like clockwork," I told him.

"I can handle all you want. I got customers buyin' thirty, forty a day! Ain't no lie! Be goin' fo twenty-five dollars apiece on the street. Some dudes be breakin' 'em into quarters and sellin' 'em fo ten dollars apiece, no jive. You can have 'em fo twenty dollars apiece," Jasper boasted to hawk his wares.

"Jasper, my man, that ain't no good. You gotta cut me some slack. I'm talkin' bout a steady thing. How my gonna make any money at twenty dollars apiece?" I argued.

"Okay, okay, gimme eighteen dollars apiece! When you coppin' heavy, I'll git you a good price," Jasper replied. Then he asked, "How many?"

"Give me five now," I ordered, like I was playing cards. Jasper took five methadone biscuits out of his jacket pocket and placed them carefully in an empty Kool cigarette package, one by one.

"Five's a good number, so I can see how they move. A sample," I added while Jasper packaged the drugs.

"They'll move like that!" Jasper bragged as he snapped his fingers and handed me the package. "Junkies love 'em, man. They know what they be getting. No burns, it's nice."

"Okay, Jasper, I can dig it." I handed Jasper ninety dollars. "Give me your number so I can call you to talk. It don't look right for two white dudes in a Cadillac to be sittin' in an alleyway with a black dude. You hear what I'm sayin', Jasper?"

"I heah ya! We be sittin' heah, dealin' an Al Forte come along an drop da net on all of us! Dat drug control unit be all over dis place," Jasper agreed.

"I'll call you in a few days and grab some more."

"You right, man. Call me, and I'll have your package ready next time," Jasper said. We shook hands, and Jasper handed me a small piece of paper with his telephone number on it and got out of the car.

"Be cool, Jasper," I called out through Ro's opened window. Jasper looked back with his wide, toothless grin.

"I gotsta be," he replied as he waved good-bye. Driving away, I could see him shuffle across the street and return to the basement apartment.

"Whaddaya think?" Ro asked.

"I think it's okay," I answered, while making mental notes about the transaction.

"Okay? It was perfect!" Ro corrected me, proudly. He made a nice introduction, and he wanted to be praised.

"Perfect," I agreed.

"We make a good team, Sully," Ro declared. We drove back to the morgue and met with Chris and Danny again. They walked up to meet us. Chris came to Ro's window and Danny to mine.

"How'd it go?" Chris asked.

"It went good!" Ro answered enthusiastically.

"Here it is," I answered, holding up the Kool cigarette pack. Chris smiled and so did Danny.

Ro turned out to be an excellent informant, and he introduced Danny Santarpio and me to a number of midlevel heroin dealers. We usually eliminated Ro after the initial introduction and made several other buys on our own. Chris directed us and conducted most of the surveillances.

When you are working undercover, you obviously have to adopt a role to play, and you play it. There are many different types of people from many different backgrounds selling drugs, and an undercover man has to adjust to them all. He has to be a chameleon, the lowest common denominator. He has to fit in everywhere. An undercover man often has to conceal his identity and his true feelings in order to make the case. Sometimes that is very hard to do. In fact, in one instance, it was impossible for me.

"Sully, you ain't gonna like this guy, Nelson, but he can get you ten bundles, no sweat. I know you ain't gonna like him, I know right now." Ro gave me a wide-eyed look and filled me in on the background of our next target as he wheeled the Cadillac outbound on Washington Street toward the Shanty Lounge. I blessed myself self-consciously as we passed the Cathedral of the Holy Cross, home base for the cardinal of Boston, which prompted me to think about Cardinal Cushing and Cardinal Madieros, the only two cardinals in my lifetime. It seemed so ironic that the seat of the Catholic Church in Boston was located in the highest crime area of the city, immersed in a sea of drugs.

"You Catholic, too," Ro copied me and made the sign of the cross, also.

"Yeah," I answered.

"Alright," Ro reflected out loud, happy to discover another common element between us.

"What do you mean, I won't like him? I like everyone," I said, directing my thoughts back to Ro's earlier declaration.

"He's a racist, man, a real hater. I'm tellin' you. Rememba those overdoses round Christmas time?"

"Yeah?" I thought back to those dark days before Christmas.

"Whole time, Nelson was braggin' it was his stuff. Kept tellin' everyone, he gots da best!"

I soon found out that Ro's observation was right. His description was perfect. We met Straight Razor Nelson on the corner of Northampton and Washington Streets. As soon as he walked up to the window of Ro's car, he began speaking to me in the most arrogant, obnoxious manner.

"Whatchoo mean, you want tin bundles, now? You want tin bundles, you wait! That's right, you wait, boy!" he shouted, while pointing his finger at me, to impress his ready-made, hostile-looking street audience, standing around the front of the Shanty Lounge. Nelson ranted and raved and moved around theatrically on the sidewalk like he was on a Broadway stage. He made it clear that he had no use for white folks, and he said everything that he could to ridicule and demean Ro and me. I bit my tongue and stared at him.

"You want tin bundles, you pay my price! Unnastand, boy?" Nelson lectured. He turned around to face his audience, and laughed derisively. He stepped back up on the curb and swaggered over to the group of hustlers who were taking more than a curious interest in the presence of Ro and me in our Cadillac.

"How can you stand it?" I whispered to Ro, out of the corner of my mouth, while Nelson was out of hearing range.

"I told you," Ro whispered back, without moving his lips.

"He's sickening. I find this hard to take. Do you think he may try to burn me?" I asked under my breath, worried that Nelson might try to rip me off by selling me "turkey," which is what we called a counterfeit substance. It was common for dealers in this area to pass off a substance like milk sugar or lactose for heroin. The average white junkie would have no recourse. He wouldn't stand a chance in this all-black crime-infested neighborhood. There was no money-back guarantee here. So let the buyer beware. I was also thinking that at any minute now someone in Nelson's group could pull out a sawed-off shotgun from under one of those long leather coats.

"I don't know," Ro answered again without moving his lips.

"If he burns me, Ro, we're comin' right back, and I'm gonna kick his big bubble ass all over the sidewalk. I might need a little help with the crowd control if all these brothers are still here when we get back," I said, to test Ro's mettle. Ro didn't hesitate.

"I'll come back with you," he answered automatically, without missing a beat. Ro was solid. He was that sort of guy. If he was with you, he was with you all the way. He was not afraid to take a beating. I could see Nelson swagger back toward us with his nose up in the air.

"Open the damn gate, Ro!" Nelson ordered, impatiently. Ro opened the back door and Nelson slid in.

"Take me fo a ride, and we'll talk bout it. Now, let me see, you want tin bundles. How much dust you got?" Nelson began.

"Well, that depends on the price that you give me, Straight." I started to negotiate, when Nelson cut in rudely.

"I sayed, how much money you got, boy? Now, I gots the dope. Don't be tellin' me what price it bees, I don't care what you want!"

Nelson really was obnoxious. He must have figured that I was a live one. I took a deep breath in an effort to control my anger, but my thoughts kept drifting back to that young girl with the black beret from Lucifer. I could picture her now. It made me want to smack him, but I kept breathing slowly and deeply.

"I've got a thousand dollars, Straight. I figure that's a pretty good price," I offered.

"Whatchoo mean, sounds like a good price? I told you, boy, I gots da dope! You pay what I say!" He ridiculed me in rhyme.

That jingle was the straw that broke the camel's back. Straight Razor Nelson pressed the wrong button. I spun around and reached over the seat back, grabbing him by the lapels of his navy pea coat. In one swift motion, I pulled Nelson toward me, banging his head against the roof of the car as I did so. Holding him inches away from me, I sprayed saliva all over his face as I screamed at him.

"I ought to break your head, you asshole! You're a shitbum! You're scum! Do you understand that, boy? I wouldn't buy a fuckin' thing from you, you asshole!" I shouted, out of control.

Nelson's eyes bugged out, and all I could see was his bewildered stare. I thought about the young kids who died from his heroin just before Christmas, and I was overcome with rage. I let go of his collar with my right hand and I pulled it back into a fist, then I smashed him as hard as I could on the bridge of his nose, right between the eyes. I knew as soon as I connected that it was a nice hard punch. Nelson fell back against the seat like a ragamuffin, with snot all over his lips and blood pouring out of his nose onto his face. The bright red blood spilled down his chin and neck and soaked into his pea coat. His eyes were glazed over, and my instinct was to follow up with a knockout punch, but I held back. I spit on him to initiate a response so that I could finish him off, but he didn't make a move. I slapped him hard across the mouth in frustration, and he pulled away from me, cowering into the far corner of the backseat. All the bravado was gone.

"Ro, stop the car and let me out! Get rid of this shitbum now, and come back and pick me up. I don't ever want to be in the same car as that scumbag, ever!" I hollered.

Ro stopped and let me out on Washington Street under the elevated trains, and I slammed the door behind me. I watched as Ro drove to the corner of Northampton and Washington Street to drop Nelson off. Then he made a U-turn and came back for me. I could see the surprised look on Ro's face as soon as I got into the front seat.

"Man, you scared that niggah white!" Ro said.

"I don't want to do business with him, Ro. He pisses me off," I announced.

"I thought you were puttin' on an act, man," Ro said with a smile. Then he added, "You really are crazy!" Ro stared at me with raised eyebrows. His response made me laugh. I was all wound up inside, but Ro's reaction defused my anger. It is a crazy world, this undercover scene, I thought to myself. I don't want to buy drugs and lock this guy up because he pisses me off! Figure that one out.

Ro later brought Danny Santarpio in and introduced him to Nelson. Danny made a series of heroin buys from Nelson and eventually arrested him. Ironically, several days after Danny arrested him, and while Nelson was out on bail, I had another meeting with him. I was standing in the first floor hallway of an apartment building while a team of Boston Police detectives and DEA agents were executing a search warrant on a drug dealer's apartment on the third floor. I had a perfect view of the entranceway to the building. My job was to follow any late arrivals to the drug apartment and block their escape path when the raiding party confronted them.

I watched a number of innocent apartment dwellers come and go, and I am sure that it made them a little nervous to see a stranger lurking in their building. I tried to appear as non-threatening as possible. I had recently shaved my beard and moustache and cut my long hair, so I looked fairly clean. I shifted my weight from one foot to the other as I checked out the people who came and went. When they met my eyes, I smiled and nodded. I even helped an older lady with her bundles of groceries. There was no real action since I had taken my post, and I was beginning to get bored. I was more preoccupied with looking friendly to the neighbors in my blue barracuda jacket, tan khaki pants, and loafers. All of a sudden, I spotted a black male as he strutted up to the buzzer and spoke into the speaker. I could not hear what he said, but he looked very much like Straight Razor Nelson. Two clicks came over my radio, which I had hidden under my jacket. That was the signal that the person in the doorway had buzzed the apartment being raided. I started to get that familiar rush that comes just before the action starts. My senses were all on heightened alert.

I heard the buzzer unlocking the inner door, and I took several steps toward it and stopped. I watched the dark figure through the dirty glass panel as he opened the heavy oak door. It was Straight Razor Nelson! His eyes met mine with a cold, contemptuous stare, and I knew that he did not recognize me. I stood directly in his path, and he bumped into me arrogantly, chest to chest, with his head down. When he raised his head, he looked at me disdainfully.

"Get out my way, white boy," he barked, and I ignored his command. I stood solidly in front of him. A sudden warm feeling came over me. It was the feeling that you get when you know that everything is going right for you. I knew that it was fate that brought us together again.

"Nice to see you, Straight," I welcomed him with a smile. My overly friendly greeting confused Nelson and caught him off guard. I shifted my weight to my right foot, which was slightly to the rear of my left, just as Nelson began to raise his right hand to throw a punch. I blasted a crushing right-hand punch to his jaw. As he began to crumble, my instincts as a prizefighter took over, and I fired off a series of straight punches that all landed very hard on Nelson's nose and chin. I continued to throw punches as he dropped all the way to the hard wood floor, hurting my knuckles as they cracked on his skull. I was unaware of anything but the two of us. There was no noise, no sound, and no smell. All I could see was my opponent, and I was fighting for my life. I felt someone grabbing me around the shoulders, and I thought for a moment that it was the referee forcing me to a neutral corner. When I looked back, I realized that it was Danny.

"Whoa, what are you doin'?" Danny asked, baffled at the sight of me punching a dead heap. I stood over Nelson breathing heavily from exhaustion after throwing so many punches, and I looked at Danny. Raising my right hand to gesture as I began to explain, I noticed that my knuckles were covered with blood.

"It's Straight Razor Nelson, that piece of shit," I said, continuing to breathe heavily. I looked down at Nelson, still unconscious from the knockout punches, and then I looked at Danny. A couple of Boston detectives came down the stairs and walked up to us, to look at the scene.

"Winner by a knockout!" Jerry O'Dea laughingly mimicked a fight announcer. His rendition made me laugh.

"I hope I killed him," I said. Still panting and out of breath, I looked down at Nelson's inert body once more. Jerry O'Dea, Al Forte, and Danny Santarpio looked at each other with concerned expressions.

"I think you might have," Al said with a worried look.

"Paulie, get out of here, and let us take care of things," Jerry said. I looked at all three of them, and they were looking back sympathetically at me.

"Go ahead. We'll handle it," Danny assured me.

I skipped out the front door, and I turned my head to take one last look at the scene. Al, Jerry, and Danny were all kneeling down around Nelson's body. Danny looked up and our eyes met. He waved me on impatiently with a look of assurance. I turned and hurried into the night. I walked a long way thinking about Nelson and visualizing the pounding that I gave him. I unleashed a flurry of punches so fast that he never had a chance to respond. After Nelson made his first move, it was all over. I never let him get a punch off. The people he killed with his heroin didn't have a chance, either. He killed a lot of people with his hot shots of heroin whom I never even knew, but I will never forget the beautiful girl in the black beret.

After Jerry, Al, and Danny revived Nelson, they placed him under arrest for possession of heroin with intent to distribute. He was subsequently charged with multiple sales of heroin to federal agents and was sentenced to fifteen years in federal prison. Straight Razor Nelson was never charged with the deaths by overdose.

What do you want to do today?" I asked Danny, who was leaning back in a chair next to me with his feet up on his desk, studying a surveillance report.

"I don't know," Danny answered unenthusiastically.

"We got to get something going. This paperwork is killin' me, it's so boring," I said.

Danny and I had just finished up a couple of big cases and were writing arrest reports, evidence reports, and surveillance reports for days on end. We felt like a couple of government file clerks, and were both getting itchy. It was time to get out on the street again. I made up my mind that today was the day.

"Dan, why don't we just jump in a shitbox, and drive out to the Washingtonian? One of my old informants called yesterday, and said that they were dealing drugs like fools out there!" The Washingtonian was a methadone center, and the junkies were crawling all over the place according to my informant.

"Are you all right?" Dan asked, sarcastically. "You wanna buy street shit?"

"Danny, I don't want to buy street shit any more than you do, but at least it'll get us out of the office. You never know where it might lead. Maybe we'll end up with some stoolies out of the thing. Nobody talks more than a good old junkie stool pigeon." I struggled to sound enthusiastic in an effort to pull us out of our funk.

Dan and I were beginning to get on each other's nerves. It was the natural result of working too closely for too long. Our recent inactivity intensified our already volatile relationship from having worked so closely for such an extended time.

"Yeah, okay," Dan agreed reluctantly. "Maybe we can come up with some stoolies."

We changed into sneakers, jeans, army jackets, and caps, appropriate attire for the methadone clinic. Then we signed out a couple of hundred dollars in official government funds and headed to the methadone clinic in a beat-up Ford Pinto. It seemed like things were getting better for us already as we drove through the city.

Dan and I arrived at the drug clinic a little before noon. The Washingtonian is located on a knoll near the Forest Hills MBTA station. As we drove up the hill and into the parking lot, we knew immediately that we were in the right place. All eyes were on us. Some junkies stood around conversing in groups in different areas of the parking lot, while others sat huddled in cars. Their paranoid looks questioned our presence.

"Pull over here, Danny, and I'll hit on this dude," I ordered anxiously, turning the radio off.

"Nah, let's park and get out," Danny countered.

The adrenaline started pumping. We were in their world now, the world of the junkies. Danny and I had no need to discuss the manner in which we would approach the situation. We worked together so well, so naturally, that our moves were automatic. Danny parked to the side of the lot, and we both got out. I evaluated the situation while Danny approached the most promising prospect, a junkie in her early twenties with frizzy, dirty-blonde, shoulder-length hair, who turned to look at us when we ambled up to the group.

"Who's holdin'? We wanna score," Danny demanded.

"Who's holdin?" she repeated. Then she asked, "Who are you?"

Danny ignored her question rudely, and turned his back on her. He exchanged hellos with a skinny, pimple-faced kid who thought that he knew Danny from somewhere. I jumped into the conversation by asking about two junkies, to break the ice and ease the tension.

"Tinker or Richie around?" I asked. Tinker was our stool pigeon, and Richie was a junkie who overdosed on heroin the night before and died. It was a good way to introduce ourselves to the group. Knowing Tinker and Richie gave us credibility.

"Nah, Tinker just left. He comes around ten, and then leaves. Richie OD'd, man. Richie won't be around no more." I could see that the skinny, pimple-faced kid relaxed as he answered the question.

"You shittin' me, man. Richie OD'd?" I asked, feigning concern.

"Yeah, he checked out for good, man. It's a bummer," the skinny kid answered philosophically.

"A bummer," I repeated, sadly.

"If you guys want to score, go see the guy standin' by the van. He's got some dyno shit," the skinny kid suggested.

Danny and I thanked him simultaneously, then started walking toward the guy in the black leather jacket near the van, surrounded by seven or eight other junkies. Danny and I walked up to the guy, pushing brusquely past the others, who were standing around. We both nodded to him, and he nodded back without saying anything. We stood and watched while he took money from the few remaining junkies in line and handed them bundles of heroin wrapped in folded pieces of blue-lined writing paper. Finally, the guy made his last transaction and looked up at us.

"What can I do for you, dudes?"

"We're here to cop," Danny answered bluntly.

"How much?" he asked.

"Half bundle," Danny replied.

"I'm out now. I have to get it from my van," the guy said. "Follow me."

We followed him to his beat-up old van, when suddenly he turned around and confronted us with a stare.

"Hey, who are you guys, anyway?"

He stood by the van, looking at us suspiciously and waiting for an answer. He was paranoid.

"We're friends of Tinker and Richie. We usually score from Tinker, but we missed him today," I answered quickly.

"Hey, man, I never saw you guys before," the guy blurted out as his eyes darted back and forth between Dan and me.

"Everyone knows us," Danny assured him. "We're righteous. We just need a little somethin' to hold us over till tomorrow when we see Tinker again."

I could see that the guy was getting "hinky," or nervous. He was now so paranoid that he probably wouldn't sell to us under any circumstances. Then, he said nervously, "You guys could be cops."

"What did you say?" Danny shouted angrily as he moved toward the guy, pointing his index finger at him accusingly.

The guy in the black leather jacket made no response.

"How'd you like a slap in the mouth, you maggot?" Danny continued moving forward and taunting as he gave the guy a stiff shove.

"Stick the dope up your ass," I yelled at the guy while grabbing Danny by the shoulders to pull him away.

The guy recovered from Danny's shove and stood there, embarrassed.

He looked away from my stare, and then looked down at the ground. Dan and I turned and started to walk away when the junkie with the frizzy hair put her hand on my arm. We stopped.

"You dudes friends of Richie and Tinker?" she asked softly, with a renewed interest in us.

"Yeah, that's right," Danny answered defiantly.

"Well, you must be okay, then," she smiled, surprising us completely.

"Listen," she whispered as she moved closer to us. "I have the best dope around."

Danny and I nodded to show our approval.

"If you want to score, see me tomorrow. I go to the HoJo's every morning about eleven, right after the clinic," she continued in a low, husky whisper.

"We'll need a bundle," I said.

"Yeah, no sweat. Anything," she promised.

"How much?" Dan questioned.

"Uh . . . ," she hesitated. "Two-fifty a bundle."

"You got it!" I replied.

"See you tomorrow," said Danny.

"Eleven at HoJo's. I'll be there," she assured us, and then added, "Believe me, I've got the best."

Dan and I got into our wreck and waved as we pulled out of the parking spot. We remained quiet for a while as we pulled out of the driveway of the Washingtonian and proceeded around the rotary. We could see the surveillance as we drove away. One car followed behind us, and one remained in place with an eyeball on the parking lot of the methadone clinic.

"There's the HoJo's, set back from the road. That's where we meet her," I said.

"Yes, indeed," Dan replied. I could tell by the tone of his voice that he was now in a good mood. We could hardly wait till tomorrow! We were finally coming out of our funk.

"Do you believe it, Dan?" I asked rhetorically.

"Right on, brother!" Dan answered loudly, with a laugh. "We can buy dope anywhere!"

"That's a weird scene up there, Dan. All those junkies, it's like the Twilight Zone! They all had dogs, too. That was a weird scene alright," I thought out loud.

"Ain't it, though," Dan agreed.

"It's another world," I said.

"She digs our act, doesn't she?" Dan laughed.

"She sure does. I couldn't believe her, though. She doesn't fit. I almost wanted to ask, what's a pretty girl like you doing in a place like this?"

This girl was atypical, I thought to myself. Junkies are usually easy to spot; they jump right out at you. This girl with the dirty-blonde hair was a little different. She was almost wholesome looking. She was plain but pretty, with no makeup, the all-American girl-next-door type. Something about her told me that this case was going to be different.

The next day, Danny and I went back as arranged. We drove into the parking lot of the HoJo's and waited. We waited for about a half hour, and still the blonde didn't show. Danny and I started to get a little "jiggy." Finally, at approximately 11:30, I walked into the restaurant, and I spotted her. She was sitting in a booth with a guy and another couple. They all looked like junkies, except the blonde. She waved and smiled, and I nodded and walked outside. Standing in front of the entrance, I winked at Danny, who was seated in the parked Pinto facing the restaurant. When the girl with the dirty-blonde hair came out of the restaurant, I could see her approach in the reflection of the windshield. I turned around to greet her.

"What's happenin', babe?" I asked.

"Hello," she answered with a ready smile.

"You got it?" I asked.

"Yeah, I got it," she faltered. "I only got half, though. Let's go to your car."

She walked next to me to the car, and we both got in. The girl sat in the backseat behind Danny, and I sat shotgun.

"Here it is, twelve bags," she said tentatively, as she unwrapped the package carefully and offered it to us.

"Twelve bags!" Danny hollered. "We ordered a bundle!"

"I know, I know you did. My old man and me did the rest of it up last night. It's a bummer, I know," she apologized, matter-of-factly.

"It's a bummer, alright! We got people waitin' and we only get twelve bags? We made a deal for a bundle! What's wrong with you?" Danny continued hollering. "What's wrong with you?"

"Alright, I know. I'm sorry, I screwed you guys up. My old man and I were up all last night," she tried desperately to explain as we both turned around to look at her. "We B and E'd this house last night," she continued. "We were both going through the drawers, and I heard this noise. I told my old man, but he said, Don't worry, it's nuthin'. I told him again when I heard it, and he told me to shut up. All of a sudden, there was this scream, and there was this fuckin' old lady standin' in the doorway. I mean old. She musta been seventy! My old man punched the old bag in the mouth, and we ran as fast as we could. I thought we'd never get out!"

"You mean you go into houses when the people are home?" I asked naively.

"Oh, yeah, all the time. But no one ever woke up before," she answered with a nervous laugh.

"What about dogs?" I asked. "Don't they scare you?"

"Dogs are no problem. The other night we rifled a joint, and they had this big German shepherd. The sign outside the house said Beware Attack Dog. Fuckin' dog sat and watched us steal everything! My old man carries dog biscuits," she boasted.

I stared into her eyes as she described the robberies, careful not to reveal the feeling of disgust that welled up inside of me. So much for the girl next door. I wondered how someone could be so hard-hearted and ruthless. She looked like an angel, but she was more like a devil.

Meanwhile, the junkie whom she had been sitting with in the restaurant appeared in the entranceway to HoJo's. He was pointing toward us, shouting something and motioning with his arms.

"What's this?" I asked, pointing to him.

"Oh, that's my old man. Roll down the window," she answered, gesturing frantically at the junkie to wave him off, and he went back inside the restaurant.

"He's worried about me," she said proudly. "Don't want me gettin' ripped off."

"What's he gonna do if we decide to rip you off?" I laughed.

"He's got a gun," she said ominously, without emotion.

At that point, I handed her the money, and she handed me the dope.

"I don't worry about gettin' ripped. I worry about the police. You should worry about getting caught, dealin' like this in the open," I said.

"I don't worry about the law. You deal out in the open, right under their noses, and you're better off. Besides, whadda they gonna do to me? I have four kids. I don't have a record. I mean, really," she reasoned.

"We want two bundles, tomorrow," Dan interrupted abruptly. "You gonna have it?"

"Yeah, I'll have it. I promise. See you tomorrow," she assured us as she got out of the backseat.

"Hey," I called out, as she walked away, "What's your name, anyway?"

The blonde turned around with a big smile and answered, "Emily."

"Okay, Emily," I smiled back. "See you tomorrow."

I put a test on the heroin as Danny drove out of the HoJo's parking lot.

"It's positive for heroin," I said.

"We got junk!" Danny advised the surveillance agents over the walkie-talkie. When he turned on the radio, "Smoke Gets in Your Eyes" by the Platters was playing.

"We saw her arrive in a blue Chevy, about a half hour before you arrived, 203 and 204," Sergio Santini, a surveillance agent, advised us. The registration comes back to a Robert Parker, Centre Street, Dorchester. He's in our files."

"Thanks, 205," Danny replied.

When we returned to the office, we discovered that Robert Parker was a pretty bad character. He was a junkie, and he had done time for the sale of heroin, breaking and entering, assault, and possession of a firearm. He had a substantial criminal record. He was married to Emily Parker, our subject, who had no criminal record.

Over the next couple of weeks, Danny and I made a series of heroin buys from Emily and a number of other junkies at the Washingtonian methadone clinic. We had about twenty defendants, so we would surely be able to develop some informants after we rounded them all up, which made this low-level heroin case a little more interesting. Things were going pretty well up to this point, but suddenly, some strange things began to happen.

Danny and I developed such a good rapport with Emily that she suddenly proposed a business venture to us one morning. She would introduce us to her source if we would in return give her a percentage of the profits from our business. Danny and I agreed immediately to the terms, and we made a deal. Emily then got into her car and signaled us to follow her. We followed her out of the HoJo's parking lot, onto the street, and around the rotary near the Franklin Park Zoo, when a car cut in front of her and forced her off the road. Danny pulled in behind her, and we began rushing out of our car. Emily signaled us from her car to wait, and we stopped our charge. Two junkies whom we had seen earlier that morning got out of their car, walked up, and leaned over to speak to Emily through the car window. One of the junkies was her old man. He kept looking nervously in our direction, then back at her. They appeared to be engaged in a very spirited conversation. Finally, Emily got out of her car, and all three began walking toward our car.

"They make us, Danny?" I asked.

"We'll find out soon enough," Dan answered.

"Remember, she said he has a gun," I said.

"I remember," Danny answered quickly.

"What do you want to do? Arrest 'em right now? Talk our way out of it? What?" I quizzed Danny anxiously as I opened my car door to get out.

"Let's play it by ear," Danny concluded as he opened his door.

I got out and Emily approached, while the two junkies stopped in their tracks and remained in the background. I kept an eye on the two junkie guys, looking for signs of a weapon.

"You're cops," Emily said. "The deal is off. I'm sorry I ever met you."

"What?" I screamed.

"They said you're cops. Some guy up at the clinic says you busted him a few months ago. He said you're undercover feds," Emily explained reluctantly. Both junkies nodded in agreement.

"That maggot!" Danny yelled.

"Where is he? Who is he? I'll kill him, that piece of shit! Crossed us? He's dead! Who is he?" I screamed as I went into a rage. The two junkies and Emily backed off defensively, and watched us nervously.

"Are you cops, or what?" Emily asked almost apologetically, in a quiet voice.

"Are we cops?" Danny screamed at her.

"Do we look like feds?" I yelled.

"If we were feds, you'd be in jail, you stupid bitch! How many times have we copped from you? Huh?" Danny continued, screaming in her face.

"Okay, okay, I know you're not feds. I'm confused. That's stupid, I know. I'm all shook up, though. I'm too nervous now. I can't do the deal today cause I'm too nervous. I know you're not feds, though," Emily rambled on.

"Emily," I assured her in a calmer voice, "some asshole is trying to hurt us. I don't know what his reason is, but he is tryin' to hurt us. Maybe we're cuttin' into his business. Maybe he wants to eliminate his competition. I don't know what it is, but I have to find out. This is important. We gotta know who this asshole is. We gotta straighten his ass out. You understand, Emily?"

"It was that Jew kid, that kid with the Chevy. He always has his princess girlfriend with him. I think he's a hairdresser or something," Emily confessed, quickly giving up the informer.

"That dirty little Jew son of a bitch did this?" hollered Danny.

"You know him?" I asked Danny.

"Yeah, you know him too! It's that little bastard we saw the other night! That fag!" Danny fumed. He acted so well that I wondered for a minute if he was really serious.

"Oh, the hairdressa," I joined in, pretending to catch on. "That little weasel piece of shit! Let's go get him now and give him a beatin'! Follow us, Emily, and we'll make him apologize to you before we croak him. Is he still up there at the clinic?"

"Please, guys, I believe you. I'm just too nervous to do anything else today," Emily begged.

"Relax, Emily. It's not your fault. We gotta straighten this out ourselves. It's between us and him. We'll see you tomorrow," I said.

"Okay, guys, okay. I'll wait to hear from you. I'll see you tomorrow," Emily answered with a sigh of relief.

When we drove away, Danny told me who the rat was. He was a junkie named Harvey whom we had arrested about a month before for sale of heroin. Danny recognized him earlier at the methadone clinic, but did not think that he had seen us.

In the drug business you can never afford to underestimate anyone, not even a junkie. One mistake as undercover agents or a chance occurrence could literally cost us our lives. Needless to say, I was truly furious. We had recently attended the funeral of a New York DEA agent who was shot to death in a hotel room when his true identity was discovered by drug dealers. The tragedy was still fresh in our minds. Danny and I were becoming increasingly paranoid, much like many of the drug users and dealers with whom we worked.

We began a frantic search of every possible junkie hangout to locate Harvey. Finally, after several hours, we found him in the parking lot of an exclusive apartment house in Brookline, where he lived with the beautiful young daughter of a very prominent and wealthy Bostonian. The girlfriend, walking with her arm around Harvey's waist, became nervous when she saw me approach them, and she clutched him tightly. I walked up to him, grabbed him by the shirt, and gave him a hard slap in the mouth with my open hand. His knees buckled and he fell to the pavement, with the girlfriend still struggling to hold onto his arm. I reached down and picked him up by his shirt, snatching him away from her. When I stood him all the way up, I let go of his shirt, and gave him two open-handed slaps—one with my left hand and one with my right. Harvey stumbled backwards like a rag doll, and fell in a heap. He lay there in the fetal position, cowering.

I stood over Harvey, shouting "Harvey, you scum! You gave us up, you scum! You told them who we were! Harvey, you could cost us our lives! Do you know that? Do you care?"

Harvey stayed down on the pavement, whimpering. He refused to get up. He would not respond in any way. He just kept crying. Finally, I picked him up and dusted him off and looked into his eyes. He would not look back in mine. He stared at the ground, denying that he betrayed us. Harvey's girlfriend put her arms around him and comforted him. She stood there next to him, petrified, with tears streaming down her cheeks as we walked away. I never forgot the look on that young girl's face as she consoled him that afternoon. She had a look of innocence. Physically, the girlfriend appeared frail, but she showed more strength and courage than a lion as she rushed to protect Harvey. I thought to myself, this horse is hitched to the wrong wagon. My intuition, unfortunately, proved to be right. Little did I know at the time that within a few weeks, she would be dead. Harvey's girlfriend was murdered for the sins of her lover. She was shot in the head as she sat in the passenger seat next to Harvey while he drove around the rotary on the Jamaicaway between the Faulkner Hospital and Jamaica Pond. A white male with long hair, a moustache, and a beard fired the fatal bullet from the window of a stolen car. The killer wore sunglasses, gloves, and a black stocking hat pulled down tightly over his head. Boston Police homicide detectives believe that the bullet was meant for Harvey. Was the murder related to our case? Who knows? The murderer has yet to be found.

Undercover agents assume a criminal identity and then enter into the secretive, hazy world of the drug dealer. The danger, mystery, and uncertainty add to an already strange existence. It is a lonely life. The agent must leave his family and friends and live in an environment where values are different and morals do not exist. The undercover guy comes from one side of society, and he must cross over to the other side. However, the undercover guy must operate in this milieu without compromising himself. This task is much more difficult than anyone could imagine. At times, he must overlook crimes committed in his presence so as not to risk exposure and imperil more important, ongoing investigations. In addition, undercover people are alienated in many ways from other law enforcement officers because of the shadowy nature of their duties, forcing them to live with a great deal of anxiety and frustration. Undercover people are often hassled and even arrested and jailed by the police. It is not a job for the faint of heart.

When Danny and I returned to the methadone clinic, we were able to convince Emily that we were not cops, and that she should continue to sell heroin to us. Emily was so convinced that she agreed to introduce us to her source for the heroin. On December 23, 1973, a cold, snowy morning, Danny and I followed Emily in her 1964 Chevy through Franklin Park, where she took a left onto Blue Hill Avenue. The Chevy traveled slowly through Grove Hall, past the Black Muslim temple, and turned right at Saint Patrick's Church onto Dudley Street, deep in the heart of Roxbury. When the Chevy stopped at the curb in front of the 600 block on Dudley Street, a Spanish guy appeared, almost mysteriously, and walked mechanically out of the doorway. After hesitating to look directly at Danny and me, he got into the front seat of Emily's car. A moment later, the Chevy pulled away from the curb and moved slowly along Dudley Street. They took a right turn, and then continued straight for a short distance. The tires of Emily's car left tracks in the freshly fallen snow. After several more turns, the Chevy pulled over to the side of the curb and parked on Howard Avenue. We waited for a few minutes until Emily got out of her car and signaled us to join her.

"Here we go," I said apprehensively.

Danny looked at me as he took the keys out of the ignition, and we both got out of the car and walked toward the Chevy.

"Get in," Emily said as she got back into the driver's seat of the car herself.

Danny got in through the rear door on the driver's side, and I entered the rear on the passenger's side. Our eyes met one last time across the roof of the car before we got in. I was surprised to see two young boys, approximately four and six years old, sitting quietly in the backseat.

"These are two of my kids," Emily said with no further explanation.

"Hello, guys!" Danny said to the youngest, as he patted him gently on the head with his hand.

"Hi, handsome," I said, feigning a gentle punch to the chin of the older boy.

Both boys smiled unconvincingly and looked alternately at Danny and me. Danny and I looked at each other, trying to read each other's mind. We were thinking about our own kids.

"This is my man," Emily said directly, interrupting our thoughts and drawing our attention to her and the Spanish guy in the front seat. He nodded on cue, but said nothing.

"I'm Sully," I said.

"I'm Dante," said Danny.

"*Dinero*. Money," said the heavily muscled, middle-aged Spanish guy in a heavy accent.

"It's two thousand, like we said, for the ounce," Emily explained politely to us, interpreting for him.

"We have the *dinero*. We wanna see the *heroína*," I said, as I looked from the Spanish guy to Emily.

"*Heroína*," Emily said in an exaggerated, affected voice as she looked at the Spanish guy. Robotically, he produced the ounce of heroin, wrapped in a bundle of wax paper and sealed with a small piece of scotch tape. He removed the tape and opened the package to display the white heroin powder as he handed it to me over the back of his seat.

"*Gracias, señor*," I said as I carefully took the package from him with two hands.

"*Dinero! Dinero!*" the Spanish guy interrupted urgently as I examined the heroin.

"*Sí, sí*," I responded immediately, and I passed the heroin, over the little boys' heads, to Danny. I then took the money out of my pocket, and counted out two thousand dollars, and handed it into the front seat to the Spanish guy. He carefully counted the money again, very slowly, then he folded it once and put it into his pocket.

"*Quiero comprar mucho heroína en el futuro*," I said, letting the source know in Spanish that I intended to buy a lot of junk, but he did not reply.

"Does this guy speak English or Spanish?" I asked Emily as I looked from him to her.

"Spanish," Emily replied, flatly.

"*Señor, el jefe, me gusto mucho conocerlo*," I tried again to get a conversation going, but he did not respond.

There was a strange silence, as if we were in a vacuum. There was no sound, and there was no movement. It was as though everyone else in the car but me knew what was going on. The sensation in my stomach told me that I was in a very serious situation, but I could not distinguish what it was. I remained motionless like everyone else for a very long time, then I leaned slightly forward and saw that the Spanish guy had a 45-caliber automatic pistol on his lap, and it was pointed directly at Danny. He was staring hard at Danny without blinking, and he had absolutely no expression on his face. My 45-caliber pistol was stuck in my belt, and I could feel it in the small of my back, but there was no way I could get to it now. I leaned back, ever so carefully, and reached into the right front pocket of my woolen navy pea coat, and slid my fingers around the stock of my 38, with my index finger on the trigger, and my thumb placed firmly around the stock, just below the hammer. No one moved. My 38 is really no match for a 45, but I have no choice, I thought to myself, as I contemplated my next move. Should I shoot him through my jacket and the backrest, without removing my pistol? Should I warn him first that I have a pistol pointed at him? What about the kids? What if he shoots Danny? I made my decision boldly. I deftly pulled my 38 out of my coat pocket, and I pressed it against the Spanish guy's head.

I shouted, "*Soy la policía! Ponga la pistola en la silla!*" trying to get him to put down the pistol, but the guy did not move.

I repeated, "*Soy la policía! Levante las manos!*" He still did not respond even after I said I am the police.

I reached with my left hand, under my right hand, and opened the car door, while continuing to press the pistol to the back of the Spanish guy's head. I got out of the car, and told him to drop the pistol and get out of the car with his hands in the air. He sat still, as if he were deaf. He did not move or respond to any of my commands. Suddenly, he burst out of the car, and spun around and hit me along my right cheekbone with the flat side of his gun. I felt the cold steel of the 45 as it banged into my face, and I instinctively grabbed his wrist. I struggled to force the pistol into the air and away from my face. The Spanish guy latched onto my wrist at the same time, immobilizing my gun. It was a standoff.

We struggled like two bears, dancing in the snow. Each time I began to overpower him, he would knee me in the groin or kick me in the shins. I hung onto his gun hand, and kneed him back. We continued the deadly dance.

"I'm the police, man, the police. Don't you understand? *Soy la policía. No entiende?*" I yelled desperately in his ear.

The Spanish guy just stared at me with absolutely no expression on his face at all. How could he not hear me? Was he deaf? Were no words coming from my mouth? His only response was to knee me in the groin and kick me in the shins. I prayed that the surveillance agents would arrive and end the stalemate. The surveillance agents never came. They had made a wrong turn and did not know where we were. It seemed as though the two of us were struggling forever.

We stood still long enough for me to realize that my grandmother lived a block away from where we were struggling. I had walked this same sidewalk and crossed this same street as a kid. I thought it ironic that I would die in a place where I had played with toy soldiers. I thought of my mother and father. I thought of Pam, and how I would miss her beautiful smile. I thought of our brand-new daughter, Stacey. It would be her first Christmas, and I wouldn't be able to give her the presents that I had stored in my locker. My life passed, in an instant, before my very eyes. I asked God to have mercy on my soul. I asked Him to help me. Several times during this struggle, I found myself looking down the barrel of the Spanish guy's gun. Each time, I summoned up the strength to force the barrel away again. The thick snowflakes continued falling quietly down on us, covering everything. I felt like we were figures in a scene of one of those glass paperweights that you shake up and snow falls. It was surreal. Finally, drawing on all the strength that I had left, I forced the Spanish guy's gun away from me once again, and I pointed my gun at his face. All I could see was the cold, expressionless face of the Spanish guy, staring at me.

I looked into his eyes, and I tried one more time, *"Ponga la pistola en la calle! Lavante las manos! Soy la policía!"*

His only reply was a deadly gaze, a chilling, emotionless stare. All my attempts to reason were ignored. There was no way to stop this muted monster that pushed and pulled relentlessly to overpower me. He wanted to kill me.

I pulled the trigger ever so slowly, and bang! The deafening noise of the blast echoed in my right ear. The guy's grip loosened on my wrist, and I stepped back with my right foot, and crouched down in a police shooting position, with the barrel of my gun pointed at his head. I watched the Spanish guy standing, as if he were drunk, waving his 45 slowly from side to side while continuing to point it at me. If the 45 goes off, I will be dead, I thought. Why is he still standing? Did I miss him with my bullet? I foolishly ducked down, like a boxer, bobbing and weaving to avoid a punch. Then, realizing the futility of this move, I popped back into a shooter's stance, and I quickly fired the remaining four bullets of my gun into the Spanish guy's head. He swayed from side to side, then he spun around slowly to his right, collapsed, and fell on his face. I could hear gurgling and intestinal gas escaping as he defecated. I watched a dark stain appear on the bottom of his pants. Steam was coming from the large jagged opening in the back of his head, which drew my eye to the gooey river of brain and tissue that flowed from it in spurts of dark red blood.

Muffled sirens sounded in the snowy distance, growing louder and clearer, until they were right next to me. I stood, straddling the Spanish guy's body as I noticed the smoke rising up in streams from my pistol, which was pointing toward the ground. It was a cold December day. In my peripheral vision I saw two uniformed Boston Police officers get out of their marked cruiser with guns drawn and approach me in slow motion, cautiously. The officers came closer, with their guns pointed directly at me.

"What's goin' on?" one of the officers asked carefully as he evaluated the scene.

"I just shot this guy," I answered simply, standing still, careful not to move my hands.

"Yes, I see," the same officer answered as he continued to study the scene.

"I'm a federal agent. We were doing a drug deal and he tried to shoot my partner. My badge is in my right rear pocket," I told the officer. I could see the surveillance agents pulling up, and bounding out of their cars.

"Federal agents! He's an agent!" I could hear Tom Batten announce to the police officer, as he walked toward us, holding his badge high in front of him.

"Sounds good to me," the officer said as he holstered his pistol.

"Another one for the good guys!" the other officer quipped.

"Would you guys take those kids away from the scene, please?" I asked the cops, motioning toward the Chevy with my head. The cops went over to the Chevy, and I remember relaxing when I saw one of the officers walking away from the scene carrying both boys in his arms. No kid should ever have to witness a shooting like this.

I looked at the guy at my feet. Tom Batten rolled the dead body over with the toe of his boot and bent down to get a closer look. After he examined the body, he stood up again and looked at me.

"His 45 is cocked, Paulie," Tom said. "He would've killed you."

We looked at each other with the same horrible thought in our minds. A lost grip, a slip, or any number of things could have resulted in a very different ending. I was alive by the grace of God and the other guy had five bullets in his head. I turned to look for Danny, and I reached out to hug him as he approached me, his arms stretched out with palms up. I realized that I was still holding my empty pistol in my hand as we hugged and patted each other's back. We stood next to the bloody body, studying each other's eyes. Danny's turned and cast a cold stare down at the dead man.

I learned that Danny had been engaged simultaneously in an equally precarious encounter. As the Spanish guy bounded out of the car at me, Emily drew a pistol and pointed it at Danny, but he could not bring himself to shoot her while her young sons looked on. Danny and Emily, guns at each other's faces, remained in a stalemate until the sound of my gunshots drew her attention. At that moment, Danny twisted the pistol from Emily's hand and placed her under arrest.

Police cars continued to arrive, and the noises of sirens and police talk filled the air as detectives and uniformed cops milled around the scene of the shooting. Danny and I got into a car with Tommy Batten and drove to Boston Police, District Two, in Roxbury. When we entered the station house, the desk sergeant signaled to us and pointed to the rear of the station, where a group of officers waved us in. As we walked through the labyrinth of uniformed police officers, they stared at us. I could hear them talking:

"Good guys, one; bad guys, nothing."

"He deserves a medal from the city."

"Wish he got a couple more."

When we arrived at the group that was waiting for us, one of the officers asked which one of us shot the perpetrator, and I raised my hand. He asked if I would give some details to an officer who was seated at a nearby desk. I nodded, turned to the officer, and began answering routine questions for the incident report, which he was typing slowly, "hunting and pecking" with his index fingers.

"Name? Date of birth? Rank? What police department do you work for?"

In the middle of the questioning, the telephone on his desk rang, and the officer picked it up and listened. With the phone still to his ear, he called out in a loud voice to another officer, seated at a desk across the room, and anyone else who was interested.

"The perpetrator expired at 12:44 p.m."

An icy chill went up my spine, but I consciously looked around to make sure that no one else noticed my reaction. I never thought that he would live after being shot in the face with five hollow-point bullets. I knew from weapons training that those bullets burst inside of his skull, and tore everything inside apart, including his brain, before leaving through that gaping, bloody hole in the back of his head. Still, that sergeant's announcement had a chilling effect on me.

In the middle of the interrogation, I felt someone putting a friendly arm around my shoulder, and giving me a gentle hug. I knew immediately that it was Lieutenant Eddie Connolly, the head of the Boston Police Drug Control Unit. His voice was very distinctive and gave him away when he spoke.

"You did good, kid. Thank God you are all right," the lieutenant said to me with sincerity.

"That's enough. These are my guys," the lieutenant announced to the officer who was asking me questions. He pointed to several of the agents standing in a huddle, who had been on surveillance, and said, "These guys will give you the rest of the details."

"You guys come with me," Lieutenant Connolly said as he motioned to Danny and me. We followed the old lieutenant into an office and he closed the door. He stopped and turned around to face us. He looked at us like an understanding father would look at his sons when they were about to explain a difficult situation. We looked back with trust and openness.

"How're you guys doin'?" the lieutenant asked caringly. We both responded that we were all right. Considering his many years of experience, he most likely knew that we were lying.

"If you need anything, call me. I'll do anything that I can for you. If you want to talk with me, I am always there for you," he said as he continued looking at us. The door opened and a uniformed sergeant walked in briskly and said that ballistics needed a make on my gun, right away.

"Let's go. I'll go with you," the old lieutenant said, nodding his head to the sergeant as he plopped his crumpled felt hat on his head and moved toward the door. We headed for the exit, and I saw Fred Borne, our supervisor, Ed Class, the regional director, and Todd Downs, my former supervisor, now the assistant agent in charge, approaching us through the crowd of police officers and detectives.

"Good job!" Ed Class said with an approving smile. Todd Downs and Fred Borne stood on either side of Class with concerned expressions on their faces.

"Any alcohol involved?" Downs asked out of the corner of his mouth. I shook my head, no.

"Was it a justifiable shooting?" Borne asked. I somehow wanted to laugh, but I didn't. I answered by nodding yes.

"Good," Downs and Borne both responded, very officiously.

"I'll give you and Danny a ride back to the office," Borne added, self-importantly.

"No, they're coming with me. Pick them up at headquarters in about an hour," Lieutenant Connolly replied, leaving no room for discussion.

"Uh, okay, yeah. I'll pick you up at police headquarters," Borne called out to us as we walked outside, through the back door of the station house.

It felt nice to be outside in the cold air again, away from all the excitement and hubbub the shooting had created. I felt a quiet peace, walking to the car with Danny and the old lieutenant, two guys that I trusted with my life. I was like the Spanish guy, in a way. I was at peace, but I was alive. It really felt good to be alive today, too.

"This way you get away from all those questions, and you can get some peace and quiet," the lieutenant explained, as we drove toward Boston Police headquarters on Berkeley Street. We pulled up in front of the station, and I could hear the noise of the police cruiser's rubber tires squeezing up against the curb as we parked. We got out of the lieutenant's command staff car, and Danny and I followed him up the stairs, past the lobby, and onto the elevator. All along the corridor, cops, secretaries, and even the janitor said hello to Lieutenant Connolly, and they smiled at Danny and me as we followed him. Connolly was a cop's cop, and we were both proud to be with him. When we arrived in the lobby of the ballistics section, an old cop with a squirrelly face peered at us from behind a caged window.

"Hello, Lou," the cop in the cage said, using the shortened version of lieutenant.

"Hi. This guy just shot that dope dealer on Howard Avenue," Lieutenant Connolly said in his nasal voice, getting right to the point.

"Okay, I'm gonna need your gun for some tests. I'll return it in about two weeks," the cop said flatly as he looked out at me through the cage. I began to nod my understanding.

"Bullshit! He ain't handin' his gun over to no one! He needs his gun! Some son of a bitch drug dealer'll kill 'em." Lieutenant Connolly cut us both off.

"Lou, that's procedure," the squirrelly cop explained apologetically through the cage.

"Bullshit! What kinda proceedja's that? Fire a couple of rounds, and give him his gun back, or you don't get it at all!" Lieutenant raised his nasal voice on my behalf.

"Okay, boss, I suppose I can do that," the cop conceded, reluctantly.

The lieutenant nodded at me, and I opened the chamber of my pistol and handed it through the window to the cop in the ballistics room. He took the pistol from me, placing it in a white towel that lay opened in the palm of his hand, and he turned and walked out of my sight. I joined the lieutenant and Danny, who were leaning against the wall, talking.

"These guys have been off the street so long that they forget what you have a gun for. I'll stay until he returns your gun, then I have to get back to my unit. If you guys need anything, call me," Lieutenant Connolly commanded. The ballistics cop appeared in the caged window, and I reached in and took my pistol from him.

"All set," he said.

"Thanks," Lieutenant Connolly responded. Danny and I shook hands with the lieutenant, thanked him for the special treatment, and jumped onto the elevator. When Danny and I got off at the lobby, Fred Borne was there as promised.

"So, how's it goin'?" Borne said when he saw us.

"Okay," Danny said, and I nodded in agreement as we followed Borne out the front door of headquarters to his car.

"So, you guys want to get a bite to eat?" Borne asked as we got into his car and began our drive. Eating was the last thing in the world that I felt like doing. Danny and I looked at each other and responded with noncommittal shrugs.

"How 'bout Brigham's?" Borne persisted.

"Sure," I answered, looking at Danny.

"You won't get much of a chance to eat because Inspections is on the way up from Washington," Borne announced.

"Inspections? Why?" I asked.

"Procedure," Borne answered, like a true bureaucrat. I wondered what Inspections had to do with the shooting of a drug dealer. Why would they fly two inspectors up from Washington? What was going on? Again I looked at Danny, and we shrugged our shoulders. Borne parked the car on Boylston Street, in front of Brigham's, and we all got out of the car and walked inside. We sat at the counter and a teenage waitress came over and handed us the luncheon menus. Borne and Danny opened their menus, but I was not interested in eating. I watched the waitress draw water into glasses and bring them back to the counter for us, and I noticed that her name tag read Carrie.

"That's a nice name," I said.

"Thanks," she giggled.

"Carrie Nation was a very famous woman. Do you know who she was?" I asked.

"No," the waitress replied, absently.

"She was a leader of the temperance movement, and she spoke out against pornography," I said. I could tell by her response that she was clueless, so I smiled, and told her that it was really not that important.

Borne ordered a hamburger and Danny ordered a cheeseburger. The waitress looked at me, and I told her that I was not hungry. Borne reminded me that I hadn't eaten all day, and I would not get a chance later on. Reluctantly, I ordered a well-done hamburger and a coffee. The waitress left, and Borne, Danny, and I made small talk. Borne wanted us to discuss the shooting, but I didn't feel like it, and neither did Danny. Borne just was not the kind of guy that either of us warmed up to. He was a transfer from the FBI and he brought all their worst qualities with him. He once asked me what I thought was an agent's most important weapon. As I paused to consider my response, he answered for me.

"The telephone; remember it." A telephone really would have come in handy for me today, I thought.

The waitress delivered our sandwiches, and Borne began eating immediately. Danny took a sip of his coffee, and I looked straight ahead, thinking of the shooting incident. When I picked up my hamburger to bring it to my mouth, I saw the juices oozing from the meat as blood, and it made my stomach nauseated. I stopped before I reached my mouth, and as I looked at the sandwich, I noticed spattered, dried blood on my hands. My fingers and the backs of my hands were dotted with blood from the Spanish guy. I put the sandwich down and took a sip of coffee. I became self-conscious thinking about the blood on my hands.

"Aren't you gonna eat your sandwich?" Borne asked, looking greedily at my hamburger.

"Nah, I really don't feel like it," I answered.

"I'll eat it," Borne volunteered eagerly.

"Yeah, sure," I answered, as he reached over, picked up my sandwich, and began stuffing it into his mouth. I watched Borne's face as he gobbled up the hamburger, and I realized that he had no idea how Danny or I felt. Like the waitress, he was clueless.

After our dinner stop, we went to the office. Todd Downs met us and nervously told us that the inspectors were in the regional director's office talking with him, and they wanted to speak with us alone; first me, then Danny. I was puzzled at first, then I began to get angry. I thought to myself, why do they want to separate us? That is like an interrogation. Did we do something wrong? Whose side are they on?

As I was thinking about the situation, Peter Fenton, a fellow agent, walked up to us and whispered that we should hire lawyers. I looked at him, but I didn't understand. Why do we need a lawyer? I wondered. While Fenton was still there, Chris Regan leaned over and mumbled that we should tell the inspectors nothing. A tall, lanky, neatly dressed man whom I had never seen before appeared in the entranceway to Group Two and looked directly at me.

"Hello, Doyle, my name is Inspector Richardson, and I would like to talk to you, alone," Richardson said seriously, and he emphasized "alone." He alienated me with his opening sentence. I don't like people who address me by my last name. I really don't like people who try to bullshit me.

"Just you and me, man to man?" I responded.

"No, my partner is inside," Richardson clarified his request.

"Oh, then my partner will join us," I replied.

"No," Richardson laughed, impatiently, "that's not the way we do things."

"Oh, yeah, then you talk to me alone, and your partner can talk to Danny alone, and then we can switch. That's the way we do things, too," I countered. Richardson, angered by my noncompliant response, looked at me in disbelief.

"Okay, okay," Richardson said with a condescending laugh, "Danny can come with you."

Danny looked at me and knew how angry I was getting. We followed Richardson into the regional director's office, and he introduced us to his partner, Inspector McGinley.

"Relax, guys, you did a great job today. There's nothing to worry about. We're here to help you," Richardson began.

"Help us? We don't need any help, do we, Danny? We could have used some help this morning when Bonnie and Clyde pulled the guns on us, but we didn't get any. We don't need any help now," I said angrily.

"C'mon, guys, we're on your side. You guys are probably going to get the Administrator's Medal for this." McGinley tried feebly to soft-soap us.

"A medal? Really? Then why are you here? Where's the administrator?" I said sarcastically. "We have made some pretty good cases over the years, and all of a sudden we get a medal for shooting a small-time heroin dealer. That makes a lot of sense."

"Listen, why don't you cut the shit, and tell us what you want," Danny demanded.

"Okay, we understand. It's been a long day for you guys. We need to ask you a couple of questions, and we're out of here. It's normal procedure to be interviewed by Inspections after use of lethal force by an agent. Fair enough?" Richardson proposed.

"Shoot," Danny said. I laughed nervously at Danny's choice of words.

"Tell me what happened," Richardson requested as he turned on a tape recorder and pointed it at us. Danny and I recounted the entire incident from beginning to end, exactly as we remembered it. Richardson and McGinley took notes the entire time we talked. We finished by describing the shooting scene. When we were done, the inspectors studied our faces, but said nothing for a long time.

"So, the guy pulled the gun on you, and you blasted him. Then you walked over and emptied the gun into his head and finished him off," Richardson said, disregarding everything that I had just explained to him. I was so angry that I wanted to punch his head in. I looked over at Danny, and he gave me the signal with his head to leave.

"As I said before, we don't need your help or anyone else's," I informed him angrily as I stood up and moved threateningly toward the inspectors.

"C'mon, Paul," Danny said, and he put his hand on my shoulder.

"Go help someone that needs it," Danny said sarcastically, and we walked out of the room, leaving the inspectors alone with each other.

Danny and I hung around the office, trying to look busy at our desks, but our minds were somewhere else. It was obvious that we were both preoccupied with the shooting. It was a few nights before Christmas, and all the agents were going over to the Bell in Hand, a little bar across the street from the federal building, for a little holiday cheer. I picked up file folders, made believe I was reading, and then I put them down. I was trying to stall until everyone left the office, so I could get my daughter's Christmas gifts out of my locker and go home. I had no desire to sit around a bar, but I didn't want to tell the guys that. Time suddenly seemed so precious to me.

"C'mon, I'll buy you a beer," Chris appeared and said thoughtfully, looking down at me, over the top of my desk.

"Thanks, Chris, maybe later," I said, but he knew that I would not be joining them.

"Okay, Paulie, you did the right thing today. I'm glad it was him and not you. If you change your mind, the offer is still good. Merry Christmas." Chris smiled and left with a salute.

Chris was about the last one to go. Danny said that he was going to head over to the Bell in Hand for a beer and would catch a ride home with Chris. After Danny packed up and left, Borne called my name from his office, and I answered from my desk. He called me in, so I got up from my desk and walked into his office. He was seated behind his desk, playing with a pencil in his right hand. He pointed to Ron LaGuerre with the pencil.

"Ron will drive you home tonight," Borne said.

"Why?" I asked, looking over at Ron for a clue as to why. Ron and I both smiled.

"Procedure," Borne answered.

"Okay, we better follow procedure then," I said sarcastically.

"Whenever you are ready," Borne added.

"Okay, thanks." I turned to Ron and asked if he would mind waiting a few minutes while I got some things from my locker. Then I took out the Christmas gifts that I bought for Stacey, my eight-month-old daughter. No one could ever understand how thankful I was that I was alive to do this. My locker and the presents looked so beautiful to me. I removed the gifts from my locker, and I wobbled down the hallway to Borne's office, my arms full of packages. Ron laughed when he saw me, and he got up and took a couple of the bags from me.

"You know Santa don't do this alone. He got helpers!" Ron grinned widely as he adjusted his arms around some of the presents, and we walked out of the office together.

"How many people did you buy all these presents for?" Ron laughed.

"One," I answered. Ron's laugh caused me to laugh.

"One? Who's the one?" Ron asked in a high-pitched voice, with raised eyebrows.

"My daughter," I said.

"She's only a baby," Ron laughed, and continued in the high-pitched voice. "The presents are bigger than she is!"

Ron was a brand-new agent, but he was a real good guy. He had recently graduated from Boston College, and was very motivated. Borne assigned him to work with Danny and me because he wanted him to get started right away, and Ron did. He was a self-starter. Every morning I drove, picked Ron up at his apartment building across from Franklin Park, and drove him to work. We usually talked all the way into the office. He was black and I was white, but that was not important to either of us. We had some of the deepest conversations about God, religion, morality, right and wrong, and life in general when we were together. We had so much in common. It was a good choice, after all, to have Ron drive me home tonight, I thought. Borne can't be wrong all of the time.

"Ron, would you mind stopping by the Arch Street shrine while I run in for a minute?" I asked. I wanted to go to confession. I wanted to tell God that I was sorry for what I had done, to ask forgiveness for having taken a man's life.

"Hell, no, I don't mind," Ron answered. He talked with energy and enthusiasm, and he always made me feel good.

We parked directly across the street from the Arch Street shrine. The giant crucifix on the shrine's façade loomed over us as we got out of the car and walked across the snow-filled street. Last-minute Christmas shoppers were rushing to Jordan Marsh and Filene's Basement, and the Salvation Army Santa was ringing his bell on the corner. There was a Mass going on at the street-level chapel of the shrine, so we went down the stairs to the chapel in the basement. Ron and I both sat in a pew and waited as the people in place before us filed in and out of the confessional. We sat silently, praying to ourselves as we slid down closer and closer to the end of the bench. When it was my turn, I pushed the drape aside and ducked into the tiny cubicle. I knelt down facing the dark screen in front of me. I prayed silently, and I asked God's forgiveness, until the tiny door on the other side of the screen suddenly slid open. Straining my eyes to see through the tightly woven screen, I could barely make out the shadowy profile of a priest.

"Fatha, forgive me, for I have sinned. It has been about six months since my last confession." I began to recite the format that I had learned in the first grade at Our Lady of Perpetual Help Grammar School. Then I stopped. There was a long period of silence, while I tried to verbalize my thoughts.

"Are you all right?" the priest asked.

"Yes, Fatha," I answered, and then confessed. "I am an undercover agent, and I killed a man today in a shoot-out."

"Are you a policeman? Were you on duty?" the priest asked.

"Yes, Fatha, he sold me drugs, and then he pointed a pistol at my partner," I began to explain.

"Son, I know that it must be a traumatic experience to take another man's life, but in the eyes of God, you did not sin. You took the man's life because you had no other rational choice. It was kill or be killed. If you didn't shoot him, he would have killed you or your partner. That is self-defense, and that is not a sin."

"Thank you, Fatha, I appreciate your kind words, but what bothers me is that I don't believe that. I took a man's life, and I have to wait until I die for God's judgment."

"Son, that is not so. You are already forgiven," the Father told me.

The priest was concerned and I know that he wanted to ease the pain I felt that I could not disguise, but I truly believed that the matter was between God and me. I did not think that the priest had the power to forgive me in this instance. I wanted the grace of confession, but I somehow could not relate to the sacrament.

I completed my confession and went to the altar at the front of the chapel to pray my penance. When I was finished, I walked to the back of the church and waited for Ron. While I waited, I watched all the other people coming and going to confession, kneeling and praying, or just sitting quietly in the pews, and I wondered what they were praying for. What brought them there? How could God handle so many requests for mercy and pleas for forgiveness? When Ron was finished, he joined me and we walked up the stairs and out of the church. The snow was falling steadily, and it stuck to our heads as we crossed the street. We got into the car and pulled out of the space into the snow-filled street. After Ron turned onto the expressway and headed toward 128, he looked several times in my direction, and I sensed that he wanted to say something.

"I'm glad you made it, man," Ron said with sincerity.

"Thanks, Ron," I answered, looking sideways at him.

"I don't know where the hell we were, but we lost you, and it would have been our fault if that dude killed you," Ron said very seriously.

"Nah, that's not true. It's difficult to follow someone through the streets of Roxbury without burnin' up the surveillance. It happens all the time, you know that. If I got killed it would be because that Spanish dude shot me before I shot him. It always comes down to one on one. You know that from training school. There are only two kinds of people in the world, the quick and the dead," I explained.

"Yeah," Ron answered thoughtfully, "but I would never be able to live with myself."

"Yeah, but you wouldn't have to share the car with me anymore, either. You have to think on the bright side," I joked.

On the radio, the news commentator was jabbering on about the local news. Suddenly, his voice became very serious and he announced, "A federal agent shot and killed a drug dealer today in Roxbury. The agent acted to protect the life of his partner. Ed Class, the regional director of the Bureau of Narcotics and Dangerous Drugs, commended the quick action of the agent for saving the lives of his partner and two small children, who were present at the time of the shooting." I asked Ron if he would pull over, so that I could call my wife from a pay phone. We stopped at a gas station at the East Milton exit ramp. I walked over to the pay phone, dialed my telephone number, and waited for Pam to answer. As I listened to the telephone ringing, I pictured Pam. I thought how worried she would be if she heard about the shooting on the news. I listened as the telephone rang on and on. I finally hung up and rejoined Ron, who was finished gassing up the car.

"How'd it go?" Ron asked, inquisitively.

"She didn't answer."

"She's probably out Christmas shoppin', buyin' you a great big present!" Ron joked, in an effort to take my mind off of things.

"Would you mind stopping by my parents' house?" I asked. "I am worried about them, too. They would be upset if they heard the news. Plus, Pam might be there with the baby, visiting."

"Anything you want, Paul. I'll take you anywhere," Ron said in his exaggerated, high-pitched voice.

"Thanks, I appreciate it."

"No, problem," Ron answered.

We drove along the expressway and merged onto Route 128, passing the Braintree Shopping Plaza, where we could see the parking lot overloaded with cars full of last-minute Christmas shoppers. The snow was falling faster as we drove past the Blue Hills, and I thought about how cold and dark it was tonight. I thought about the guy I killed earlier in the day and how he was lying on a cold slab in the morgue. I didn't even know his name. I couldn't get him out of my mind, the ice-cold stare.

"Paulie, which one is your parents'?" Ron asked as he pulled into the trailer park, waking me out of my trance.

"This one here," I answered, while Ron drove slowly toward a white mobile home that appeared to be vacant, except for the light of a television set that illuminated the inside sporadically with uneven splashes of light. I knew that they were home because my father's car was parked outside their trailer. Ron followed me up the platform while I knocked on the door. I knocked harder when no one answered. I could see my parents inside, watching the television, but they did not move. Finally, I saw my mother get up and walk to the door. She opened it a crack. Obviously, she did not want company.

"It's Paul," my mother shouted to my father in an aggravated tone.

"Hey, hey, Merry Chrishmish," my father said. He sounded drunk.

"Hi, Mom." I kissed my mother on the cheek.

"Hi, Dad," I said, looking into the trailer to see my father struggling to stand up. I looked back at Ron and shook my head in disbelief and disappointment. It was the first time that Ron had ever met my parents. When my father got up from the couch, he stumbled toward the open door. He had an exaggerated, plastic smile on his face, and he seemed surprised to see me standing on his doorstep with a black guy.

"Come on in," he said loudly, almost barking.

"C'mon, Ron," I said, turning toward Ron, putting my arm around his shoulder and stepping aside, to let him enter first.

"Mon in," my father said, sounding more drunk than before, as he struggled to focus his eyes and get a closer look at Ron.

"Hello, Mr. Doyle," Ron said enthusiastically.

"You're a good boy," my father said, completely unaware that it was an insult to address a black man as boy. I was embarrassed for my father and for Ron.

"Dad, I stopped by to tell you that I was involved in a shooting, and I killed a man. I didn't want you and Mom to be worried if you heard it on the news," I explained. My father blinked slowly, and tried to focus his eyes.

"One a those goddam niggas?" he said, slurring his words. It wasn't my father. It was the booze talking. He looked at Ron and said, "Not you, I didn't mean you."

I felt sick to my stomach when he spoke. I came looking for my father to save him from worrying, but I also really wanted to talk to him about the shooting. I needed to talk about it with my father, but he was drunk. Ron did not let my father's comments bother him, and he somehow managed to smile throughout the embarrassing visit. He knew what I was going through, though, because he grew up in very similar circumstances. As we finally drove away from the trailer park and headed for my house, a wide grin spread over Ron's face. When he looked at me, I apologized.

"Ronny, I apologize for my father," I said.

"You don't have to apologize," said Ron sincerely with a sparkle in his eye. Then he added, "At least you got a father."

When he said this, a giddy feeling came over me, and I wanted to laugh. Ron started to laugh that funny laugh of his, and I broke out laughing, too. The absurdity of the visit, and our attempts to muffle our laughter made the moment even funnier. We were both being overly concerned about each other's feelings. He understood what happened because he grew up in the same kind of environment; only the color of our skin was different. The tension evaporated with our laughter.

Ron took a left turn into my street and headed toward my house. I could see from a distance that Pam was not at home. I wondered where she was, and I pictured her driving alone along the highway and hearing the news flash. I wanted to be the one to tell her what happened.

"Would you like me to come in with you?" Ron asked, again startling me out of my thoughts.

"Yeah, come on in and have a drink or something to eat," I said.

"You better put Black Jack away first," Ron reminded me with a smile, and he cuffed me on the arm. It was really ironic and funny because Ron trained Black Jack, my pit bull terrier. As a result, Black Jack hated Ron. He was always the aggressor in the training sessions, sneaking up to the windows of the house like a burglar. Black Jack became an excellent guard and attack dog, but he had a special hatred for Ron, and black people in general.

Ron waited at the front door while I put the dog away. When I returned to let Ron in, I saw his face through the glass top half of the storm door. He was smiling again, and it made me smile automatically. Ron came in and walked to the kitchen with me, then watched while I poked through the refrigerator.

"I can heat up some spaghetti and meatballs, or I can make you some hot dogs and beans," I said, looking into the refrigerator. When I glanced over at Ron, he was laughing again.

"No, thank you! You ain't got no chitlins or black-eyed peas?" he joked.

"A glass of milk, or a cup of tea?" I persisted.

"No, thanks, man," Ron said, warmly, with an exaggerated seriousness. "I better be going, so I don't get buried in this snow."

"Okay, Ron, thanks." I grabbed his hand and shook it, and looked him in the eye. "Be careful."

"Okay, man, I will. You take care," Ron said, and then he went to the car. We both wanted to say more, but we didn't know what to say. I watched through the windshield as he started the car, and the windshield wipers cleaned the snow away. I waved, and he waved back, as he backed out of my driveway and drove away. I hated to see him leave.

I went back into the kitchen and I stood there for awhile, moping around in the silence, until I heard Black Jack bark from down in the cellar. I turned the doorknob and Black Jack charged with excitement through the opening and almost knocked me over. He jumped up, bumping my nose with his head and licking my face. He was like a bull in a china shop!

"Good boy," I said, patting his head and face with two hands. He pushed away from me with both paws and rushed from room to room. He was looking for someone. I realized that he was on to the scent of Ron, because he was growling.

"It's okay, boy, it's okay; he's gone. It's all right," I assured Black Jack as I knelt down and hugged him. Black Jack quickly turned his attention back to me, and he bowled me over with his head. I fell over backwards onto the floor, Black Jack pushing me with his head and lapping my face. I played with him for a few minutes and then I thought about this afternoon, and how close I came to getting killed. This moment, playing with my dog, never would have happened, I thought.

I scrambled back to my knees, and then I got up and went into the gym that I had built in the garage. I turned on the light and looked at the punching bag dangling on the chain from the ceiling. I faced the heavy bag and started throwing light punches at it. Jab, jab, right cross. I faked a left, then threw a right hand, and followed up with a left hook to the body. I focused all of my attention on the bag, and I began to throw harder, more powerful punches. Finally, I threw a furious flurry of punches meant to knock my imaginary opponent out. Black Jack growled, and I turned to look at him. He leaped through the air at the bag, with his teeth showing. The interruption caused me to miss the bag completely with my right cross, and I hit Black Jack squarely on the snout. He fell over and landed on his back and banged the back of his head on the floor. He got up immediately, poised and ready to go again, but I stopped punching the bag, and I stood quietly, looking at him. The bag was swinging slowly, back and forth on the squeaky chain, and it no longer appeared the fearsome threat, as it had moments earlier. Black Jack was confused, but he was ready to attack. He wanted to protect me, but he didn't know from whom. I kneeled down again and hugged Black Jack. He started once again to lap my face and wag his tail. He began licking my hands and nibbling on my knuckles with his teeth. When I pulled my hands away, I could see that my knuckles were bleeding. I had punched the bag so hard that I shredded the skin. I thought about how my blood was now mixed with the blood of the Spanish guy. I began to think of the last moments before I pulled the trigger. Could I have prevented it? Did I have to kill him? Black Jack crashed into my face again and put his paw on my shoulder to get my attention. I hugged him again and I told him that everything was all right. I wished that I could assure myself that everything was all right! I stood up and I went to the kitchen and fed him some dog snacks. When they say that a dog is a man's best friend, I know what they mean. There aren't many friends whom you could punch in the face without dampening their spirits and straining their friendship.

As I was feeding Black Jack, I could hear someone putting a key in the front door lock, and he was gone. He rushed to greet Pam, who was carrying baby Stacey and bundles of presents. She put Stacey into her crib with her snowsuit still on, then she walked into the kitchen. Pam had a beautiful smile on her face, as always, and as she walked, she told Black Jack that he was a good boy. She was surprised to see me leaning against the wall when she came around the corner.

"Hello!" Pam said enthusiastically, and she put the bags down on the counter and put her arms around me.

"Hello," I said tentatively, trying to appear unconcerned, while trying to figure out what she knew about the shooting.

"How did you manage to get home so early?" she asked, and I realized she was oblivious to my ordeal as she greeted me with a kiss.

"It's Christmas," I answered. I could tell by her manner that she did not know about the shooting.

We made tea, and we began talking about Christmas and how we were both so excited because it would be Stacey's first. Pam showed me all the presents that she had bought for Stacey, and then I showed Pam all the presents that I had bought. We were worried that we wouldn't have enough for her, but now our house looked like a toy store! We began to laugh, and then we couldn't stop. We hugged and laughed until we cried. We were blessed, I thought. We could not have been happier. I was the happiest man in the world because I was married to the most beautiful girl in the world, and we had the most beautiful baby girl in the world. I knew how lucky I was, and tonight, I knew it more than ever. I didn't want to tell her about the shooting. I didn't want to talk about it.

"Wha! Wha!" Stacey yelled loudly from her crib, at the top of her lungs.

Pam and I looked at each other and laughed again. Our time alone was too good to be true. Stacey had slept for some time while we talked, and now she wanted some attention.

"Paulie, good night, I am pooped," Pam said to me with her sleepy eyes, then added with a kiss, "I love you."

I laughed and told her good night. She could not stay up for anything. When it was bedtime, she was gone. An atomic bomb could go off, and Pam would not hear it. She slept like a baby. That's why I always got up when Stacey cried at night. Pam went to bed about eleven o'clock that night.

"Whatsamatta, Stacey baby?" I whispered, and bent down to pick her up. What trust, I thought to myself. This beautiful baby is counting on me for everything. She is inherently trusting. She smiles so beautifully, and she makes the cutest faces. It's after two a.m. and we are smiling at each other in the dark. I held the tiny baby in my arms and rocked her back and forth, thinking about her natural beauty, a miracle, I thought. She stopped crying and I finally realized that she was asleep, so I gently put her back in her crib, bundled her up in her blanket, and kissed her good night. Then I stumbled through the dark into my bedroom. It was around one o'clock in the morning, and I was beginning to feel tired from the day's events. I thought to myself, how ironic it seems, Stacey trusts everyone, and I trust no one. Stacey is my daughter, but she is also my antithesis.

I pulled my gun out of my waistband and put it between the mattress and the box spring, right below my pillow, so I could reach it in an emergency. I pulled the covers down, and I tried to slip into bed as quietly as I could so I wouldn't wake up Pam. I couldn't help but think how beautiful Pam was as I watched her sleep. I pulled the covers up to my chin, rested my head back on the pillow, and looked up at the ceiling. I thought about the shooting and the Spanish guy. I recited my prayers to myself, and I asked God to forgive me and to have mercy on my soul.

I closed my eyes, and a movie clip began to play. I was standing face to face with the Spanish guy, and he was staring at me. It was as though he was really there. I opened my eyes to get out of the movie. My nerves were strained, and my heart was beating fast. I could feel the blood rushing to my neck and head. I looked at the ceiling, my chest was heaving, and I tried to think about something else. My eyes were heavy, but I fought to keep them open. I could hear the seconds tick away on the alarm clock. My eyelids got heavier and heavier, and then they closed, and the movie began again, clip by clip. The Spanish guy and me, face to face, the stare, the words, the shots, the drunken stance, the collapse, the hole in his head, the blood, the shit, the smoke coming out of the barrel of my gun. I opened my eyes to get away from the scene, but my body had a life of its own. I had no control. My head was spinning and my heart was pounding. I was scared. My body was hot and the sheets around me were soaked with sweat. I looked over at Pam to make sure that she was asleep. I prayed for God's help. The never-ending movie went on all night, frame by frame. The fatal heroin buy played over and over in my mind, endlessly. I was very tired, but relieved to see the sun come up after the long, dark night. The sun would light up the darkness, I thought, and everything would be all right again. The shooting was finally over.

I rolled over and slid out of bed. As soon as my feet hit the floor, I knelt down beside my bed and reached under the mattress for my gun. I took it in my right hand, and I lifted up the shade with my left hand just enough to enable me to peek out. The snow was still falling and I could see that there was already an accumulation of about thirty-six inches. But that is not what interested me. I was looking to see if there was anyone there, any possible threat. I strained my eyes to see through the frosted window and the thick snow, but the visibility was poor. I could only see to the end of my driveway. The streetlight made a yellow tunnel of light to the street, but it was hardly visible in the dim morning light. When I stood up, Black Jack approached and nuzzled me. I scratched him behind the ears and ushered him out of the bedroom so we wouldn't wake Pam. I closed the bedroom door, and Black Jack jumped up excitedly and put his two front paws on my chest. I pushed him away and whispered that he was a good boy. He got more excited as I pulled on my jeans and flannel shirt. I had to stop and pat him to calm him down, so he wouldn't wake Pam and Stacey. I put my pistol in my waistband, and put on my socks and boots. I walked over to the living room window, and Black Jack bumped his head into mine as I crouched and leaned over to peek out below the shade. I put my arm around him as I looked out, but all I could see was the snow blowing in the wind and whipping into the windowpane, and I could feel the draft streaming in between the sash and the sill. I went over to the coatrack and pulled on my hooded parka and snapped the short leash on Black Jack. I opened the front door, and I had to force the storm door with my boot to open it against the accumulation of snow. My dog and I squeezed out together, into the dark morning storm. I stood silent listening, while Black Jack pulled his ears back and raised his nose and squinted his eyes to search for any adversaries. I stood there for a long minute with Black Jack tugging on the leash. Finally, when I was convinced that there was no one moving, we began to make a search of the perimeter. Black Jack burrowed through the deep snow, and he dragged me along. I struggled to hold him back. We walked slowly around the entire house searching through the deep snow, but we found nothing, no footprints or sign of any kind. I was still not convinced. I walked up the crest of the hill and checked behind every telephone pole. When I reached the top, I looked as far as I could see, but I could see nothing but the falling snow. I looked down at Black Jack and he seemed to wonder what I wanted. I smiled slightly when I realized that there was no one around, and I praised him. We walked back down the hill and went into the house. I could hear that Pam was already awake and talking to baby Stacey.

"What are you two crazy guys doing, going out in this storm?" Pam called out, teasing me.

"What storm?" I joked, while Pam and baby Stacey laughed out loud at Black Jack and me, standing in the doorway, covered from head to foot with snow.

I unleashed Black Jack, and he almost knocked Pam over as he rushed to her with his tail wagging like a whip. She laughed and patted him with one hand, while she held our giggling baby girl in the other. I took off my parka and sat down next to them and began taking off my boots, and I wondered how I could be sitting here in this warm, beautiful place. It was so peaceful. Is this real? I wondered. Am I really here? Am I dreaming?

"Pam, would you like a cup of coffee?" I asked as I began to measure out the coffee into the basket of the percolator.

"No, thank you. I'm going to have a cup of tea," Pam answered.

I walked into the gym while I waited for the coffee to perk, then I walked into the dining room and gazed out the window. The snow seemed to be falling faster and faster. I was "jiggy" and I wanted to get out of the house, but I didn't want to alarm Pam or draw attention to my fears. I walked back into the kitchen and poured myself a cup of coffee. I stood up while I slowly sipped from the coffee cup. I tried to look out the kitchen window without being seen by Pam. Paranoia was taking over my mind.

"Pam, I think I'm going to go to Mass this morning," I said, trying to look as natural as I could.

"There won't be any Mass today. It's a blizzard!" Pam laughed.

"There will be Mass. There's always a Mass," I said self-consciously.

"Paul, look outside. Everything is cancelled. Listen to the radio," she said to persuade me.

"I don't care, I want to get some exercise, anyway," I answered as I put on my parka and headed for the door.

"You're crazy!" Pam called out good-naturedly, as I shut the door behind me. She knew that it would be futile to argue with me at this point.

I was beginning to wonder if what she said was right, though. I wondered if I was going crazy. I wandered through the heavy drifts of snow, trying to see as well as I could. I purposely left Black Jack home because I was convinced in my mind that I would be ambushed and killed. I wanted him to stay at home to protect Pam and Stacey. I thought that it would be better for me to walk away from the house, so that the killers would not harm them in order to get me. I was forced to lean into the wind so as not to be blown backwards. I reached the top of the hill, and I turned left onto Washington Street toward Norwood. I did not see any cars, but I could hear a solitary snowplow. Then in the distance I noticed what appeared to be two headlights moving slowly toward me. The lights got closer and closer. Butterflies began in my stomach, and my heart began to pump faster and faster. As the lights approached, I began to make out the silhouette of a car. I could feel the moisture in my palm as I held the pistol grip tightly, deep down in my parka pocket. The car drove near, and I aimed the pistol at the driver, without taking it out of my pocket. The blood was rushing to my head, my heart was pounding, and my stomach danced out of control. The car appeared to pass, and I tensed up and tried to act as if I didn't notice it. Then it stopped. I hesitated and turned, as if to cross the street. I could see the passenger window retract slowly, and I waited for the barrel of a gun to appear. Instead, I saw the face of an old lady, and she called out to me.

"Is there a gas station up this way?" the old lady yelled as the snow rushed in her window.

I approached the window cautiously, and I could see the old lady seated in the passenger side and a sad-faced old man driving. The blood began to leave my head, and I relaxed a bit and watched the nervous look in the old lady's eyes. I wanted to help them.

"There is a twenty-four-hour gas station straight ahead, about two miles," I directed them. I took a deep breath and let it out to calm myself down. What's wrong with me, I wondered.

"Thank you, son. You don't know how happy you made us! Thank you. Do you need a ride?" they asked.

"No, I don't need a ride. Thank you, I am okay. You just be careful," I answered with a wave.

"You are a nice boy," the old woman said, and she rolled up the window. I watched the car drive through the snow until it was out of sight. I wondered who they were, and where they were going on a stormy day like today.

A ten-wheeler went by with its plow blade lifted in the air, but I did not see another car on my walk all the way to Saint Denis Catholic Church. As I climbed the steps of the church, I noticed that my footprints were the only ones. The stairs were not shoveled. I had to yank the heavy wooden door to open it against the snow that had drifted against it. I stepped inside the church and stomped my feet to clean off the snow. I flipped my hood back, and I shook my head from side to side to clean the snow and ice from my face and hair. The church was empty, save for a white-haired priest staring at me from the altar as he snuffed out the flame from the last candle. He stared, but didn't speak, as I walked, like the abominable snowman, to the front of the church. I stopped at the foot of the altar and said hello. The priest continued staring apprehensively, trying to discern what I was doing.

"Good morning," the priest managed.

"Good morning, Fatha. I guess I missed Mass," I said.

"No, I was getting ready to close up the church. No one came," the priest explained.

"Okay, Fatha, I'll see you another time," I said.

"No, no, we'll have Mass," the priest insisted.

"No, that's okay, don't say Mass just for me," I told the priest.

"No, please, I'm glad that you are here. We will have Mass," the priest said, quickly realizing that I had walked through a blizzard for a reason that was unknown to him, but surely important to me.

I genuflected while simultaneously making the sign of the Cross, and I knelt down in the first pew. I blessed myself again and began to pray silently, while the priest prepared the altar for Mass. He made several trips, moving silently from the sacristy to the altar, placing the cruets of water and wine, the chalice, and the Bible in their designated places. I continued to pray while I followed the movements of the priest with my eyes. He walked to the center of the altar and stood solemnly for a few moments, then he looked directly at me.

"In the name of the Father, the Son, and the Holy Spirit," the priest began the Mass.

I realized that the priest and I were the only people in the church, but I remembered the words of Jesus from the Bible: "Whenever two or more of you are gathered in my name, I am there." I was deeply moved by the thought. I struggled with my emotions while kneeling in the presence of Jesus. The priest continued reciting the liturgy of the Mass, and I asked God to help me. I thanked God for sparing my life, and I petitioned Him to forgive me for taking the life of another. I asked God to have mercy on my soul.

Breathing in deeply through my nose, I could feel the cold, salty air burning my lungs while I tried to keep pace with my colleagues Danny Santarpio and Jason Germano. They both ran like deer. The ground was covered with hard, crusty snow, and our feet made crunching sounds as we jogged along Pleasure Bay toward the Sugar Bowl and Castle Island. The three of us clopped along, wearing stocking caps pulled down over our ears, scarves wrapped around our necks, and parkas over our sweat suits. White vapor spilled from our mouths as we jogged in the darkness. Police sirens sounded in the distance.

"They're playing my song, again," I said.

"Don't you know anything else?" Jason joked. "I find that song very hard to dance to!"

"It doesn't matter," Danny joined in, "he can't dance anyway, he's Irish."

"What are you talking about? I'm dancin' right now," I laughed. "I'm doin' the airborne shuffle."

"Was that what you were doing the other night, when you knocked that door down with your head?" Jason quipped.

"Yeah, and that was the 'Ali shuffle' when he knocked Straight Nelson out cold in the hallway on Beacon Street with a left hook!" Danny joked again. We all laughed out loud while we ran. We fell quiet for a while as the airplanes approaching Logan Airport, one after another, roared raucously overhead.

"Where should we begin tonight?" I asked between jet engine noises.

"Let's begin with a bowl of fish chowda at the No Name, and take it from there," Jason answered.

"I second that emotion," I joked.

"I third," laughed Danny.

Jogging along the jetty in Boston Harbor, we could see the fishing boats anchored off the coast. Seagulls glided along beside us while the wet salty air blew into our faces. We began to pick up speed, pumping our legs faster and faster as we ran over the bridge from the jetty to Castle Island.

"Why don't we check out Father's, Daisy's, Zelda's, and Clarke's?" I suggested. "The usual nightclub tour."

"Sounds like a plan to me," Danny agreed.

"It's a deal," Jason concurred.

We ran faster than usual around the periphery of Castle Island, and we kept up the fast pace all the way back to the L Street bathhouse. My lungs felt like they were about to explode. The wind was blowing strong against us on our return route, forcing us to lean into it so it wouldn't blow us over backwards. The wind resistance turned our three-mile run into an endurance test. It was us against the elements, and we liked that challenge. We practically sprinted the last half mile of the course, running hard and racing, neck and neck, past the South Boston Yacht Club and the M Street beach. The three of us slowed down to a trot and stopped running when we crossed the invisible finish line at the intersection of L Street and Day Boulevard. Breathing deeply and sweating, Danny, Jason, and I swaggered, three abreast, on the sidewalk in front of the brick bathhouse building as we cooled down after our run. We walked to the end of the building and stopped for a while to stretch and bend on the snow-covered sand at the edge of the black saltwater of Carson Beach. After regaining our breath, we walked back into the bathhouse to shower and change into our undercover clothes.

Jason and Danny were leaving the shower room just as I was entering. I hung my towel on the rack, walked into the open tiled shower area, found one of the only showers with a nozzle, and turned it on. I tested the water with my hand, and stepped into the stream of water when the temperature seemed right. I rubbed the bar of soap over my body and stared at the ceiling while I thought about our strategy for the night. Suddenly I looked across from me, and I noticed that Willie White, a young man with Down syndrome, was also taking a shower.

"What time is it, Willie?" I asked matter-of-factly.

"Don't know," Willie answered immediately in his gruff-sounding voice.

I looked over at Willie thoughtfully, and he smiled at me. I realized that it was a dumb question for me to ask of Willie. It seemed that Willie realized it before I did by the way he kept smiling and looking at me.

"Willie, you don't care about time, do you?" I asked. A more appropriate question, I thought.

"I don't know, I don't care," Willie answered, staring up at me from under his hairy, gnarled brow.

"But you know that you're my friend, Willie, don't you?"

"I'm your friend, Paulie," Willie assured me unequivocally with a grin.

As I looked at Willie, I thought about the complicated nature of my life and the lives of others, particularly the deviousness and deception of the people involved in the drug business. It was virtually impossible to know what the people I was dealing with were actually thinking, and I don't think they knew themselves. I confuse myself sometimes. But Willie, who doesn't even know what day it is, knows that we are friends. He smiles and tells me so every time I see him. People sometimes say that when a woman gives birth to someone like Willie, with Down syndrome, she gives birth to an angel. It makes sense, because Willie doesn't have the capacity to do anything wrong. He couldn't possibly commit a sin. I am lucky to have an angel for a friend, I thought to myself. Willie is definitely going to heaven when he dies, but people like me can never be sure where we will go.

"Bye, Willie," I said as I stepped out of the shower and grabbed my towel. Willie had a very thoughtful look on his face when I called out to him, and my farewell jarred him from his peaceful state. He straightened up and turned to face me.

"Bye, Paulie, be good," Willie answered me abruptly. I'll try to be, I thought to myself. It was like a reminder from an angel.

Danny, Jason, and I left L Street and headed to the No Name Restaurant on the waterfront. After a bowl of chowder and a cup of coffee, we began our undercover rounds of the nightspots. We decided to start at Father's Bar on Charles Street at the bottom of Beacon Hill. Father's was a very popular place and had an interesting clientele. The avant-garde atmosphere attracted a youthful mix of college students, artists, and hip professionals, as well as the Beacon Hill regulars. Father's was known as a dynamite singles bar and pickup joint. It also provided a steady flow of customers for the dope peddlers who hawked their wares.

On this particular Friday night, the place was jam-packed and the music was blaring. We walked in the front door and nodded to the doorman, who waved us by. We were never bothered by the usual identification check. The doormen, bouncers, and bartenders in most of the places where we worked knew us, and we were always welcomed like celebrities. We spent so much money buying drinks, and we tipped so well, I guess we were celebrities of a sort to them. I made my way to the bar through the crowd, while Danny and Jason followed in my path. We waved hello to a number of people and smiled at a few of the girls as we eyeballed the crowd. The bartender had our drinks on the bar before we got there.

"That's on me, guys," he announced with a smile.

"In that case, we'll have to drink 'em," I declared with a laugh. Danny and Jason nodded thanks and raised their beers in recognition of the bartender's goodwill.

"Nice crowd," I said, looking at the bartender while I sipped my beer.

"It certainly is for nine o'clock," he answered.

I looked around the bar discreetly to see if I recognized anyone who could compromise our identity. Danny and Jason did the same. After completing the circle of observation, our eyes met, and we lifted our beers up high and tapped them together. We saw no one in the bar who could blow our cover. I decided to check out one more place.

"Mind my place at the bar," I ordered jokingly. "I have to see a man about a horse."

I put my beer down and headed for the men's room. As soon as I opened the door, I could hear a gasping, guttural sound, like someone was trying to talk while he was being choked. I saw a black man with dreadlocks leaning forcibly against a white man with long blonde hair, holding his shirt collar with his left hand and pressing a shiny stiletto to his throat. What I saw confirmed what I thought I heard when I first opened the door. I walked through the doorway, proceeded past the two men, and stood at a urinal out of their view. The man with the knife continued his assault as if I wasn't there, but before I was finished, he decided to talk to me.

"Hey, punk, you ain't seen nuttin'; this ain't none o your bizniz. Unnastand?" the man with the knife said in a deep, threatening voice.

"I hear ya," I answered quickly.

"You betta heah me, punk!" he threatened, louder and braver this time.

"Yes, sir," I answered immediately as I zipped up my fly. I flushed the urinal, and I reached into my belt and grasped my 45. Then I turned around and took a deep breath.

"Y'all betta walk on outta heah, punk! And forget what you seen," the man with the knife commanded loudly.

"Yes, sir, that's right. I ain't seen nuthin'," I answered again, and I walked slowly toward the exit. When I reached the end of the stall, I could see the man in the dreadlocks straining to look back at me while he continued to press the knife to the blonde guy's neck.

"I'm goin', man, I'm goin'," I said, heading for the exit. When I was abreast of the two guys, I stopped and whirled around, grabbed the man's knife hand in a jujitsu hold, and bent it backwards toward his wrist while simultaneously jamming the barrel of my pistol under his chin. He was in so much pain that he let go of the blonde guy's throat with his other hand, and I shoved him up against the wall next to his victim. I had his right hand bent over with my left hand, my forehead up against his, and my 45 pressed into his neck. My right forearm was under the blonde guy's chin, pressing him to the wall.

"What's goin' on, fellas?" I asked.

"Me?" the blonde guy inquired, politely.

"Yes, you," I answered facetiously.

"I sold this gentleman a kilo of hash, and now he wants his money back," the white guy managed to explain as my arm pressed against his neck.

"That so?" I asked the guy who formerly held the knife.

"Dat shit's no damn good!" he complained.

"That so?" I asked the blonde guy.

"The stuff's the best. I brought it back from Amsterdam myself," he explained. I wanted to laugh, because it seemed so funny to see these two talking heads defending themselves like school kids in front of their principal.

"But the customer's always right," I added. "If he don't like it, he don't like it."

"Right on, man." The dreadlocks agreed enthusiastically with my observation.

"Don't be movin' around so much, brother, cause if this 45 goes off, your brains'll be all ovah the ceiling."

"Alright, man, alright," he responded cautiously with eyes bulging.

"Now, don't you agree with my conclusion?" I asked the blonde guy.

"Yeah, but shouldn't he return my hash?" he asked logically.

"Of course he should. You didn't return his hash, brother?" I politely asked the dreadlocks.

"No, man," he answered testily.

"No, man? What do you mean, no, man?" I mimicked him.

"It's gone, man, it was no good, so I got ridda da shit," he responded, in an attempt to explain the matter away.

"You jivin' me, man. Don't jive me. Your first mistake was to call me a punk, now you gonna jive me. You get nothin', brother, and be happy. Case closed! End of story. Walk out of here, and forget you ever saw me, brother. And don't ever make another mistake, brother, because it'll be your third, and three strikes you're out around here," I said angrily, pushing the barrel of my pistol tightly under his chin. I stepped back with my gun still pointed at the two men, and I slipped his knife carefully into my waistband. I told them both to straighten themselves up and to march out of the men's room like nothing ever happened, and I took my foot away from the door. As soon as I opened the door, the man with the dreadlocks stepped out quickly, and the blonde man followed like he was stuck to him. When he was a few feet away from the bathroom, the dreadlocks veered off to the left and took another dude by the elbow and led him through the crowd toward the door. When they got to the door, they turned around momentarily and looked toward the back of the room where I was standing. As soon as our eyes met, they turned around quickly and left. I knew they were trouble. I watched the door for a moment to make sure that they did not double back inside, and then I walked to the bar and joined Danny and Jason. I picked up my beer and sipped it without saying anything. Then I looked around the room, and I leaned forward like I had something important to say. Danny and Jason took my cue and watched me closely.

"Jason, follow the two dudes that just left and see where they go," I whispered, as Jason looked directly into my eyes. Jason handed me his beer and moved quickly out of the bar to follow the two black guys.

"What's up?" Danny whispered, with a look of concern on his face.

"I'll tell you later, D. Someone's watching us right now," I answered.

I could see the guy with the blonde hair sitting down at a table with another long-haired hippie type. They were trying to get a look at me without being obvious. Our chance meeting in the men's room saved him a couple of thousand dollars, and maybe even his life. I wanted to leave him with the impression that the encounter was no big deal to me. Several minutes later Jason returned and stood between Danny and me, and I handed him his beer.

"You were in that men's room an awful long time," Jason remarked humorously, and I smiled.

"We've been wonderin' about you lately, Sully," Danny joked, raising his eyebrows.

"Now which one was it that you liked, the cute hippie with the pretty blonde hair or the handsome dude in the dreadlocks?" Jason laughed, and I shrugged my shoulders.

"He couldn't make up his mind. He'll take them both," Danny said, and we all started laughing.

"Did you see where they went?" I asked seriously.

"They got into a maroon Mercedes with tinted windows, and they drove off like they were in a hurry," Jason reported.

"You get a license plate?" I asked.

"Uh huh," Jason replied.

"Dynamite, Jason, let's get outta here," I suggested.

"And leave all these beautiful women?" he joked.

"C'mon, we have to check out the rest of the joints," Danny agreed.

"And miles to go before we rest," Jason quipped.

We finished our beers and tipped the bartender. After reminding him to take messages for us till next time, we shook hands and left the bar. As we walked out, I sensed that the blonde hippie guy and his friend were watching us. Before I went out the door, I stopped and looked back over my shoulder. The hippie with the long blonde hair was smiling and looking at me, and he raised his drink and mouthed the words "thank you." I nodded to him, and then I followed Danny and Jason. We walked quietly along Charles Street in the snow in the light of the old Beacon Hill gaslights until we reached our powder blue Cadillac. Jason whisked the snow off the windshield and then opened the door. Danny sat in front next to Jason, and I got into the backseat.

"Touché!" I joked as I pulled the stiletto from under my coat and waved it like Zorro. Jason and Danny turned around to look at me.

"What the hell is that?" Jason asked.

"I'm lucky I didn't stab myself to death when I got into the backseat," I laughed.

"There's enough people that would like to kill us, let's not give them any help," Danny joked.

"I took this away from the soul brother in the bathroom," I told them.

"Oh, you guys were playing show-and-tell in the bathroom," Danny quipped.

"What did you say? Hey, pal, no playing with knives," Jason kidded.

"It was something like that," I laughed, and then I explained what actually happened. While I completed my story, Danny and Jason stared at me in puzzled amazement.

"What are you, nuts?" Jason replied.

"Why didn't you come out and get us?" Danny asked, concerned about the incident. "He could have killed you."

"I didn't have time. It happened so fast," I explained. I knew that Danny and Jason were worried about me and wanted to be there, but it wasn't possible. I just reacted. I also knew that they would both die to protect me if they had to. It was one for all, and all for one with us.

"He wants to keep all the fun to himself," Jason joked, trying to camouflage their anger. "Next stop, Daisy Buchanan's," Jason continued. We drove inbound on Charles Street and turned right onto Beacon.

"Jason, pull over right here. I have to make a quick call," I piped up from the backseat.

"Can't you wait till we get to Daisy's?" Jason complained.

"No, it's too loud in that place. Pull over here, quick," I ordered, and I hopped out and hurried into the downstairs bar at the Hampshire House. I went directly to the pay phone in the entranceway, put in my dime, and dialed the telephone number for the Boston Police Drug Control Unit. I knew that there was one cop who could help me right now, and it was Al Forte, one of the sharpest drug detectives in the Boston Police Department. Forte had spent the early part of his career in uniform in Roxbury, Dorchester, Mattapan, and the South End, and he knew every drug dealer in that area. He had a photographic memory, and a knack for names and faces, especially blacks. Forte had an uncanny ability to remember criminals and connect them with investigations. He also had the largest cache of informants.

"Drugs," a dull voice answered.

"Hello, is Al Forte working?" I inquired.

"Forte, pick up the phone," I could hear the dull voice say.

"Hello, Forte here," Al Forte answered, enthusiastically.

"Al, am I glad I caught you," I said with relief in my voice.

"What's up, Paulie boy?" he asked affably.

"I need a little help. I just took a stiletto away from a black male, approximately six feet tall, dressed like a Rastafarian. He had a partner, looked like O. J. Simpson. They got into a maroon Mercedes, Massachusetts license plate 456-789."

"That's Punky Wilson and Green-Eyed Jack. They're bad. They're rippin' guys off all over the city. They walked into that after-hours place off of Dudley Street the other night and blasted the owner in front of everybody. Bronco Fitzgerald gets there minutes after the shooting, the guy's laying dead on the floor, and nobody saw nothin'. The whole town is petrified of these guys. They're rip-off guys, and they're stone killers," Al enlightened me. Then he added lightly, "Don't piss 'em off!"

"I think I already did, Al."

"Well, we'll go with plan B then," Al answered humorously.

"Do you know where they hang, Al?"

"I know where they be right now," Al answered coyly, "cause my snitch be right next to them. My guy's scheduled to call at ten."

"I need a quick favor, Al. Get the word to them that they were seen at Father's Bar on Charles Street," I explained as fast as I could.

"Charles Street, that's a little out of their area," Al mused.

"They were tryin' to rip off a hippie type, and I walked in and broke it up," I continued. "I put my gun to his head, and took his knife away."

"I guess you did piss 'em off, Paulie," Al laughed.

"So would you put out the story that a mob hit man, Sully, that's me, is not the guy to mess with. Let him think that he was lucky to lose his money and not his life," I instructed.

"You got it, Paulie, I'll make sure that they get the word. They'll stay away after I'm finished with 'em. They're crazy, but they're not stupid. The brothers are still bashful around the mob. It's that old mob mystique. Those guineas still have everyone bullshitted, " Al assured me.

"Ok, Al, I appreciate that. I gotta go. Danny and Jason are waitin' for me in the car."

I hung up the receiver and ran up the stairs. I let myself into the car again, and Jason and Danny looked over the front seat at me.

"Are we finally ready? Do you have to go to the boys' room? Anything else you want me to do?" Jason teased.

"Yeah, can you get me an office job?" I answered.

We were extremely successful in our undercover work that cold, snowy night. After Father's we hit Daisy's, Zelda's, and Clarke's, just like we had planned, and we set up some very good cases. The most important event of the night, however, proved to be that incident in the men's room of Father's. Tales of that chance encounter in the men's room developed into folklore and spread throughout all the bars on Beacon Hill. The young hippie became my best advertisement. He relayed the story that I saved his life, and I became known as something of a Robin Hood because of him. We were well known prior to the men's room incident, but now we were folk heroes. Danny, Jason, and I became modern-day Three Musketeers!

Danny and I returned to Father's the following week. We were having a beer and getting our messages from the bartender, when I sensed that there was someone behind me. I carefully turned to look; it was the hippie from the men's room.

"Sully, I want to thank you for sticking up for me last week. You saved my life, man," the hippie praised me while holding out his right hand. "The name's Ted."

"Nice to meet you, Ted," I answered as I shook his hand. The bartender had probably told him my name. "It was no big thing. Did you hear him call me a punk?"

"Yeah, that sure was a big mistake on his part, and it was almost his last mistake," Ted acknowledged and smiled. Then he asked courteously, "Would you and your friend care to join me at my table?"

"We're kinda busy right now, my man, but thanks anyway," I replied.

"I will make it worth your while, Sully," Ted said. Danny and I paused for a moment before we looked at each other in agreement, and accepted the hippie's invitation.

"After you," I said with a sweep of my hand, motioning for Ted to go first. Ted led us to his usual, very private table in the rear of the bar.

I introduced Ted to Danny. "Ted, this is Dante."

"Very pleased to meet you, Dante," Ted answered deferentially. "Your friend, Sully, went to the wall for me last week."

"Nice to meet you, Ted. Sully looks out for everyone. No one messes with Sully," Danny said.

"Well, now I want to help you guys out. I already know what you guys are into. I owe you big time, so if I can help you out, I will. Everyone knows me in here in this bar and on this street. I have the best connections in town. As of now, my connections are your connections," Ted informed us very seriously. Danny glanced at me from across the table with a look of approval, trying to mask his excitement.

"Thank you, Ted, but we're pretty well connected ourselves." I brushed him off with an air of self-importance.

"No, Sully, you don't understand. I have connections all the way to Amsterdam, Hong Kong, San Francisco," Ted boasted. "I can get anything."

"Like what?" I asked. "We're into a little different thing than you, man. You're a hippie, you got a little different clientele than us. You're dealin' smoke, and we're dealin' junk to the ghetto."

"I told you guys, I can get anything. I deal smoke, but I can get anything I want. I have sources for heroin, coke, acid, meth, you name it," Ted explained.

"You know, man, Dante and I been thinkin' 'bout branchin' out, diversifyin'. We got a nice junk business now, but we could spread out," I said.

"Now you're talking, man. You should diversify," Ted agreed.

"These college kids are really deep into LSD. With all the schools in Boston, I could move mountains of LSD if I had a source," I bragged.

"Sully, I got the best source of acid in the world. My guy goes all the way to the factory," Ted boasted. "I can introduce you to him."

I cut him off. "Hey, Ted, wait a minute. We got enough friends. We don't need to meet any more people. That's how you end up in jail; meetin' people."

"Oh, yeah, I understand," Ted answered.

"This guy could be a narc," I cautioned.

"Sully, I've known him all my life. He's not a narc. I would never do that to you," Ted explained sincerely, and then added cautiously, "plus, I don't want to get killed."

"That's right, Ted, you're too young to die," I agreed for emphasis.

"Sully, I don't like guns, and I never have. I love peace. I would never fight with anyone. It's not my thing. That guy was going to slit my throat the other night, until you walked in! You saved my life, man, and I will never forget it. I owe you my life. I'm your friend forever, man." Ted extended his hand across the table. I reached across and shook it, and he reached over with his left fist and tapped it on top of our clasped hands.

We drank a few more beers, and I told Ted that we had to leave to make some drug deliveries around the city. We shook hands again and thanked him for the beers, and then put on our leather coats and gloves and left the bar. It was cold outside that night, and we walked toward our car briskly with our shoulders hunched.

"What about Ted?" I asked.

"He's ours," Danny answered.

"Is he ever," I agreed.

"He's our best friend," Danny added.

"Do you think he can do what he says?" I asked.

"We'll soon find out," Danny mused.

"If we let him, he would have shaken hands with us till three in the morning!" I joked.

Danny and I laughed thinking about that. There was no doubt that Ted was now on our side. He would prove to be the classic "unwitting dupe," as the Agent's Manual defined the informant who was unaware that he was acting in the government's interest. Danny and I decided to call it a night and go home and get some rest.

Over the course of the next few months, Ted introduced us to one source after another. We bought marijuana, hashish, cocaine, methamphetamine, amphetamines, and barbiturates from an assorted group of midlevel dealers and smugglers. Then one day in February, while sitting with Danny, Jason, and me in his booth at Father's, Ted reminded us of his acid connection.

"My man, the one with the LSD connection, is coming to town next week, and he's bringing you a sample," Ted stated suddenly, out of nowhere.

"The guy with the connection to the factory?" I asked, picking up the cue.

Ted nodded affirmatively, and added, "They call him the 'Acid King.'"

"Cool," I answered.

"Cool," Ted repeated, and then sipped his beer while he drifted off, immersed in thought. I signaled Jason and Danny that it was time to go, and we all got up.

"Sayonara," I said, intruding on his thoughts.

Ted looked up at us and answered, "Sayonara, Sully, right on." We each gave Ted a parting hippie handshake, and we left the bar.

"What do you think?" I asked.

"I think we're gonna meet the Acid King!" Danny laughed.

"Should I give him a pack of Rolaids when I meet him?" Jason quipped. "Or will we need the Rolaids after meeting him?"

"I'm the one that needs Rolaids, after working with you two guys! I think this guy is dealin' anotha kinda acid!" I joked back as we got into the car.

We drove over Beacon Hill and back to the DEA (Drug Enforcement Agency) headquarters at the JFK Building to meet Chris Regan. We were going to help Boston Police Detective Bronco Fitzgerald and his squad to carry out a search warrant in downtown Boston. When we got to the base, Chris was already there, waiting impatiently for us.

"Shall we go?" Chris said immediately and slipped on his midlength black leather jacket. We fell in line behind him and piled into his government-issue Plymouth Fury. Chris quickly stuck the blue light on the dashboard near the windshield. Then we pulled out of the garage and drove directly to police headquarters with the siren going and the blue light flashing.

"We don't want to make Bronco wait," Chris joked, as he zipped over Beacon Hill and cut across the Boston Common. When we turned right onto East Berkeley Street, Chris turned off the flashing light and switched off the siren. He pulled over at the curb in front of police headquarters and parked. We jumped out of the car and ran inside, climbing the stairs two at a time till we arrived at the drug unit.

"Gentlemen," Bronco Fitzgerald directed his attention toward us with a smile. The greeting seemed incongruous, coming from Bronco and directed at us. He was seated on a desk with one foot on the floor facing his audience: Chris, Danny, Jason, me, and four men from his squad, who were gathered around him. We gave Bronco our strict attention. Bronco Fitzgerald could have been a poster boy for the Boston Police. He was six feet tall and looked like a middle-aged linebacker. His masculine features seemed to be chiseled out of his reddish face, and even when he smiled, you knew that he wasn't fooling around. Bronco was the epitome of a cop. He was born and raised first in Roxbury and later, the Savin Hill section of Dorchester, and he walked the streets of the Boston neighborhoods like he owned them.

"Tonight I am going to knock on the door myself, and tell the bastard that he is under arrest. Once I have him cuffed, you can all run in to tear the place apart for the drugs," Bronco instructed us.

"Why the special treatment?" Chris asked with a sparkle in his eye.

"Because this bastard is my daughter's boyfriend," Bronco answered stoically, cocking his head slightly to one side.

"Sounds fair enough to me," Chris responded lightly, sensing the stress in Bronco's remarks. Everyone laughed and nodded in agreement.

Bronco's youngest daughter, twenty-one-year-old Colleen, the apple of his eye, worked as a hostess at the Parker House Hotel on Tremont Street. She was stunningly beautiful, with long red hair, and she attracted a lot of attention while greeting customers at the fancy restaurant. One customer whom she attracted was the subject of our raid this evening. Colleen quickly lost interest in the young businessmen and lawyers she was dating after she fell for this drug dealer. She was beginning to sample some of his drugs and was staying out later and later. It was a nightmare for Bronco Fitzgerald.

"You and your boys will come up the front stairs with me, Chris. My guys will hit the back door. I have a key to the entranceway. We will go in, and you and your guys will wait while I go up to the third floor and place him under arrest. You will be able to see me almost the entire time because it is a beautiful open stairway. It looks like a prop from a movie."

"Should we expect any resistance? Are they known to have weapons?" Chris asked.

"All these assholes have weapons, don't they?" Bronco answered rhetorically. "But no, they're not shoot-'em ups. The main guy is scheduled to deliver the dope at a certain time. When we are called, we head over there and take him and everyone in the place. I already have an arrest warrant for him in my pocket and a search warrant for the apartment."

It was Bronco's case and Bronco's search warrant. We were there at his invitation to help him. When you worked with the local police, you followed their lead, especially when the leader of the raid was Bronco Fitzgerald, one of the best cops in the city. Bronco's squad knew Bronco better than anyone, and they were very quiet tonight. I sensed that this raid meant a lot to Fitzgerald. It was not going to be the usual routine drug bust. I just knew it, and so did everyone else.

Bronco dispatched the four guys from his squad to set up surveillance on Tremont Street with an eyeball on the location, while we waited with him in the squad room. We made small talk and thumbed through the day-old newspapers that were lying around to help allay the preraid jitters. Then the telephone rang.

"Fitzgerald," Bronco answered. "He's goin' up? Okeedokee." Bronco looked at us and put down the receiver. "Let's go," he said, and we all got up and went to Chris's car.

"Someone just went in . . . looks like our guy," a voice transmitted over the walkie-talkie.

"That's him, that's our guy. He just went in? We're on our way," Bronco answered confidently, speaking into his walkie-talkie.

Chris turned right onto Boylston Street from East Berkeley and then went left onto Charles Street, right on Beacon, then right again onto Park Street. When we came to the intersection of Park and Tremont, we could see the doorway that we were going to raid, and we could see the other detective's car parked in front of a Dunkin' Donuts. Our target was almost directly across from the Park Street subway station, in the shadow of the State House. Chris slowly pulled the car across Tremont Street, turned left onto Winter Street, and parked. We all got out of the car and headed for the doorway. Walking down Tremont Street, we could see the other detectives slip into an alley to get to the back entrance of the apartment building. I reached the front door first, and I stood aside while Bronco opened the door with the passkey. We followed him into a large open foyer lighted by chandeliers hanging from the high ceiling, and we stopped again. Bronco signaled us to wait, and he went on, climbing the staircase with his head up, stepping deliberately. As he approached the second balcony, we could hear a squeaky door open and close and footsteps moving quickly. Bronco stopped and listened. We saw a shadowy figure moving briskly down the stairs from the third balcony toward Bronco. Then the plan suddenly went awry. The shadowy figure was our subject, and he came face-to-face with Bronco, who was standing on the second balcony. They stared at each other momentarily.

"Well, well, fancy meeting you here," Bronco said sarcastically.

"I'm on my way to pick up Colleen," the guy said.

"I don't think so," Bronco said, standing with his feet spread apart in a wide stance and reaching for his handcuffs.

"Fuck you, Fitzgerald!" the subject replied angrily, and loud shouting echoed through the open stairway. We could hear struggling and punching as we raced up the stairway to help Bronco. As I approached the second balcony, I could see the guy kick Bronco in the groin. Bronco leaned forward and grabbed the guy by his groin and by the front of his shirt and pulled him down the stairs toward him. The guy sort of hopped on one foot as he and Bronco reeled forward toward the railing. Bronco swung to his left and lifted up the subject in the air. Bronco's strength, together with the subject's momentum, propelled him over the railing. We rushed to grab Bronco to prevent him from falling, and we could hear the sickening thud as the guy fell headfirst onto the first floor black-and-white-tiled landing. Breathing heavily, Chris and I hung onto Bronco, who was draped over the railing, exhausted. We leaned on him until we could each catch our breath. The guy, spread out on the landing below us, did not move. We leaned over the railing together, our arms around Bronco's shoulders, and looked at the guy lying silent and still.

"Are you ready to go, yet?" a muffled voice could be heard crackling over the two-way radio.

Fitzgerald burst into a loud, husky laugh. "For Christ sake, those guys are still waiting to hit the joint!" His barrel chest was still heaving from the exertion of the fight. He pulled the walkie-talkie from his jacket pocket and transmitted, "Go ahead, hit the door. We're out front."

We could hear the crashing sounds as the other detectives knocked the back door in, and we looked at each other nervously.

"C'mon, Paulie, we'll hit the front door," Chris ordered, and we began running up the stairway.

"Take his pulse, and stay with him so no one robs him," Fitzgerald called down to Jason with his left hand cupped to his mouth. Then he said to Danny, "Let's go. I don't think that guy's goin' anywhere." Danny followed Fitzgerald up the stairs and joined Chris and me on the landing.

Chris gave me the signal to hit the door, and just as I began my approach, the door opened.

"Thought I'd make it easy for you guys!" Jerry O'Dea, one of the detectives who hit the rear door, greeted us. We filed into the apartment and found two guys already in handcuffs standing against the wall in the hallway while the detectives searched their apartment. I overheard one say to the other that the guy who sold them the drugs set them up. They were convinced that the guy who had left the apartment moments earlier set them up for the bust. I told the guy he was a genius for figuring out who the informant was. I also told him that the guy must have been very remorseful, because he committed suicide by jumping off the balcony after leaving the apartment. The two guys looked at me like I was crazy. I left the apartment and joined Jason and the subject on the first floor.

"How's he doin', Jason?" I asked.

"He ain't," Jason replied tentatively, looking alternately from me to the guy on the floor.

"He ain't?" I asked.

"Unless he's a pretty good faker," Jason laughed nervously. "He's got no pulse, and he's not breathing."

I knelt down to take a closer look at the subject's face. He had a bruise on his forehead, but that was all. He looked like he was sleeping. I reached over and touched his cheek with my hand. He was still warm, but I knew that he was dead. Ten minutes ago he was trying to kill Bronco Fitzgerald, and now he was dead. It didn't seem real to me. I wondered why I was chosen to share this moment with him. Where were his parents, his brothers, his sisters, and his friends? I wondered. I wouldn't want to die like this, I thought. While I was looking at him, I heard steps, and I looked up to see that it was Bronco Fitzgerald.

"This is Detective Fitzgerald. We need a meat wagon at 197 Tremont Street," Bronco announced into his radio.

"197 Tremont?" a voice questioned.

"Yeah, that's 197 Tremont," Bronco repeated, and pulled the radio away from his face.

"On the way!" the voice replied.

Bronco put the radio down by his side, and leaned back against the railing. Danny, Jason, Chris, and I stood silently in a circle around the body. We stared at the corpse and glanced at each other. None of us knew what to do or say. The drug dealer was dead, so any attempt at resuscitation would be hollow. We all stood in silence like self-appointed mourners.

The muffled sirens wailed in the distance until, suddenly, the ambulance was at the entrance, and the EMTs were filing in and kneeling around the body. Within seconds, they exited with the body, and we were left standing alone—Danny, Jason, Chris, Bronco, and me. I looked across the circle at Bronco just as he was putting a Tums antacid tablet into his mouth.

He looked at me without blinking, and said sullenly, almost morosely, "Bad acid."

All the cops that we worked with had stomach problems. It wasn't hard to figure out the reason why. They worked till all hours of the night and into the early morning. They ate greasy foods and washed them down with coffee, and they smoked one cigarette after another. Most of them would have a few beers in a cop joint before going home to sleep for a few hours. They all had to be in court early the next morning for arraignments and trials that could last all day. Sometimes they got a chance to go home to change clothes and get a warm meal, but more often than not, they stopped for a meal in a diner and went directly to work to begin the entire process all over again. The stress of the job, coupled with family responsibilities, made life very difficult for these guys. When Bronco, with the white residue of the Tums antacid tablet on his lips, said that he had bad acid, I knew exactly what he meant. I was beginning to feel it myself.

I thought about that handsome young dope dealer lying dead on the cold marble tiles. More than ever, I realized that the drug business was absolutely evil. The kid had so much going for him that he probably could have been successful in anything that he tried. He just had a bad attitude. He was a handsome kid. Unfortunately, he chose the easy way to make money. I'm sure that his ending wasn't easy for his family, or for Bronco's daughter.

I watched Bronco telephone his daughter from the apartment to break the news to her. He looked over at me with the receiver still next to his ear.

"She hung up on me. She said that I killed him," Bronco said with hurt in his eyes. Colleen refused to speak to her father ever again.

The next day we were sipping coffee in the Group Two office area of the DEA and discussing our new developments with Fred Borne, the group supervisor, when the undercover telephone rang. We all hesitated and looked at each other as the phone continued to ring. Danny ran to the booth and answered the call. Jason, Borne, and I watched Danny's animated conversation through the glass panel in the door of the booth, and Jason and I laughed. We knew that it must be Ted, our hippie friend, and we were excited that we would be making another case. Borne stood in front of us, holding a piece of paper in one hand and a cup of coffee in another and looking back and forth at Jason and me. Borne's beady eyes seemed to search suspiciously for some clue from us. He always doubted us. No matter how many cases we made, he was always negative and skeptical. I think that because he was so methodical and dogged in his approach to drug investigations, he couldn't understand our spontaneous undercover encounters. In addition, I think it bothered Borne that we seemed to have so much fun while we were working. He believed that drug investigations had to be boring and tedious. A drug investigation, Borne style, revolved around file checks, telephone records, and paper trails.

Danny came out of the undercover booth with a wide grin and hurried back to join us. Jason and I both smiled because we could see that Danny had good news. Borne watched us glumly.

"We're all set, brothers!" Danny said, as he slapped us high fives, inadvertently ignoring Borne.

"All right!" Jason and I answered simultaneously.

"Ted's man, the Acid King, is coming to town to meet us!"

"The Acid King?" Borne repeated sarcastically, rolling his eyes and walking away while we continued laughing with each other and enjoying the good news.

"Let's go to lunch and decide what we're gonna do," Danny suggested, and Jason and I agreed. I could see Borne peering at us suspiciously over his half-frame reading glasses as we walked out of the office noisily. We walked to the Italian North End and turned left onto Hanover Street. When we entered the European restaurant, the maitre d' stood at attention and saluted us with the menus. He walked briskly, like a drum major. We followed him to our table while he talked in a very confidential manner over his shoulder to Danny. After we sat down and the maitre d' handed us our menus, he lingered for several minutes, looking at Danny for further instructions. Danny ignored him.

"Gentlemen, have a nice meal," the maitre d' said to Danny, and then nodded at Jason and me before walking back to his post at the front of the restaurant.

We studied our menus for a while, and then I said, "Danny, that maitre d' treats you like you're the Godfather!"

Jason and Danny laughed together with me because it was true. He was a casting director's dream for an Italian mobster. Everywhere we went, people reacted the same way to him, whether we were in Boston, New York City, or New Orleans. People assumed that Danny was a mobster, and some thought they knew him. It was all vague, under the surface, but understood. Danny went along with the charade so naturally that it was easy for him to be an undercover guy. He never had to convince anybody of his role.

"I'm getting' the veal parmesan," Danny announced after serious deliberation. Jason and I ordered the same. The maitre d' kept looking over at us nervously from his post at the front of the restaurant. Leaning over the table, we discussed our plan for meeting with the Acid King in whispers, so no other diners could hear us. We decided to arrange the meeting for a nightclub in Revere so that we could make a solid impression on the Acid King. A childhood friend of Danny's owned the nightclub, and he would set it up like we were the owners. During our discussion I looked up from the table, and I could see the maitre d' briskly approaching us with a very officious look on his face. He stopped at the end of our booth and whispered something in Danny's ear. The maitre d' straightened up and looked around surreptitiously.

"Thanks," Danny replied, confidentially.

The maitre d' winked slyly at Danny, and walked away straightening his collar.

Jason and I looked at Danny so he could tell us what the secret was. He sat back dramatically and spread his arms out over the back of the booth and looked around suspiciously, the same way that the maitre d' had, while we waited for an answer.

"Two FBI agents, Johnny Connolly and someone else, are having lunch in the other room. The maitre d' wanted us to know, in case they were lookin' for us," Danny revealed to us out of the corner of his mouth, while he struggled to keep from laughing.

"Isn't it beautiful? We're federal agents setting up an undercover drug deal on our lunch hour, and this guy tips us off that the feds are in the next room! This entire thing is crazy!" Danny continued in a whisper.

When we finished our dinner, we walked by the maitre d', and Danny deftly slipped a sawbuck into his hand as they shook.

"Be good," Danny said to the maitre d'.

"Ahm always good," the maitre d' countered and said "*ciao*" as he smiled knowingly.

We walked back to the JFK Federal Building circuitously, finalizing our plans for our meeting with the Acid King, stepping in and out of traffic and walking under the expressway in the cold afternoon air. We rounded the corner into the Group Two office, laughing and discussing the maitre d'. Fred Borne looked up from his paperwork and stared at us from his desk. He was right where we left him over an hour ago, doing the same thing.

"Is that the same cup of coffee, Fred? It must be cold by now!" Danny remarked, unable to resist the temptation to tease Borne. Lost for words, Borne smirked and shook his head. He looked back down at the paperwork on his desk to appear to be busy. We took our coats off and sat down at our desks to continue our conversation about the maitre d's remarks and the undercover meeting that we were planning.

"You didn't tell me that a guy got killed on that raid last night," Borne called out to us sarcastically. He obviously overheard some hushed office conversations.

"We didn't know you cared," Danny answered wisely.

"You told us that all you wanted was arrest statistics, so we didn't think he counted. He died before we had a chance to arrest him," I added.

"Fred, this guy was so scared when he heard that we were after him, that he jumped to his death," Jason teased.

"You guys probably threw him off the stairwell! You probably killed him! You or one of those wacko cops from the drug control unit," Borne yelled out from his office. He didn't realize how close he really was to the truth. I forgot to tell him about the telephone call I had received from Bronco Fitzgerald earlier in the day.

"Paulie, that piece of shit woke up in the wagon! Can you believe that?" Fitzgerald declared lightheartedly in his loud, harsh-sounding voice.

"What are you talking about?" I answered.

"That arsehole I tossed off the balcony last night. He came back from the dead!" Fitzgerald stated callously, through subdued laughter.

"No way!" I remarked incredulously.

"Doctor says it happens; shock. The concussion shut his system down, like he was dead. He came to in the meat wagon, like nothing happened. He walked away when they got to the hospital. I got the bastid this morning, though. Put the cuffs on him at Bulldog's, then drank the beer he ordered. He escaped death, but he can't escape Bronco Fitzgerald!" The call ended with a burst of laughter. That was a true statement. You can't escape Bronco Fitzgerald. He keeps coming. He's relentless.

A feeling of relief came over me as I hung up the receiver and stared off into space. We were all completely convinced that the young man had died. How could that be? After I had killed the Spanish guy in Roxbury, I dreamed that he got up off the slab at the morgue, where I last saw him, and walked away. Now I was getting confused about what was real and what was not.

We decided to meet with Ted the hippie later that afternoon to make final arrangements for our rendezvous with the Acid King. Danny called his friend, Jay, the owner of Jacob's Ladder, the nightclub in Revere, to set up our undercover role as owners. Jacob's Ladder was an "in place" on the North Shore where all the small-time hoods and wanna-bes hung out and loved to be seen. The place was virtually packed almost every night of the week. It was especially good for this particular case because there were never any hippie types there. Ted and the Acid King would have no connections there to check us out. It looked like an Italian gangster joint, and that's exactly what we wanted. Everything was falling into place.

After it got dark, we drove down onto Charles Street and parked at the corner of Charles and Chestnut Street. We got out of the car and began walking toward Father's Bar, past a couple of restaurants, a pharmacy, and a bakery, until we came to the Yankee Bookstore. It was basically a pornographic bookstore, thinly camouflaged with some art books to preserve the dignity of the customers and not offend the blue-blooded residents of the very proper Beacon Hill neighborhood.

"Hey, Sully, there's your friend inside," Jason said.

The over-the-hill, obviously gay clerk was a sad but humorous character. I had originally walked into the store in the fall in search of a get-well card for an agent who was in the Mass General Hospital recovering from a heart attack. I soon realized that I was in a dirty bookstore and not a card store. I was turning to leave, when the clerk gave me a come-hither look and a wink. I hesitated for a moment and looked at him, then I noticed drug paraphernalia displayed on the counter. I had recently received a memo from DEA headquarters in Washington stating that stores selling drug paraphernalia like bongo pipes, coke spoons, and roach clips should be targeted in order to obtain intelligence information about drug users. Since that initial visit, I made more cases out of this dirty bookstore than anyplace else.

"Think he's hiring?" Danny quipped.

"C'mon, let's go in and see," I said. Jason opened the door, and Danny and I followed him inside.

"Well, hullo, boys." The guy behind the counter welcomed us in from the freezing cold. Jason and Danny split up and went down different aisles looking at magazines, and I went over to the clerk.

"One of these days," he said to me wistfully, rolling his eyes and bending his head back.

"Yeah, one of these days," I answered quickly. "Have you seen my hippie friend, Ted, around?"

"Ted just went by. He's going to get a coffee, and he's coming back," the clerk answered eagerly, brushing his eyebrows out with his pinky fingers.

"When?" I asked.

"In a couple a minutes. Geez! You guys got no patience," the clerk said.

"He's coming here in a few minutes!" I shouted toward the book racks at Jason and Danny.

"Good, now I can finish reading the interesting articles in *Penthouse*!" Jason quipped from the aisle as he opened up the centerfold.

"People really buy these books?" I asked incredulously.

"Buy them? Honey, I can't keep them on the shelves! I sell the real porno ones for twenty-five dollars, and they sell like hotcakes. Then I buy them back for five dollars, and I wrap them again in cellophane and sell them again for twenty-five bucks," the clerk laughed.

A buzzer went off, and the front door opened. It was Ted, the hippie, entering carefully with two paper coffee cups. When he looked up, he smiled at me. He put the two coffees on the glass countertop in front of the clerk and motioned for me to follow him to the back of the store.

"My man is coming tomorrow. When can you meet him?" he asked anxiously.

"I'll meet him tomorrow."

"When?"

"Have him meet us at our nightclub," I said. I could see that the hippie was impressed.

"Okay," he answered simply.

"Tell him to meet me at midnight at Jacob's Ladder in Revere, man," I said.

"Right on, right on," Ted repeated and motioned for me to follow him back up to the front of the store. He put his arm around me, and I knew that he was happy. Jason and Danny had already joined the clerk at the counter.

"You guys havin' a good time?" Jason joked, looking at Ted and me.

"Yeah, a good time," I answered casually. Then I turned to Ted and added, "Midnight at that place."

"I'll show them what a good time is," the clerk interjected, trying to sound sexy. We all scoffed at him and continued our conversation.

"Right on, man," Ted answered and made a fist and hit it on top of my right fist, and then I did the same. I signaled for Jason and Danny to follow me as I left the store.

"Later," Jason and Danny said, nodding to Ted and the clerk. Walking away, we could hear the muffled sound of the buzzer ringing. We all laughed as we approached our car.

"Sully, when your friend saw the hippie and you go down the aisle together, his nose went so far out of joint!" Danny joked.

"The icing on the cake was when the hippie put his arm around you," Jason added.

"Will you guys get serious?" I asked. "We have a meeting with the Acid King!

"Yeah, and that guy in the bookstore is liable to commit hari-kari," Jason teased.

"Is that what those guys do? Hari-kari?" Danny asked, and we all laughed. We were feeling good, in spite of the cold weather, because we knew that we were developing a real good case.

The following night, Jay, the real owner of Jacob's Ladder, set us up in a private VIP room off to the left of the main club area. It gave us enough privacy to conduct our drug deal, but also provided some of the flavor and excitement of the disco. The room drew attention to us, in a way that suggested our importance. We could see the entire club from our vantage point, including the bar and the dance floor off to one side. The ocean inlet was visible through the insulated glass wall on the other side of the club. The contrast between the cold, ocean weather on the outside and the heat of the disco beat on the inside was striking, and we felt as if we were right in the middle of it. Sitting in oversized leather chairs, Danny, Jason, Jay, and I tapped our open hands on the table and bobbed our heads to the disco beat while we waited for the "marks" to arrive. We looked at each other self-consciously and sipped our drinks.

I noticed the hostess, a tall, very pretty girl with dark hair, moving gracefully toward us. She appeared to be leading someone through the crowd. As she moved closer, I could see that she was leading the way for two hippies with long hair. They looked totally out of place as they trailed in her wake. The hostess stopped in front of our table like an army orderly reporting for duty, and the two slightly built, shortish hippies lined up obediently next to her. She smiled courteously. One of them was our mark, the Acid King, but we weren't sure which. The hippies glanced at each of us timidly, without making eye contact, while we looked them over.

"If I can get anything for you gentlemen, just send for me," Jay said, shaking hands with Danny, Jason, and me as he got up to leave.

"Baby, get these gentlemen a drink," Danny ordered the hostess.

"We're Ted Palmer's friends. He couldn't make it tonight," one of the hippies said apologetically while the other ordered.

"Good ta know ya," I said, motioning them to sit at the table. They both sat across from us, looking nervously at each other and then at us.

"Nice place," one of the hippies said.

"Thanks, we like it," Danny answered, grinning slyly.

"What's the deal? What can you do?" I questioned.

"We can get you all the acid you want. That's what Ted Palmer said you were interested in," one began.

"Whoa, whoa, who's we?" I interjected.

"Oh, sorry, I mean me and him. I'm Norman and he's Ralph," Norman answered very politely. I knew by the way that he answered the question that we had them under our control.

"Well, how do you know how much I want?" I quizzed Norman coldly.

"Oh, sorry, I mean we supply everyone, so I know that we can get you all that you need." Norman was deferential, almost apologetic.

"You supply everyone?" I asked skeptically, while Danny and Jason laughed.

"We supply LSD to all the cities from San Francisco to Boston," Norman answered casually. This guy is serious, I thought to myself, as I measured his responses to my questions. He's the real deal.

"Well, let's get it on, then," I said.

"Here," Norman said, handing me a plastic baggie, through which I could see white pieces of perforated paper with colored symbols on them.

"This is it?" I asked, holding up the baggie to get a closer look at its contents. I could see tiny Mickey Mouse figures, smiley faces, and cartoonish suns.

"The sunshine is the mainstay. That's our flagship brand. The kids also like the Mickey Mouse and the smiley faces. In any case, it's the best acid around, the best quality. Drop one hit, and you're gone for hours. You'll see it all, man, you'll see it all. It's God, man, the truth." Norman waxed on about the virtues of his brand of acid. I thought to myself, bingo, agents have been looking all over the country for the source of this "orange sunshine" acid, and here he was standing right in front of me.

"Yeah, man, I can dig it," I answered, after listening to his description of the acid. "We'll get back to you in a couple of days."

"Here's my number, man. Right on, man," Norman said, handing me a piece of paper with his telephone number on it, and then reaching out to tap fists with me.

"Right on, Norman," I agreed, tapping his fist. Then I added, "You want to meet some broads?"

"No, no, we have to be going. Thanks anyway, man," Norman declined.

"That's what I like, man, a real businessman! You're a real businessman, Norman. No messin' around! I like that," I commended him. Norman and his pal smiled shyly and nodded at my compliment. The pair shook our hands and got up to leave. Jason followed them to the parking lot and took down the license plate of the car as they drove off.

When Danny and I were certain that Norman and Ralph were gone, we hugged each other and whispered that this case was going to be a big one. Jason walked back, and we all hugged again. We were feeling good. We raised our bottles of beer to toast our success, just as Jay walked in.

"Everything go okay?" Jay asked, nervous and concerned.

Danny quickly thanked Jay. "You were great. We're putting you in for an Oscar! Thanks for everything. You made us look like the Godfather."

"Hey, anything I can do for you guys. You guys are crazy. I wouldn't know what to do undercover. I would get too nervous. You guys got nerves of steel," Jay laughed.

"Nerves of steel after a few beers, maybe," Jason joked.

"Where does it go from here?" Jay asked inquisitively. Danny, Jason, and I smiled at each other.

"How does San Francisco sound?" Danny asked.

We finished up our beers and said good-bye to Jay. Then we turned and pushed our way through the thick disco crowd, bouncing to the beat as the loud disco music reverberated over the speakers. I waited near the telephones and watched the waitress with the dark hair clear our table and pick up the fifty-dollar bill that we left her for her tip. Her eyes met mine as she put the money into her apron, and she walked across the dance floor holding my gaze until she stood very close to me.

"Hey, who are you guys, anyway?" she asked curiously.

136

"What kinda question is that?" I asked her evasively.

"I mean, like I know you're somebody," she struggled, as Danny and Jason came out of the men's room one after the other.

"Baby, I'm no one. I'm just with him," I added, referring to Danny.

"And if I tell you who I am, I gotta kill ya!" Danny said, pointing his index finger at her playfully, almost touching her nose. She rolled her eyes, and threw her head back, smiling at us.

"Bye, baby," I said as I began to leave.

"And don't forget, you don't know nuthin'," Danny added jokingly.

"I don't know nuthin' bout nobody," the pretty waitress answered straight-faced, then added quickly, "Thanks for the tip, guys!"

We got the results of the drug analysis back from the DEA laboratory, and we were ecstatic. The tests indicated that our LSD sample was the same LSD that was flooding the country, and it originated from the same source. In other words, all of the LSD was made in the same illicit laboratory. Ted the hippie told us that Norman was known as the Acid King, and that he ordered directly from the laboratory. If Ted was telling the truth, then we were on the verge of cracking one of the biggest LSD cases ever. It was up to us now to develop the case and get to the laboratory itself.

"Paulie, what do we do now? How do we get to the lab?" Danny asked.

"We order up a load. We go to his place to pick it up, and then we order up big and insist on going to the lab." I was beginning to formulate a plan.

"You think he'll go for it?" Danny wondered.

"We'll never know if we don't try," I answered.

"Let's do it," Jason said. We all walked over to the undercover telephone booth and squeezed in together. Danny took the piece of paper from Norman out of his pocket and began dialing.

"Hello, Norman! That's some dynamite shit, man! We can make some real money with that shit, but we want it all, man," Danny said. Danny held the speaker away from his ear so that we could hear Norman's response.

"All right, man, good! You liked it, huh? That's good," Norman answered enthusiastically.

"Right on, man, our people liked it! Now that I know I can move it, I want to wipe out everyone else. I want to wipe out my competition. How much can you deliver?" Danny asked.

"How much?" Norman repeated Danny's question, nervously.

"Yah, how much?"

"Do you want like a hundred or a thousand hits?" Norman asked. His quantities were in line with what hippies and college kids usually wanted. LSD degrades quickly, so dealers liked to buy it in amounts small enough that they could turn them over quickly. It was unusual for someone to order larger quantities of LSD.

"I mean like about twenty-five thousand hits! I'm no sucker. I want to buy big to save, man. I don't want to diddle around. I want to make some money." Danny got right to the point. Norman didn't answer.

"Hey, you still there?" Danny pressured him.

"Yeah, I'm still here," Norman answered, then paused for a moment before continuing. "Give me a couple of days."

"A couple of days? I thought you were the Acid King?" Danny belittled him.

"Yeah, I need a couple of days to put it together," Norman answered tentatively. Danny was definitely in control of the negotiations at this point. I could feel it.

"All right then, go do it. I need the shit," Danny ordered and hung up the phone. Jason and I looked at Danny, trying to interpret his assessment of the conversation. He was smiling.

"What do you think?" Jason and I asked at the same time.

"I think I shook him up with the big order. We dazzled him! I think he expected us to order a hundred or so hits, like everyone else," Danny said.

"Do you think we spooked him?" I asked.

"No, I just think we surprised him by doing something out of the ordinary. How many people take a sample, then order twenty-five thousand hits?" Danny asked rhetorically, then answered his own question. "None! The hippies and college kids buy a couple a hundred, a thousand a whack, budda-bing, budda-bing. We order twenty-five thousand! Now he knows we're not playing around," Danny explained.

"The next step's the lab," I said.

"You got it, baby," Danny agreed.

Jason, Danny, and I decided to update the group supervisor on the status of the case and get approval so that we could move ahead. At each stage of an investigation, we had to get the support of a group supervisor before we moved on to the next level. Securing the supervisor's approval was often more difficult than the undercover work itself. Fred Borne didn't want us to make the buy. He wanted us to arrest the dealers and seize the twenty-five thousand hits of acid when they delivered it to us. Borne told us that he didn't think we could justify spending so much money for a buy. He liked to go by the book. The book, the Agent's Manual, recommended that certain procedures be followed. The problem with many of the supervisors was that they followed the procedures in the Agent's Manual like it was the Holy Bible. The supervisors were the hard-line managers, and we were their antitheses. As undercover guys, we had to adapt to ever-changing situations. The ingenuity of the undercover agent is pushed to the limits because of the complex dynamics of a dope deal. This case was no different.

"This is the man, Fred. His acid matches up with the stuff that Washington is concerned about. It's everywhere," Danny explained to Borne as the four of us stood in his office.

"Yeah, sure," Borne interjected, sarcastically.

"Fred, it's a fact. We got the report from the lab," Danny continued.

"And you think that this guy Norman can come up with twenty-five thousand hits of acid?" Borne asked skeptically.

"Fred, I really think he can. The guy said all the right things when we met him undercover, and he knows all the right people. The telephone tolls link him up with the biggest names in acid! The office in San Francisco is still working on our leads, and they all check out," Danny tried.

"Okay then, set it up for as much as you can, and we'll knock him off," Borne ordered obtusely.

"Fred, are you all right?" Danny challenged, sarcastically. I could see that he was getting very angry at Borne's lack of insight. "Fred, this is a big one. We think we can get the lab. All our intelligence indicates that it is the same lab that is spewing out the orange sunshine all over the country. This guy can take us there. We know that there are no more than a handful of chemists in the world who can make this stuff, and we know that they are located in Northern California and Oregon. Our target is in the San Francisco area. If we can get to this lab, we can make a real difference," I explained, trying to defuse the confrontation between Danny and Borne. Borne stared at me as if he was thinking, and then looked at Danny and Jason.

"Fred, I promise, this is big. We can do it," I added, smiling, because I sensed that he was wavering.

"Get me all the documentation. I'll call Washington and see if they'll go for it," Borne ordered reluctantly. Then he added playfully, in his feeble attempt to be friendly, "Get out of here!"

"You won't regret it, Fred!"

"Amen, brother." Danny congratulated me on my apparent success in converting Borne. We left the office excited to be moving the case another step closer to the clandestine lab.

Over the next couple of days, between undercover telephone conversations and strategy planning, we documented everything we found on Norman and Ralph and the LSD sample. As a result, we received approval from Washington, and we made arrangements to go to Norman's house in the Berkshires to buy the twenty-five thousand hits of acid. We were excited because no one had ever bought this much acid before, and no one from Boston had ever gotten close to an illicit, clandestine lab. We were getting close.

On a sunny day in March, Danny was driving and I was sitting shotgun, admiring the scenery as we approached the end of the Mass Turnpike. I was thinking about all the LSD-induced tragedies and deaths that I had read about while documenting this orange sunshine case.

The official U.S. government reports that we read indicated that the problem was even more serious. The fallout from LSD use was now reaching astronomical proportions. Although no one ever actually died from an overdose as a result of ingesting LSD, the mind-altering experiences that it caused sometimes led to death. Panic reactions induced by LSD caused subjects to run into oncoming traffic and trains in an attempt to escape from imaginary demons that were chasing them. Others experienced euphoria and dove out of dormitory windows, convinced that they would float on the clouds. The problem was that different people reacted differently to the exact same dosage unit of LSD, and no one knew why. In addition, the LSD high was uncontrollable because there was no known antidote to it.

It occurred to me that Norman and Ralph were responsible for many of these deaths. These two meek little hippies were murderers. It was difficult for me to imagine, and I was dealing with them. It is no wonder that the average person didn't see it that way. Hippies espoused peace, free love, and the freedom to "do your own thing." I wondered if Norman and Ralph ever considered themselves murderers when they read the newspaper accounts of these LSD tragedies.

"What are you thinking about?" Danny asked.

"I was thinking about this LSD," I answered.

"It's crazy shit, isn't it?"

"I don't understand why people want to see colors and hallucinate," I responded.

"Who knows?"

"They say they see God. It's like a religion," I said.

"Yeah, they see God when they get run over by a truck! I'll wait till my turn comes to see God. I ain't gonna rush it," Danny said jokingly. I laughed at his philosophical response.

"Look at these trees, man. Isn't it beautiful, Dan?"

"It's beautiful, man. We need to do a case like this every once in awhile to get us out of the cities, to see trees. It's like a vacation. We haven't been out of the ghetto in years," Dan remarked.

Beep, beep, beep! A horn burst interrupted our private conversation and drew my attention to Tony Ragazzi and Jason Germano in a surveillance car, pulling up next to us in the passing lane. Jason was motioning us to pull over at the last service station on the turnpike. Danny took his foot off of the gas to let Ragazzi pull in front of us, and we followed him, cutting across lanes of traffic to pull into the service area. We all got out and went to the men's room, and then sauntered back to our cars. I hung back with Jason while Danny walked a little ahead with Tony Ragazzi. Tony was the senior man on this trip, and he wasn't happy about having to make a two-hour drive to do the surveillance on our undercover drug buy.

"This better be a good one, you guys. I got a million things to do, and they send me out here to cover a hippie LSD deal. I call that kiddie dope!" Tony complained.

"Tony, relax, enjoy the scenery. We don't even need you. We asked the boss to send you along so you could get out of the office," Danny chided him.

"Yah, yah, yah, you guys are loaded. I'm here to protect the money, I'm not worried about you guys! I'm worried about the money."

"Tony, the money's fine, don't worry, Tony, just stay out of sight. This is walkin'-around money for Paulie and me," Danny teased.

"Jason, we're gonna miss you, man," I said, because I felt bad about the situation. Borne made us cut Jason out of the deal because we were not technically partners. Having three guys was actually better for security, safety, and corroboration, but we could not convince the boss.

"The way I see it is, I lucked out," Jason said whimsically. "I get the most important job. I have to keep Tony from screwing up the deal!"

"That's right, Jason. I never thought of it that way," I laughed.

"That's why they have to trust the most important jobs to me, Paulie, and not you guys. You guys don't think, you just act," Jason teased, and I grabbed him with my arm around his neck and threw a series of mock upper cuts to his stomach. We pushed each other away, and Danny and Tony turned around to see what we were laughing about.

"What are you guys up to now?" Tony asked distrustfully.

"Just going over the plan for today," I answered.

"Yeah, right," Tony said skeptically.

In a more serious tone, I detailed the plan. "Jason comes with us for now. We drop him off someplace with the money. We go and see the dope, we get a sample, then we go and meet with Jason, put a test on the acid, then bring the money back to Norman and make the buy."

"Okay, let's do it," Tony said.

We drove out of the service area onto the turnpike, with Tony following in his government-issue police model Chevrolet. Jason, Danny, and I were together like we should be, even if it was only for a short time.

"He said he's got a million things to do," Jason said, frustrated after driving with Ragazzi for almost two hours.

"Yeah, he's got to count his paper clips and pencils, and shop for a new pocket protector," Danny joked. It relieved some of the frustration.

After a while, we came to the location of the farm where we were to meet Norman. We passed by and studied the entrance road.

"That's it, Tony," Danny announced over the walkie-talkie.

"The one with the mailbox?" Tony asked.

"Yup, that's it. It's gonna be a tough location to surveil," Danny answered. "We're gonna drop Jason and the money off at that coffee shop that we passed back there, and then go do it."

Ragazzi responded with a double click of his walkie-talkie transmitter, and he followed us as we made a U-turn and headed back to the coffee shop. We stopped, and I went inside with Jason and copied the number off the pay telephone. Jason wished me luck, we shook hands, and I went out and got back into the car with Danny.

"It's show time," I said. Danny smiled and slapped me five, and we drove away. When we came to the mailbox, Danny turned left, slowly crossed the road, and eased onto the gravel driveway.

"Tony, don't follow us in here. We'll see you when we leave," Danny cautioned Ragazzi. Ragazzi clicked back in response. We shut our radio off, and continued down the long, narrow, brush-covered drive.

"Danny, these hippies like the country," I remarked.

"I guess so," Danny answered, straining to see where the drive would lead us. After about a half mile we came to an opening, and we could see a broken-down farmhouse and several vehicles parked at odd angles.

"Looks like they have company," I observed as Danny drove up to the side of the two-story house and parked. We got out of the car and looked around for signs of life, and then began to climb the wooden stairs leading to the front porch. We stopped to listen through the front door, which was unlocked. We could hear several people talking inside, but their voices were muffled, and we could not understand what they were saying.

"Hello! Hello!" I called loudly, while knocking on the door. Danny and I looked at each other, trying to evaluate the situation, and then we heard feet shuffling. We could see through the window that someone was walking toward us. When the door finally opened, it was Norman.

"Peace," Norman said, smiling, as he tapped his fist on mine and then on Danny's. It was obvious to us from his slow reactions and his mellow demeanor that he was under the influence of drugs. We followed him down the hallway toward a kitchen. I could see people in several of the rooms as we passed by. In one there was a middle-aged man in a business suit laying on the floor, straddled by a cute little "flower child," wearing a sarong and halter top. It looked like they were wrestling. A couple of long-haired hippies were squatting down around the guy in the suit, and they appeared to be examining him. When we entered the kitchen area, there were several people already there, drinking tea and smoking pot. They all nodded and smiled.

"Norman, we got business to do," I reminded him coldly.

"Yeah, right on, Sully," Norman answered slowly, and taking the cue, motioned with his head for us to follow him into a room off to the side.

"Norman, we don't like to mix business with pleasure, my man. You know what I mean? Now let's get goin'," I admonished him, walking closely behind him into the next room.

"I can dig it, man, I'm sorry," Norman apologized as he stumbled.

"There's so much smoke in this house, I'm getting high just bein' here! You got a love-in goin' on here or somethin'?" I said.

"Looks like an orgy goin' on in the room down the hall," Danny added.

"No, man, the dude's trippin', man, that's all. The lady's guiding him through it, that's all," Norman explained.

"What dude?" I asked.

"The dude in the suit, man, he dropped some good stuff," Norman answered.

"The dude in the suit? He looks like someone's father. He could be a cop, dressed like that," I said.

"No, man, he's just a dude, that's all," Norman said, smiling dreamily.

"Well, where's the shit?" I demanded.

"It's right here, man," Norman answered absently, opening a leather sack that he took from a bureau drawer and displaying the contents to me. I took the sack from him and looked inside.

"That's it?" I asked.

"That's it, man, it's all there," Norman assured me, opening and closing his eyes slowly. I stood there holding the sack, unsure of what to do next, and Danny sensed my confusion.

"All right then, let's go get the money," Danny said forcefully.

"Like, you don't have the money, man?" Norman asked sleepily.

"Yeah, we got the money. We just wanted to see the stuff first," Danny explained.

"You mean, you gotta go back to Boston to get the money, man?" Norman asked vacantly, trying to figure out what we were doing.

"No, Jason is waiting down the road for us with the money. We dropped him off with the bag of money. Now that everything looks good, we'll go get it," I explained.

"That's cool, man, that's cool," Norman replied drowsily, apparently satisfied with the explanation. Danny and I handed him back the acid and slapped him on the back.

I picked up the telephone and dialed the number of the pay phone at the coffee shop. Jason answered after one ring.

"Hi," Jason answered.

"It's a go. We're on our way." I hung up the phone and turned to Norman.

"We'll be back in five minutes," I said, heading toward the front door. Norman followed us as if he was sleepwalking. When we walked out onto the porch, I could see another car, through the bushes, coming down the driveway. I could not believe it. It was Ragazzi! Danny looked at me and rolled his eyes. Norman looked at us in muddled anticipation.

"What's this?" I asked Norman belligerently. Norman looked startled.

"I don't know, man, cops?"

"He's too goofy-lookin' to be a cop," Danny said quickly.

"Hey, you, whaddaya doin'?" I yelled.

"Who me?" Ragazzi asked from the car.

"Ya, you, stupid!"

"I'm looking for Mr. and Mrs. Jackson. I am from Prudential," Ragazzi yelled back through his opened window.

"Get outta here, you asshole! This is private property! Get outta here now, before we call the cops!" Danny yelled as he threw a rock over the roof of Ragazzi's car.

"All right, man, I made a mistake. I'm going now. Take it easy," Ragazzi answered, anxiously.

"Screw!" Danny yelled as he threw another stone. We watched Ragazzi turn the government car around and drive away.

"What a loser! Could you imagine buying insurance from him? He can't find his customer when he's alive; what happens when he dies? Forget about it!" I remarked, hoping to distract Norman.

Another close call, I thought to myself as Norman looked at us and raised his eyebrows. Danny and I got into our car and waved good-bye. It was a good thing that Norman had smoked a little weed before we arrived!

"We'll be back in five," I said through my window while Danny turned the steering wheel and backed out of our parking space.

"Right on," Norman said automatically and waved.

"Whew," I said as Danny drove away.

"Ragazzi couldn't screw up this case any more if he tried," Danny complained aloud.

"Thank God they're all spaced out in there! I think Norman bought our act, though," I answered.

"I think so, too," Danny agreed.

We passed Ragazzi on the way back to the coffee shop. He was parked on the side of the road in a very obvious spot.

"Tony, can you think of any more ways to blow this case?" an irritated Danny said flatly over the radio.

"Hey, my job is to protect the money," Ragazzi rebutted.

"Yeah, we're going to get the money now," Danny answered, pulling into the parking lot of the coffee shop. I got out and Danny followed me in to meet Jason. He was sitting in a booth with a cup of coffee in front of him. When he spotted us coming in the front door, he gave us a "thumbs-up" with a questioning look on his face. He smiled widely when we gave him the affirmative thumbs-up in reply, and he got up and handed me the brown paper bag with the cash in it.

"It's like taking candy from a baby," I said, repeating a favorite expression of Chris Regan's.

"With a few obstacles in the way! Like Ragazzi driving his car into the middle of the deal," Danny added, laughing in frustration.

"He wanted to make things exciting," I said, smiling at Jason.

"Come on, Jason, come with us to deliver the money. We'll confuse Ragazzi even more," Danny suggested. We laughed, and the three of us got into the car and headed back to meet with Norman.

When we pulled up to the house, Norman came out onto the porch looking extremely paranoid, and he walked toward us tentatively.

"Norman!" Jason called enthusiastically. When Norman saw Jason, he relaxed and smiled.

"Jason!" Norman replied, and stood still while we piled out of the car to meet him. Jason's presence had a calming effect on him.

"Here's the money!" Jason said, handing the bag to Norman. He took it and looked inside, and then closed it up again, clutching it to his body as he hugged Jason.

"Where's our bag?" I interrupted. Continuing to embrace, Norman looked through spacey eyes at me over Jason's shoulder.

"It's inside, man, I'll get it," Norman answered slowly but happily, and then jogged inside to get the bag. He returned immediately with the bag and handed it to me. I opened it and pretended to examine its contents while Danny and Jason continued their conversation with Norman. Finally, I looked up and nodded.

"Let's go," I said, turning around to leave, and Danny and Jason said good-bye to Norman and came with me.

"Bye, guys," Norman said as he waved. "I hope you like it."

Jason and I waved to Norman as Danny turned the car around and drove away from the house. It was another world, I thought to myself, as I looked at long-haired Norman in his overalls, standing in front of the big old farmhouse. We went from one world to another in the course of our work, and we had to adapt. We bought heroin, cocaine, acid, and hash from drug dealers in the projects, the ghetto, nightclubs and bars, and now the farm. I was amazed thinking about it.

"It's a hallucinogenic!" Danny announced over the radio after I tested another sample of the LSD. Tony Ragazzi responded with a click, click of his microphone and looked up as we passed him. He was still parked conspicuously on the side of the road.

"Tony, why don't you make it a little more obvious," Danny mocked Tony over the radio. "Maybe you can paint your car orange or something!"

The following week was very hectic. The attorney general of the United States and the administrator of the Drug Enforcement Administration were personally interested in our case, and they were following it from their offices in Washington, D.C. We had managed to get this far, and now the pressure was on us to get the lab. Clandestine, illicit LSD labs were almost impossible to find because LSD traffickers and the handful of chemists who could actually operate labs, or cookers as they were called, communicated secretively. It was an extremely difficult group to infiltrate. Many agents tried, but no one had ever succeeded. The difference between our case and all the others was that chance encounter in the men's room at Father's Bar, when I came to the aid of Ted Palmer. That incident impressed Palmer so much that he told his contacts around the world. Our encounter actually became sort of a legend.

The operators of the lab in San Francisco and some of the traffickers in the Northwest were having problems with the Hell's Angels motorcycle gang. The Angels were slowly taking over the drug trade in that area, and they were violent guys. The LSD people were peaceful types who couldn't fight their way out of a paper bag, nor did they want to. Ted Palmer suggested to the West Coast people that I could offer protection to them from the Hell's Angels, and they wanted to discuss that possibility with me. Danny and I were going into the deal with a little bargaining power. Plus, we were buying half a million dollars' worth of LSD!

The plane was approaching the airport, and Danny and I were very excited. The long hours of undercover work and the tedious follow-up investigation was finally paying off.

"The last time I landed at this airport, I was returning from thirteen months in Southeast Asia," I said.

"And now you are back by popular demand," Danny joked.

"Yeah, we're back by popular demand," I repeated. "Did you ever see so many people who wanted us to fail?"

"I know. What is it?" Danny asked.

"I thought we were all working to stop drugs," I complained.

"We are. The other guys get confused sometimes. They let their egos get in the way. Since no one else has been able to pull this off, they certainly don't think that two junior agents like us can do it," Danny reasoned.

"If we do, it makes them look bad. Is that it?" I asked.

"That's it!"

"Well, then, let's get off this plane and make 'em all look bad. Cause we are gonna make this case!" I promised.

When we deplaned, we walked into the arms of the drug enforcement group from the San Francisco office that was assigned to work with us. We sensed the tension immediately. A tough-looking Italian stepped forward and introduced himself.

"I'm Dom Delario, the GS, and this is my group. We are going to be working with you on the lab," he announced grimly.

I looked around, and I saw nine tired-looking guys draped around the waiting area at the gate where we arrived. They sized us up as they were introduced and shook our hands mechanically, but they remained at arm's length. It was not a warm welcome.

"Okay, you guys go home and get some sleep. We'll get together in the morning," Delario, the group supervisor, told his group. And the nine guys all said good night as they turned and ambled away from the lobby.

"I'll take you around tonight so you can get familiar with the area," Delario said, while obviously trying to figure us out. He grabbed one of my bags and started walking, and Danny and I followed behind.

In spite of the awkward welcome, I liked Delario. He seemed like a worker, and he was obviously concerned about his group. Their mutual loyalty and respect was clear by the way they spoke to each other, as tired as they seemed during our initial encounter. I knew that something was wrong, though.

"Dom, your accent is not left coast," I said as we walked.

"No, I'm from Chicago," he answered amiably.

When we drove out of the airport garage, I could feel the moist night air coming in through the open window. This is Tony Bennett's town I thought to myself, "I Left My Heart in San Francisco," and I'm here with two *paesanos*, Danny and Dom! I liked the feeling.

"We'll go back to the office first so we can go over our plans for the case. You can bring me up to date on your negotiations, and I can fill you in on our intelligence. Then I'll take you guys to your hotel, so you can drop your bags, we'll go out for dinner, and I'll show you around," Delario explained in a professional, but friendlier tone than before.

"That's great! The deal is on hold, anyway, until we telephone our guy," I said.

"My group has been working day and night. We just finished working on a wiretap, and the guys expected a couple of days off. The boss assigned us to work with you, and they are pissed," Delario said, attempting to explain the cold reception.

"We'll make it worth your while, Dom," I promised.

"You guys are onto something big. The guys will get over it tomorrow. That's why I sent them home. They need some sleep," Delario continued.

Danny and I looked around at the scenery whizzing past as we headed toward the office. The steep hills, the waterfront, and the architecture were uniquely San Francisco. We pulled into the parking lot of the San Francisco DEA office.

"The problem is that every agent in the country who buys a little acid thinks that he is going to get to the lab. They come out here, and somehow my group always gets assigned to help them out. It's a drain! We have to drop what we are doing and take care of someone else's case. We are always putting our own cases on hold and playing catch-up. None of the cases ever succeed, and we don't get any credit in our statistics. You know how that goes. We are competing with all the other groups at a big disadvantage. My guys are dragging their asses, and it's developing into a morale problem. So that's why they seem apprehensive. We have been burned so many times before," Delario continued to explain.

"We understand. We ain't out here for no vacation," I answered, sympathetically.

"C'mon, let's go," Delario said after pulling the car into a slot marked Group Supervisor. We got out of the car and followed him to his office. Inside, he went to his desk, picked up a manila folder, and offered it to us. Danny took it and began to examine the pages, one at a time.

"It's the intelligence file on the lab that you are working on. We've done a lot of legwork," Delario said, while Danny thumbed through the file.

Danny stopped reading and looked up. "This is it! You guys have done it! All our information matches."

Delario smiled. "It looks like you guys are going to break the jinx," he said.

"Dom, I promise you, this is it. I know it is," Danny replied. I looked at the two of them, Danny and Delario, and I knew that we had connected. We connected professionally and personally. The chemistry was right, and we were going to make a lab case. We were going to get the lab!

"C'mon, let's eat. What do you like?" Delario asked.

"We like everything," Danny answered as we followed Delario back to the car.

"Okay, we'll go to Chinatown. You gotta see Chinatown anyway, then we'll check out the rest of the sights." Delario was a gracious host and confirmed my initial impression that we were clicking.

"I worked Chinatown in Boston, and all the Chinese said that San Francisco, New York, and Boston of all the cities were the most like China itself," I offered.

"San Francisco is the closest, I guarantee it," Delario said. He reminded me of Phil Janaro, my football coach when I played for the Second Infantry Division in Korea. I loved Phil, and Delario could have been his twin.

As soon as we entered the elegant restaurant, we were met by the host and seated immediately at a very private table surrounded by ornate dragons and Chinese figurines.

"This is where the wise guys like to eat," Delario whispered to us. As I looked around, I realized that the waiters were glancing over at us. That's why the host was so accommodating! He assumed that we were wise guys, just like people in Boston did. I looked across the table at Dom and Danny, and I marveled at their appearance. They both had Mafia written all over them. It's amazing how much people assume from your appearance, I thought.

"How's the Peking duck?" Danny asked Delario.

"It's the best," he declared, then, moving his eyes toward several guys seated at a table across the dining room, continued in a low tone, "Those guys are with the Lanza family. Francesco Lanza was the first Mafia boss in San Francisco. His son, Jimmy, is the boss now. When Michael Abate, his partner, was convicted and deported in 1961, Jimmy took the whole thing over. The Lanza family runs everything here."

Danny and I did not react immediately, but I picked up my water glass and took a peek at the mob guys while I sipped. Danny buttered his bread and did the same. The mob guys were as curious about us as we were about them, but they were less discreet. Delario, Danny, and I looked at each other and smiled as the waiter came over to our table.

"The usual, sir?" the waiter asked Delario.

"Yes," Delario answered. The waiter disappeared and returned with a bottle of wine. Delario tasted the wine and held the glass up to the light. He took another taste, then looked straight at the waiter.

"That's fine," Delario said, and the waiter filled all of our glasses and disappeared into the kitchen again.

"The usual?" Dan repeated lightly.

"I'm working a mob case in here, so I'm a regular. You guys will enhance my undercover role. These wise guys are all wondering who the hell you are," Delario explained.

After we ordered our meal, we continued our conversation in whispers. We talked a little more about the mob in San Francisco, and we compared them to the East Coast mobsters. Later, we talked about the details of our acid case.

"Dom, my best army buddy was from Chicago, and he taught school at Saint Patrick's, right in the city. Do you know where it is?" I asked, changing the conversation entirely. Dom paused and looked at me curiously.

"I taught at Saint Patrick's," he answered nonplussed, and I looked at him surprised.

"Dick Hahner." I blurted out the name of my friend.

"Green Beret," he answered.

"You know him?"

"I know him all my life," he replied.

"My brother and Dick Hahner's brother were both killed in Vietnam on the same day. My brother was a paratrooper, 101st Airborne, and his brother was a marine. They were both eighteen years old. Dick and I met the first day of basic training and we went all the way through advanced infantry training, jump school, and OCS together. We joined the army for the same reason. We wanted revenge, we wanted to win the war for all the young kids that died. We wanted to make sure that those kids didn't die in vain," I rambled on as the memory of those terrible days overwhelmed me.

"I know," Delario answered in a whisper. I looked at him, and I could see tears in his eyes. I realized that he knew exactly what I meant. I felt very uncomfortable.

"You know?" I repeated softly.

"My kid brother was killed during the Tet Offensive in Vietnam, too," Delario answered thoughtfully, and I knew that he felt the same pain in his stomach that I did.

"They died while all the assholes in Washington, who referred to themselves as 'the best and the brightest,' kept sending more kids over," I added angrily. The memories were opening up old scars.

"C'mon, guys, let's see the rest of the town. I'll show you around so you can get a feel for the place," Delario said in a more upbeat tone, trying to change the mood. Danny and I got up and put on our jackets while Delario went over and handed the waiter the money for our dinner. Danny and I looked at each other approvingly.

"He's one of us," Danny said. I shook my head in agreement.

Delario drove us all around San Francisco that night. He gave us the Cook's tour. We went down to the waterfront and walked through the famous Fisherman's Wharf, and we stopped and studied Alcatraz island, protruding ominously out of the bay. We drove by Haight-Ashbury, the Mission District, Nob Hill, and Telegraph Hill. The "City by the Bay," illuminated by the light of the moon, was fascinating. Delario also stopped in several of the bars and clubs to give us the flavor of the nightlife.

Toward the end of the evening, we visited a trendy, upscale bar in the financial district. It was an ultramodern room, spacious, with a lot of light-colored hardwood, highlighted with plenty of shiny brass fixtures. A circular bar in the middle of the expanse was the focal point, and the stylishly dressed patrons looked like the in crowd. The bar had atmosphere. Danny and I followed Delario through the door and stopped when he stopped. The three of us gathered around a high circular table.

Scanning the room for a waitress, I noticed that there were two very beautiful women standing at the bar in the center of the room. They were looking in our direction and appeared to be whispering to each other. One woman had blonde hair, cut Farrah Fawcett style, and the other had long dark-brown hair, which hung down below her shoulders. With their striking good looks, they stood out from all the other women in the room. The blonde leaned over and said something to her friend, who then turned her gaze back toward us and laughed coyly. She appeared to whisper something in the blonde's ear, and they continued laughing and staring at us. I looked around innocently to see whom the two women were staring at, and the blonde waved at me.

"Danny, don't look now, but that blonde is waving at me," I said, dumbfounded.

"What blonde?" Danny asked.

"That one over there," I said, staring in her direction. Danny and Delario turned their heads immediately to look at her, and she pointed her finger at us and nodded yes. I responded by pointing to my chest, and the two women laughed seductively, throwing their heads back and brushing their hair away from their faces. A waiter stopped at our table and interrupted our charade by placing drinks in front of each of us.

"Compliments of the ladies at the bar, gentlemen," the waiter said dryly, and as he began to leave, Danny grabbed the waiter's shirt and stopped him abruptly. The waiter was annoyed.

"Wait a minute!" Danny said to the waiter while he held onto his shirt, causing him to stand awkwardly in front of us. The waiter simmered, but did not reply.

"You mean, those broads over there sent these drinks over to us? Who are they?" Danny continued loudly, demanding an explanation. The waiter looked at Danny with pursed lips.

"Sir, I do not know who the young ladies are. I am a waiter, and I serve drinks. It's not my business to know who everyone is," the waiter answered slowly, pausing after each sentence, and he enunciated every word as he looked defiantly into Danny's eyes. Danny shoved the waiter hard enough to cause his head to snap back.

"Get adda heah," Danny scoffed loudly, with his hands stretched out in front of him for added effect. The waiter tripped, and then gathered himself together and walked away quickly, taking short, fast steps. Danny, no longer concerned with the waiter, turned his attention toward the two women who sent us the drinks. He waved his arms, motioning for the women to join us.

"Ladies, come ovah heah," Danny ordered the women loudly from across the room, and they responded immediately. Tall and poised, the two women walked directly toward us without losing eye contact. They held their glasses out in front of them as if they were compasses leading them to our location. They walked gracefully, standing erect, like dancers, and everyone in the bar looked at them as they passed, admiring their perfect figures. I wondered why the women singled us out. Was it a case of mistaken identity? Did they think we were someone else? As I wondered, the women moved closer and closer, until they were right in front of us, and Danny reached out and hugged them both. The two women obviously enjoyed the attention, and they responded like they were his old friends.

"Do you guys believe this? Are they beautiful or what?" Danny asked as he hugged the women impishly. They cuddled closer, leaning their heads on Danny's shoulder, still smiling and laughing, comfortable in his embrace.

"Which one do you want?" Danny asked Dom and me playfully. The women looked at us demurely. I was unable to figure out what was going on. Was this some kind of joke? I wondered.

The one with the dark hair left Danny's embrace and moved next to me. She put her left hand on my shoulder and looked up at me. When I looked at her, she smiled.

"See, they aren't gay," the blonde said innocently to her friend.

"Gay?" Danny mocked her question, loudly. "Do we look gay to you?"

"Thank God! They're not," the brunette spoke for the first time, obviously happy with their discovery. Danny looked puzzled, and I realized for the first time that he didn't really know the two women, either. We laughed and looked at Dom, who was grinning and shaking his head knowingly.

"All the good-looking guys around here are gay," the blonde explained seriously as she studied our expressions. The brunette kept looking at us also. We could see Dom smiling as he continued to nod his head in agreement with her statement of fact.

"She's right. We're in San Francisco," Dom confirmed succinctly.

"You guys aren't from around here?" the blonde inquired.

"We're from Boston!" Danny boasted proudly.

"You on vacation?" she asked.

"What are you, the law?" Danny joked.

"We're here to meet with Dominic. It's business," I explained, nodding toward Dom.

"Oh, I see," the blonde said, nodding her head as she sized up Dom curiously.

"He's the main man out here, and we got a little East Coast–West Coast business to settle, you know what I mean?" I continued. The two women were now focused on me, and I could see that my explanation made them even more curious. Despite their interest, they seemed to conclude that we were gangsters and there would be no more questions concerning our business. They just wanted to enjoy themselves in San Francisco and have a good time. I saw a large number of gays in the bar as I looked around, but there were also many straight people. Regardless of sexual persuasion, almost everyone seemed to be watching and admiring the beautiful women who had just joined us.

"Hey, you! Bring us another round of drinks," Danny ordered the waiter. It was the same man who had delivered the drinks to us earlier. He looked at Danny incredulously for a moment, then smiled politely.

"Yes, sir, certainly," the waiter replied and scurried off to the bar.

"So, where are you guys staying?" the blonde asked innocently. Danny turned to face the blonde with a threatening look in his eye, and I could see that she realized her mistake. "I'm sorry. I mean, we're staying at the Fairmont, if you guys want to come back with us for a few drinks."

Danny laughed menacingly as he continued to stare at her. She stared back at him, relieved that he accepted her clarification, but also fascinated with him.

"There's a wonderful piano bar," the brunette added.

"We'd love to, honey, but we're workin'. We gotta take care of some business tonight," Danny cut her off. Both women appeared surprised that Danny declined their invitation. They reminded me of high school girls being turned down by their prom dates. Their feelings were hurt, and they could not easily disguise their emotions.

"Oh, that's alright," the bewildered blonde responded hotly.

"It's serious business, baby," I apologized.

"Ladies, it's a matter of life or death," Dom said slowly, in his raspy smoker's whisper, which served to emphasize the importance of our imaginary meeting. It was as if Dom let them in on a secret. Both women looked at Dom appreciatively, and he stared back at them. His comment immediately reassured the women, who no longer seemed hurt.

"We understand," the blonde offered agreeably, and the brunette nodded her head in agreement.

"C'mon, let's go," Dom said, finishing his drink.

"Do you need a ride? We're goin' right by the Fairmont," Danny asked.

"No, that's alright, we have our car," the blonde declined graciously.

"We'll walk you back to your car, then. That way no one will bother you," I said.

"Oh, thank you. That's very nice. I'm Dawn." The blonde was more animated now, and feeling more self-confident.

"I'm Sully."

Dawn took a last sip of her drink and picked up her purse. I motioned for her to lead the way to the parking lot. The two glamorous women walked self-assuredly out of the bar, and Danny, Dom, and I swaggered along behind. It felt as though everyone else in the bar stopped to watch our departure.

When we emerged from the bar, I breathed the crisp salt air, which reminded me of South Boston on a good night. The women led the way, stepping out like models on the runway, talking and laughing with us until we came to a candy-apple-red Corvette convertible. They stopped and smiled, and thanked us for escorting them. Then Dawn fumbled around with her purse. She took out a pen and wrote something quickly on a match cover.

"Will we see you again?" she asked Danny as she handed him the match cover with her telephone number written on it.

"Of course you will, as soon as we take care of business," Danny assured her. The blonde kissed him quickly on the lips and stepped back and took the keys out of her purse.

"In case I don't see you again, I have something for you," she said, opening the trunk of the Corvette. She reached in and took out a current issue of *Playboy* magazine and handed it to Danny. While Danny looked down at the magazine, she kissed him again on the cheek, and smiled. She paused to look at Danny while he looked at the magazine cover and then at her. Dawn went to the trunk again, took out two more copies, and handed one to Dom and one to me. I then realized what Danny was staring at. The blonde's picture was on the cover. I looked up at Danny, then over at Dom, and back to our new friends, and they laughed again playfully.

"I'm in there, too," the brunette said coyly. "You just have to look a little harder. We can't all be the centerfold!"

"You're beautiful, Donna," the blonde complimented her friend, while pointing to a photo of Donna standing naked under a waterfall. They both watched for our reaction.

"Wow!" Danny commented.

"Donna, it looks like the water must have washed your bathing suit away," I joked, and everyone laughed.

"What's the highest number? Ten?" Dom asked dryly, then he immediately exclaimed, "You're both eleven!" It was a funny response from Dom, who had been fairly quiet and unobtrusive all evening. The five of us stood around under the glare of the parking lot lights talking about nothing. None of us really wanted to end the evening, but it was getting late, and Danny, Dom, and I needed to get some rest.

"Ladies, it's been real," I said, in a halfhearted attempt to end the small talk.

"Get adda heah! We'll catch up with you tomorrow," Danny said. The blonde reached up and put her hands on Danny's chest and kissed him.

"Good night for now, handsome," she said, and smiled as she watched his reaction. Danny smiled slightly.

"For now," Danny said, following her with his eyes as she got into the driver's seat of the convertible.

Donna, the pretty brunette, grabbed my shirt with her right hand and kissed me on the cheek. She then politely looked at Dom and waved. "Good night, guys," she said sweetly, and got into the car. Danny, Dom, and I stood together, watching as the blonde started up the Corvette. The powerful roar of the engine underscored the feminine beauty that controlled it.

"Bye, girls," Danny said loud enough to be heard over the engine.

"Bye, boys," they answered playfully as they pulled out of the parking space and drove away, waving mischievously to us. We looked at each other in disbelief.

"Are my eyes deceiving me?" I joked.

"It's a dream come true," Danny laughed.

"It didn't take you guys from Boston long! Now I don't have to worry about how you are going to spend your off time," Dom said, facetiously.

"No, Helen will worry about that," Danny said, looking at me with a sparkle in his eye.

"Who's Helen?" Dom asked, looking from Danny to me.

"His wife!" I answered laughing.

"You're married?" Dom asked Danny skeptically, and then looked at me for an affirmation. I smiled and nodded.

"I'm married, too," I laughed.

"You don't think this would happen if we were single, do you?" Danny asked Dom with a quizzical look, and we all began to laugh. We were all standing in the empty parking space at two o'clock in the morning, looking at our complimentary *Playboy* magazines and laughing like teenagers.

"Hey, let's get out of here. We gotta get some sleep. I don't want you guys dozin' off in the middle of this caper," Dom interrupted humorously. We did need some sleep. It was five o'clock in the morning in Boston. Danny and I were so tired. Our surprise encounter with the Playmates rejuvenated us temporarily, but we would be exhausted tomorrow if we didn't get some rest. Dom dropped us off at out hotel and told us to call him when we woke up, so that he could make arrangements for someone to pick us up and take us to the office.

Danny and I rode the elevator to our room. As soon as we dead-bolted the door behind us, the fatigue settled in. I turned on the television set, sat on the edge of my bed, and thought about the day's events. I wondered how the LSD lab negotiations were going to unfold, and then I smiled when I thought about Dom and the Playboy Bunnies. Danny came out of the bathroom and collapsed on his bed.

"It's all yours," he said, half asleep.

"Give me five minutes to comb my hair. The Bunnies called while you were on the throne, and they want us to hop over to the Fairmont and meet them in their rooms," I joked.

"Uh huh," Danny mumbled, too tired to appreciate the humor. When I came out of the bathroom, he was sound asleep. I shut the television off and lay down myself, but my mind would not stop racing. A steady stream of possible scenarios ran through my head. I thought for a long time about the undercover negotiations that we would engage in the next day and then somehow, I drifted off to sleep myself.

Seconds later, it seemed, Danny put his hand on my shoulder and shook me roughly. "Hey, hey, wake up." I opened my eyes carefully and peeked out at Danny from underneath the covers.

"It's ten o'clock! We have to call Dom," Danny reminded me. I pushed myself to a sitting position and looked around the room sleepily, still feeling the effects of jet lag.

"That's right," I answered unconsciously.

"Where's the number?" Danny asked while fumbling through his wallet.

"I dunno," I replied, still half asleep.

"Here it is," Danny muttered as he quickly dialed the number. I looked over at him and noticed that he was already dressed.

"Dom Delario," Danny demanded into the telephone while looking in my direction. "Dom! We're ready! He did? Great! We'll be downstairs in twenty minutes," he said and hung up.

"Twenty minutes! What's the rush? I'm starving," I complained.

"He called looking for us! Norman called the undercover number and they said that we went out for breakfast. They put a trace on the call and told him to call back in an hour or so," Danny told me.

"Hey, Danny, I gotta eat. If they said that we went to breakfast, don't you think we should go to breakfast?"

"Hurry up, take a shower. We'll have coffee and a muffin downstairs in the lobby," he replied. I was always a little grumpy when I woke up, and I didn't like to change my routine. I got started slowly, and I needed to eat to get the cobwebs out, so I could think. Reluctantly, I got up and went into the shower.

When I came out of the bathroom, Danny was standing there smiling, and drinking a coffee and eating a donut. I could see that he was excited about the deal.

"There's your coffee. I got you two donuts," Danny said, pointing to a bag on the dresser. He was trying his best to appease me.

"That's great! Breakfast of champions," I said, sarcastically. I gave in, though, and laughed at Danny's best effort to accommodate me. I dried myself off and got dressed as fast as I could because I didn't want to make Dom wait. I ate a donut and drank my coffee quickly, while Danny and I discussed our plan for the day. I could see that Danny was anxious to get going. I gulped down the last of my coffee and checked my watch.

"Let's go," I said, throwing my cup into the wastebasket. Danny opened the door, and I followed him out of the hotel room.

We got onto the elevator, already occupied by a couple of perfectly groomed men, dressed conservatively in dark business suits. They were holding their briefcases by their sides with one hand and fingering their suit jacket buttons with the other. The businessmen tried not to look directly at Danny and me, but it was obvious that they wanted to. When I looked over at them, they glanced at each other and then looked up at the ceiling of the elevator.

"We'll set up a meeting. We'll show them the money, then we want to see the shit. The money and the shit don't come together." Danny recited the rules for the day out loud in a soliloquy, paying no attention at all to the businessmen next to us in the close quarters of the elevator.

The men looked quickly at us, then just as quickly turned their eyes to the ceiling. I wanted to laugh as I read the expressions on their faces, but I didn't. The elevator stopped at the lobby and Danny strode out. Gesturing with his hands and almost hitting one of the businessmen in the face as he walked by, Danny elucidated his thoughts for the day. The lobby was busy with smartly dressed business people and glamorous-looking couples, and Danny and I stood out as neither. The doorman opened the door for us and wished us well as we walked out onto the sidewalk. He watched us curiously for a moment as if to see if we needed a cab. Then the long white Cadillac Fleetwood Brougham pulled up, and Danny and I went over and got in. We shook hands with the driver, who paused for several minutes in front of the hotel, and then drove away. The driver introduced himself as Chuck Thompson. He was a big guy, a West Coast bodybuilder type of guy, with long blonde hair styled in a pompadour, a healthy tan, and a nice white smile.

"Dom said that you guys have a pretty good case cookin'," Chuck said in a friendly tone.

"We think so," Danny replied.

"I'm glad that Delario thinks so," I added.

"How do you like your undercover car?" Chuck asked, referring to the Cadillac.

"It's us!" Danny answered quickly.

"Dom don't want you guys lookin' like a couple of assholes," Chuck said with a laugh.

"We traced the phone call this morning, and it's from a place in Haight-Ashbury, right where we suspected it to be," Chuck added.

"You guys are on top of things!" I responded.

"We been workin' like dawgs on this thing," Chuck said with enthusiasm. I sensed an interest and an excitement that I hadn't sensed the night before. A little sleep can work wonders.

"Dom has a couple of guys out sittin' on the house right now. We got 'em covered!" Chuck continued in his western accent. He wheeled the

Caddy into the government building garage like a cowboy and parked next to Delario's car. We followed Chuck into the same office that we had visited the night before. When we walked inside, we saw Delario standing by his desk smiling, surrounded by the rest of the agents in his group.

"You playboys ready?" he joked. The group laughed and eyed us good-naturedly. They didn't have to wait long for our reaction. I turned red, and Danny beamed.

"Playboys? We're from Boston; we're proper Bostonians. Haven't you ever heard of the Puritans? We're conservatives. You're the playboys! We're from the right coast, you're from the left! We pahk ah cahs, we leave the California girls for you surfer boys!" I joked back. The guys were all laughing, and I could tell by their good humor that something more than sleep was kicking in. Delario must have given them a pep talk, because they were ready to go out and kick ass. They were with us 100 percent.

"Yeah, sure, it was real proper the way you blew into town and scooped the two Bunnies from under our noses! You're proper Bostonians, alright!" Delario continued to tease. It was obvious that everyone was enjoying the banter. One of the agents, a tall slim guy, walked over and handed coffees to Danny and me.

"Compliments of the surfer boys," he joked, then added in a more serious tone, "Your man, Norman, called about nine o'clock this morning, and I told him that you went out to breakfast. He sounded anxious. I asked him for his phone number, but he wouldn't give it to me. I told him to call back."

"Dynamite!" I commented.

"Our undercover phone is over there," the agent said, pointing to a telephone booth down the hall.

"Thanks," Danny and I said, simultaneously.

"My name's Jimmy," the agent said, introducing himself.

"I'm Paul; they call me Sully," I replied.

"I'm Danny, Danny Santarpio." Danny introduced himself to Jimmy, then we met the rest of the agents in the group. It was a nice feeling, considering that only the night before, they looked like they never wanted to see us again. I looked at Dom and realized that he was the magic behind the change. Dom was the catalyst. He was an agent's agent, a good supervisor. He smiled back slyly, because he understood that I knew the reason for the change in everyone's attitude.

Suddenly, the annoying sound of a telephone ringing loudly interrupted our conversation and everything stopped. Dom pointed urgently to the undercover phone as he looked at Danny, who sprinted down the hall like a halfback running off tackle. When he tried to stop, he almost slid past the booth, but he grabbed onto the doorknob and hurried inside. I looked at

Dom and we gave each other a thumbs-up while all the other agents looked pensively at us. No one said anything as we waited in anticipation. Finally, Danny came out of the booth and looked at us all with a grin.

"Norman and Ralph are meeting us at that joint in Sausalito, at nine tonight," Dan announced, reading from notes on a small piece of paper that he held in his hand.

"Why so late?" Dom asked.

"They flew in on the 'red-eye,' and they are tired. Besides, they need more time to meet with their people," Danny explained.

"Okay, then, the rest of you guys go home and go back to bed. Come back at six o'clock so we can set up. If I need you, I'll call you," Dom said to the group.

The guys nodded their appreciation. Several of them volunteered to hang around, but Dom told them to go home. He only wanted the surveillance teams that were watching the residence in Haight-Ashbury to stay in place, and he said that he would monitor them while everyone else rested. Danny and I looked at Dom as we waited to hear what he wanted us to do.

"That means you, too! See you later!" Dom ordered. Danny and I were surprised, and we stood still, waiting and staring at him.

"We'll stick around in case you need us," Danny said.

"Get out of here, I said! You got the keys to the Caddy?" Dom asked. Chuck came over and handed the keys to Danny. We looked back at Dom, who waved good-bye to us.

"Okay, then, we'll continue to check in. If you need us, we'll leave word at the hotel where we are," I said. Dom got up from his desk and walked over to us with his hand outstretched, and we each shook hands with him.

"Relax, we'll work when we have to," Dom said good-naturedly. "But don't relax too much with those Bunnies! Be back here by six o'clock!" We laughed, and promised that we would return.

Danny drove our new Caddy out of the federal building and headed back to our hotel. We were both smiling because it was fun to be working in San Francisco. It was a nice change from East Coast cities, a nice change of scenery, and the weather wasn't bad, either. When I noticed that Danny drove past our hotel, I turned to him, and he was laughing.

"Where was that photo shoot?" Danny asked, catching me totally off guard. I looked at him as I tried to remember where the Playboy Bunnies said that they were going to be working.

"Don't think too much, my man, I already got it covered," Danny answered. "It's over here."

Danny pulled into a parking lot adjacent to a long sandy beach, drove to the far end, and stopped next to a blue van. He dropped his sunglasses down on his nose and peered over the lenses toward some figures on the beach, where the sand met the jetty. Danny then looked at me and winked. He got out of the Caddy and headed toward the group on the beach. I remained in the passenger seat, watching Danny in disbelief.

"Let's go, Paulie boy," he urged, looking back at me.

"What are you, nuts?" I asked anxiously, as I got out of the car and caught up with him.

"Whaddaya mean?" Danny said as we trudged through the sand in the direction of the jetty.

"We're just gonna walk up in the middle of the photo session?" I asked, apprehensively.

"Why not? They'll love it," Danny answered confidently. As we got closer, I could tell that the people near the jetty noticed us and were glancing nervously in our direction. I could see two women and several men who were obviously photographers. We were definitely in the right place. Donna was sitting in a captain's deck chair, all bundled up with a white towel wrapped around her, and Dawn was standing in the surf, posing provocatively in a bikini while a photographer took pictures. When we approached the scene, Dawn recognized Danny, abandoned her pose, and started running toward him, laughing excitedly. The cameraman dropped his camera to his side and stopped and stared at his subject as she threw her arms around Danny and kissed him. Donna got up quietly out of the chair, shook her long, dark hair out, and walked toward me. When we came together, she reached up and kissed me on the cheek. She stepped back and looked at me without saying anything, almost as if she was trying to analyze my reaction.

"I knew that you would come back," she said cheerfully, and we both smiled. The sun was shining and sparkling on the surf, but the air was cool, and the breeze made her shiver and break out in goose bumps.

Danny's Playmate of the Month walked over and kissed me lightly on the cheek. She hugged me, and then turned around to introduce us to the photographers.

"We've got enough! It's too windy anyway," one of them whined, and they began packing up their equipment. The Bunnies got dressed on the beach while they talked with Danny and me, then they took us by the hands and started to walk, leading us along.

"Thanks a million, guys! You were great!" Dawn yelled to the photographers over the sound of the surf and the breeze.

"You were marvelous!" one of them replied and waved his hand in the air like a girl.

"I really knew you'd come back!" Donna repeated excitedly to Danny and me, laughing happily.

"What shall we do?" Dawn asked as she looked inquisitively at Danny.

"We're tied up this afternoon," he shot back quickly, and I could see Dawn's chagrin written on her face.

"But we have a nice place for dinner," I volunteered, and Danny looked at me in surprise.

"We do?" he asked.

"Yeah, that little place in Sausalito," I answered. Danny smiled when he realized where I was going.

"You're gonna love this place," Danny said to Dawn and Donna, and they looked at him.

"But what about today? We want to spend the day with you," Dawn purred.

"It's business, baby, we got business today," Danny said with finality, ending that line of questioning. Dawn pouted and Donna looked at my face for an explanation. I said nothing, and let her imagination answer her question. Donna got into the backseat with me, and Dawn sat in the front with Danny and snuggled up close to him.

"Dante, can't you postpone your business for a while?" Dawn begged. She had an obvious crush on Danny.

"No," Danny answered flatly, and she pouted again. She continued to sit next to Danny with her head on his shoulder, as if she enjoyed his moody rebuffs. Donna kept looking at me silently, pleading with her eyes for me to explain, while Danny drove toward their hotel. When we pulled up to the Fairmont, she raised her eyebrows to emphasize her annoyance. Without ever taking her eyes off of me, she leaned over and kissed me. She pulled me close to her, squeezing me tightly around the shoulders. Dawn was already out of the car and standing on the sidewalk. Donna turned to face me.

"I hope I can wait till tonight," she said. She ran her hand over my face gently, then turned the other way to get out of the car. I slid over, got out behind her, and closed the door. I gave her another brief hug, then got into the front seat next to Danny. We drove away and I watched as Dawn and Donna stood on the sidewalk waving to us, until they faded out of sight.

"Danny, are we crazy or what?" I finally spoke.

"Crazy? We're nuts! That's why we're here," Danny answered, deadpan, and we both laughed at the absurdity of the situation.

"Can you picture Norman and Ralph tonight, when they see us with our dinner dates?" I imagined out loud.

"Forget about Norman and Ralph! What about the surveillance guys when they spot us?" Danny continued.

"It's a surveillance they won't forget," I added.

Danny and I found a bodybuilder's gym that one of the agents had suggested and worked out for a couple of hours with the weights, and then we went back to our hotel room. We didn't call home because we didn't want to compromise our identity or endanger our families in the event that the violators had access to the hotel staff. Danny read the newspaper and I delved into *The Greatest Story Ever Told*. With my head propped up on my pillow, I looked over at Danny.

"Jesus told his apostles to go out and preach the good news to all the world," I said. "Just like us," I added. "We tell everyone the good news."

"Yeah, the good news that they're under arrest," Danny responded with sarcasm in his voice.

"No, we tell them that drugs are bad," I said, trying to explain the parallel I had concocted in my mind.

"Yeah, sure, amen, brother," Danny kidded me again sarcastically.

"Danny, we're the good guys. I like that," I continued.

"Whatever you say, Sully."

"That's why those Bunnies like us. They can tell that we're the good guys," I added.

"Are you alright? Those broads like us because we're macho men! We're men! They don't like us because we're good! We're good to them because we're not 'light in our loafers,' like all the other guys in San Francisco," Danny explained with his street corner philosophy.

"Danny, there's more to this than meets the eye," I said, but I could see that Danny didn't want to listen to any more of my ideas. I could tell that he was getting jumpy thinking about the case.

Later that day when we met with Dom and his group of agents, we briefed them on our proposed meeting with the LSD suppliers at the bar in Sausalito. Danny and I gave the surveillance team detailed physical descriptions of Norman and Ralph and told them what time they were going to meet us. We explained our plan to set up a visit to the LSD laboratory for the next day so that we could bust the dealers upon their delivery of the LSD and seize the laboratory at the same time. We instructed our cover team to have agents in place for a presurveillance to see if anyone arrived at the meeting place early. We also suggested that a postsurveillance team follow the subjects when they left the bar to see if they met anyone else. Finally, we suggested that a third team be designated to remain in the bar with us.

At approximately seven o'clock that evening, Danny and I were in the restaurant in Sausalito, sitting across from each other at a table in front of a window with a view of the Golden Gate Bridge. The sun had set majestically a few minutes before, and the scene from the window was spectacular. Suddenly, everything stopped and all the customers in the bar looked toward the entranceway. Dawn and Donna caused a commotion when they walked in, and customers' heads turned to follow them as they strutted across the waxed wooden floor to meet us. They flung their arms around Danny and me like they hadn't seen us in years. Dawn sat on Danny's lap, and Donna pulled a chair close to me as she reached over to grab me by my hand. I looked over at the bar. Everyone except the surveillance agents looked away, pretending not to be gawking at our gorgeous guests. The agents were openly gaping at us and trying to figure out what part the women played in our plan. They huddled together, whispering to each other with big smiles on their faces. They seemed to remember Dom's playful teasing earlier in the day, and realized that the women were the Bunnies we had met the night before. As we sipped our beers and ordered dinner, I could see the agents peering at us enviously from their vantage point at the bar. They watched very closely as we ate our dinners and socialized with Dawn and Donna.

No one seemed to notice when Norman and Ralph entered the restaurant unceremoniously and stood in the doorway to the bar. They both squinted and looked self-consciously around the room. Finally, I caught Norman's attention, and motioned for him to come over and join us at our table. He looked at Ralph with a reassuring smile and they both walked over to meet us. As Norman and Ralph approached, several of the surveillance agents who had followed them from the hippie pad in Haight-Ashbury walked nonchalantly into the restaurant behind them. The agents walked directly to the bar and ordered drinks while looking around surreptitiously to find us. They rolled their eyes when they saw us sitting with the Playboy Bunnies.

Norman and Ralph would have blended right in with the scenery in some parts of San Francisco, like Castro or Haight-Ashbury, but dressed in their hippie garb, they were definitely way out of place in this bar in Sausalito. I could see how self-conscious and nervous they were, so I made an extra effort to put them at ease. They stood next to me and kept watching my eyes like subordinates reporting to their drill sergeant, waiting obediently for orders.

"Hey, guys! The time has come," I said, as I reached out to shake hands, first with Norman, then with Ralph. They both remained standing, nodding their heads uncomfortably, seemingly unsure of what they should do next. The presence of Dawn and Donna made them even more nervous.

"We like San Francisco!" Danny quipped, draping his arm around Dawn's bare, sun-bronzed shoulders.

"Say hello to Dawn and Donna, guys," I said with a bit of bravado. They mumbled hellos and looked down at their feet. Their reactions made it more than obvious that they were out of their element and didn't know what to do or say.

"Girls, we got some business to take care of, so you'll have to excuse us for a few minutes," I said.

I got up from the table, put my arms around Norman and Ralph, and corraled them toward an empty table in the middle of the restaurant, between two already occupied by surveillance agents. Danny left the women sitting alone to join us, and we all sat down together at the unoccupied table. Danny and I leaned across to talk with Norman and Ralph, who were side by side, almost directly opposite us.

"You like *Playboy* magazine?" I asked Norman confidentially in a whisper. He looked at me as if the question confused him.

"*Playboy*! You know, the magazine," I repeated in a loud demanding whisper. This time Norman and Ralph both nodded their heads.

"Dawn is the centerfold for this month, and Donna is on page 39," I whispered to them with my eyebrows raised, and then I smiled. They looked over at the women and then back at me, and nodded their heads again.

"They like us. They help us to relax. There's a lot of pressure in our business," I explained philosophically to Norman and Ralph as I continued to examine their expressions.

"That's cool," Norman assured me, agreeing with my philosophy.

"I understand, man," Ralph added. I could see that neither one of them really knew what to say, but they wanted to make a good impression.

"Anyway, forget the broads for now. What's goin' on with us?" I asked.

"It's all set," Norman said proudly.

"Whaddaya mean, it's all set?" Danny asked.

"It's all set. We can do the deal tomorrow," Norman answered, and Ralph agreed.

"The lab?" Danny asked.

"You will see the lab tomorrow afternoon. You will get a tour of the lab, before we do the deal," Norman continued, obviously pleased with himself.

"Right on," Danny said, and he tapped his fist with Norman and Ralph, and then with me.

"How we gonna do it?" I asked.

"Just bring the money and we'll take you to the lab to give you the sunshine," Norman replied.

"Norman, that's not the way we do business," I said with a hint of annoyance in my voice. He gave me an inquiring look.

"Norman, we show you the money, you show us the sunshine. How many times do I have to tell you?" I asked, firmly.

"But you're gonna see the lab," Norman bargained.

"No buts about it. That's got nothing to do with it!" Danny said, raising his voice.

"Norman, we ain't stupid. We lived this long. We ain't gonna get killed, and we ain't gonna get ripped off," I said.

"We won't rip you off," Norman defended himself sheepishly.

"I know you won't," I said, staring coldly into Norman's nervous eyes. He looked back at me apologetically, realizing how lame his assurance sounded.

"Meet us at two p.m. at the Fisherman's Market Restaurant on Fisherman's Wharf," I continued, and Norman and Ralph nodded immediately in agreement. Danny and I stood up, and Norman and Ralph rose from their chairs. We all looked at each other, satisfied that our uneasy business was temporarily completed. I leaned over and, placing my right hand on Norman's shoulder, I pulled him nearer.

"Norman, before we do another deal, I'm gonna have Dawn and Donna get a couple of friends for you and Ralph, and we'll all spend a weekend at the Playboy mansion in Chicago," I whispered in his ear. Norman cocked his head and looked at me. He actually took a minute to think about the proposition.

"How would you like that?" I prompted him.

"Alright," he answered, like a grammar school kid accepting a challenge. We shook hands once more, and Norman and Ralph walked toward the door, followed surreptitiously by two surveillance agents. Danny and I went back to rejoin our dinner guests. In our place, we found two neatly dressed, clean-cut men talking to Dawn and Donna. The two men glanced nervously at Danny and me as we approached, and stopped talking altogether when we arrived.

"Anotha round ovah heah! Anotha drink for everyone!" Danny ordered loudly in an exaggerated Boston accent while staring into the eyes of the intruders. The guys smiled nervously, surprised that Danny was buying them drinks, but not knowing how to react. They waited self-consciously for their drinks as Danny muscled in between them and put his arms around Dawn and Donna. I stood staring at the two guys, who kept their eyes on each other. The waitress returned with the drinks and Danny slapped a hundred-dollar bill on her tray as the two strangers took their drinks. Danny glanced at them briefly and gestured with his head.

"Screw!" he said bluntly, leaving no room for misinterpretation.

The two guys immediately turned red with embarrassment. They looked at each other quickly, then turned and walked away from us in a straight line, with their heads down, until they were out of view. I looked over at the surveillance agents at the bar. One had a quizzical expression on his face, like he was trying to figure the situation out. I realized that there was some confusion as to who was who, so I covertly signaled him to follow me into the men's room. Once we were inside, alone together, he looked at me urgently.

"What the hell is going on? Who's who?" he asked, throwing up his hands.

"Those two clean-cut guys are nothing. They were trying to pick up the girls," I said.

"And the girls! Who are they?" he asked.

"They're just girls. They're nothing to do with the case. They're Playboy Bunnies," I answered with a wink.

"Playboy Bunnies? What are they doing here? I don't get it," he asked, annoyed and confused by the situation.

"It doesn't matter why they are here. They're just here. There is nothing to get! Don't confuse the issue. The only people here that have anything to do with the case are the two hippies, and they are gone. Did you see them?" I asked.

"Yeah, I saw them," he replied.

"Then that's it. Have a drink and relax."

"You guys from Boston are something else. Playboy Bunnies in the middle of a case . . ." He stopped in midsentence.

"They're nice to look at, aren't they? We didn't want you guys to call us boring," I answered. Just then, someone came into the men's room, and we ended our conversation. I followed the surveillance agent out to the bar and watched him shake his head in disbelief. He walked over and rejoined the other agents while I went back to my table.

As the night wore on, Danny and Dawn got physically closer and closer to each other, and Donna was almost sitting on top of me. We were all talking and having fun, but below the surface, they were planning to make a night of it. While Danny and I were negotiating with the drug dealers, both women had continued drinking. They were feeling the alcoholic effects of a steady stream of Harvey Wallbangers.

The sensation that Danny and I were actors in a play came over me. We were negotiating with drug dealers to buy drugs, and we were having dinner with a couple of Playboy Bunnies in San Francisco while we were onstage. Those were the facts. But we were not drug dealers, and the Bunnies were not our girlfriends. Those were also the facts. How do we reconcile that? Who are we? I wondered. I looked over at the surveillance agents at the bar, surrounded by all the other customers, male and female, and I wondered, who are they? We were each pretending to be someone he wasn't, but the people that we were pretending to be were real. It wasn't a movie or a play. We were pretending for real, with real people, with real lives. We made it up as we went along. There were no rehearsals. The immensity of it all overwhelmed me, and my mind froze. I couldn't think anymore.

"A penny for your thoughts?" Donna whispered as she put her arm around my shoulder and leaned her head next to mine.

"What?" I responded sleepily, surprised by her question.

"I wish I knew what you were thinking about." She rephrased the question thoughtfully, and I smiled at her.

"He's thinking about you, Donna," Dawn said, "so let's go back to the hotel!"

"You ready?" Danny asked nonchalantly with a smile on his face.

"I'm ready," I answered, wondering what I was ready for. Dawn and Donna were already standing. Danny and I jumped up, and we all walked out with our arms around each other. I winked at the agents, who were still sitting at the bar as we left. Donna got up on her toes and hugged me from behind as I waited for Danny to open the car door. I wondered again, what are we doing?

"Sully, you take Donna in our car, and I'll drive Dawn in the Corvette. See you back at the Fairmont," Danny said after he unlocked the door of the Caddy and handed me the keys.

I looked at him for some kind of signal, but I didn't get any. I opened the door to the Caddy and let Donna get in, and then I walked around the front of the car and got in myself on the driver's side. I put the key in the ignition as Donna slid over next to me and put one arm around my neck and the other on my leg. As I started the engine, my instinct was to look at her, but I was afraid to. I pulled out of the space slowly and drove carefully in the direction of San Francisco. Donna snuggled close to me as we crossed the Golden Gate Bridge.

"I love this city. It's so romantic, isn't it?" she said.

"Uh huh," I answered.

"Is that all you can say? Uh huh? You guys are too tough. Don't you guys ever think about anything else but business? I'm gonna show you what romantic is tonight," Donna teased, and then she squeezed me so tight that I almost drove into the oncoming traffic.

I was thinking about the drug deal that we had set up for the next day, and at the same time, I was thinking about tonight. I continued to drive without saying anything. How did this get so complicated? I wondered. She put her right hand inside the front of my leather vest. I tried to brush her away, but she responded by tickling me and running her hand across my stomach until she touched the handle of my 45, which was stuck in my belt.

"What's this?" she asked nervously, looking in my eyes as she lifted her head off of my shoulder. I continued to drive in silence. "It's a fucking gun! What do you have a gun for?" she demanded in a panic.

"Relax," I said calmly to quiet her down. "You don't have to tell every-one in San Francisco that I have a gun."

"Why? Why do you have a fucking gun?" she asked again belligerently.

"Why? Because the world is a dangerous place, that's why!" I answered brazenly.

Donna looked at me with complete surprise, and she began to cry. Tears streamed from her eyes and ran down her cheeks. The shock of her accidentally discovering my gun was probably magnified by the effects of the alcohol she consumed in the course of the night, and she became very emotional.

"Donna, relax. It's business, that's all. It's no big thing. Some guys carry a pencilbox, some guys carry a tool belt, some guys carry a briefcase—I carry a gun," I explained. She pushed herself away and sat looking at me with her head cocked to the side and a troubled look on her face. I thought it was a good time to end our make-believe relationship, so I tried to think of the right words.

"Donna, that's why I'm no good for you. You got a good life, you're a good girl, and I'm a bad guy. You live your way, and I live mine. That's just the way it is. I'm sorry." I studied her expression out of the corner of my eye, waiting for a response. She hesitated for a few minutes, and then suddenly, she threw both her arms around me and tried to kiss me. I pushed her away frantically, because I couldn't see the road.

"I don't care what you do! I'm crazy about you, Sully. I just want to be with you. I'm sorry," she pleaded, taking me completely by surprise. My plan backfired I thought as I pulled over and parked in the circular driveway of the Fairmont Hotel.

"C'mon, let's go," I said without emotion, opening my door and getting out of the car. Donna got out, walked quickly around the front of the car, and grabbed onto me so tightly that I could hardly breathe. The hotel doorman opened the front door for us, and we walked arm in arm into the ornate lobby and onto the elevator. I wondered how far this was going to go, and I wondered where Danny and Dawn were as the elevator stopped at Donna's floor. At this point, I actually began to wonder about Danny. I thought I knew him pretty well, up till now.

"This is it," I said.

"This is it," Donna repeated, not understanding my inflection. I followed her to her room, and I put my hand on her shoulder as she was about to put her key into the lock. She turned slowly to face me and looked into my eyes and lifted her chin, as if she was expecting a kiss, but I held her away.

"Donna, there's something that I have to tell you," I said gravely. She looked at me anxiously, dreading whatever it was that I was about to tell her. I tried to look as humble as I could while I searched my mind for the right words. The more I struggled to find the most appropriate words, the more tongue-tied I became. Finally, I just blurted it out.

"Donna, I'm married," I confessed, while trying to appear as concerned for her as I could. Donna's expression changed to disbelief, then relief, and finally, amusement. She began to giggle, and then she began to laugh, and her laugh got louder and louder. She grabbed the front of my shirt with both hands and pulled herself close to me with her cheek pressed to mine. Her laughter sounded even noisier because she was so close to me, and it was certainly too loud for the hallway of the Fairmont Hotel in the early morning hours.

"Shhh, shhh!" I cautioned her, but she ignored me.

"You're funny!" she said, guffawing. She was laughing so hard that there were tears coming down her cheeks again. I was confused at first, but then I began to laugh myself, and I put my index finger to my mouth to signal her to quiet down. She seemed so happy and giddy that it made me laugh more.

"I'm funny?" I asked, wondering what she meant.

"Yes! You mean that is all you have to tell me? That you are married?" she asked, out of breath from her laughter.

"Yes, that's all," I answered, thinking to myself, That's all? Isn't that enough?

"You are too much! I thought for sure that you were going to tell me that you were gay!" she said in a lively voice as her laughter leveled off.

"I am definitely not gay!" I assured her emphatically as we both leaned against the hotel room door.

"You don't know how happy I am that you told me!" she said.

"You are happy that I told you I'm married?" I asked incredulously.

"Yes," she replied quickly. "I like you so much, Sully! Thank God that you're straight! That's all I care about. I don't care if you're married!" Just then, someone opened the door and Donna and I almost fell inside. It was Danny with a surprised look on his face. Dawn, her hair disheveled, was standing next to him in a white terry-cloth robe. Her clothes had been thrown carelessly on one of the beds. The confusion and embarrassment of the moment was apparent as we all looked at each other.

"C'mon, we got work to do," Danny said to me abruptly. I looked at him quizzically, surprised at his sudden appearance. Relieved at the excuse to leave, I straightened up.

"Let's go," I said coolly, turning away from Donna and joining Danny in the hallway.

"Is that it?" Donna asked softly.

"That's it, baby, we got business," I replied, and I turned once more to see Donna's reaction. She was biting her lip, and I could see that she was smoldering. I wanted to say something to make her feel better, but I couldn't think of the right words, so I began to walk away.

"Will you come back when you are finished?" Donna asked, swallowing her pride. I stopped and turned around once more to look back at her. She was so beautiful and so vulnerable I thought.

"Yeah, sure," I lied, knowing that I would never see her again, and then I turned away and walked out.

"Whew! I can't believe we did that!" I said to Danny when we got on the elevator. Danny turned his head to look at me.

"Did what?" he asked, still staring at me.

"Walked away," I answered. Then we both laughed.

"I know," Danny responded.

"They wanted us to stay with them," I said, thinking about Donna and the way she looked at me when I left.

"I know," Danny replied, watching for my response. "I went into the bathroom, and when I came out Dawn was standing there with nothing on but a bathrobe, untied and open in front."

"Any other red-blooded guy would have stayed," I concluded.

"Yeah, sure, but they're not married to Helen!" Danny laughed.

"Helen wouldn't mind. You're on vacation," I joked.

"Yeah, vacation! Helen's Siciliano and proud of it. You know how the Sicilian women respond to that? Huh? You don't want to know," Danny continued. I relaxed when I realized that he and Dawn had not "fallen from innocence."

"Pam wouldn't care if I stayed with Donna. She's not the jealous type. She just wants me to have fun. I only left because I knew that you didn't have permission," I teased.

"Yeah, right, permission," Danny said. "Pam would give you permission alright. She'd shoot you dead and give you permission to go to heaven. You got permission alright!"

Danny and I laughed quietly for a while, and then we got out of the elevator and walked to the car without saying anything else. We went back to our hotel, scribbled down some notes about our meeting with Norman and Ralph, and went to sleep.

Too early the next morning, Danny shook me awake. I could see the light peeking in the room at the edges of the curtains when I opened my eyes.

"What time is it?" I asked.

"It's nine o'clock, time to get up."

"Those hippies won't be up yet," I said.

"We got a lot of things to do," Danny persisted. He always amazed me with his organization. Danny paid attention to the details of a case. He was good for me, because I had a tendency to assume the attitude of my under-cover role, and I needed someone to nudge me back to reality. I complied with Danny's orders and climbed out of bed. We showered, dressed, and went to breakfast. Then we called Norman and confirmed our arrangement to meet at two that afternoon. The ball was beginning to roll.

Later that afternoon at the Fisherman's Market Restaurant, Danny and I finished lunch and Danny lit up a cigarette as we drank our coffee. I sat in a straight-backed booth, comfortably upholstered with soft red leather, staring at the people who filled the restaurant. I kept my left hand on the black leather briefcase that rested on the seat beside me, and made sure that I would be able to reach with my right hand and draw my pistol in a split second if the occasion arose. The briefcase contained one hundred thousand dollars.

I glanced briefly at Danny, who was leaning back on his leather-upholstered captain's chair as he took a long drag on his cigarette. Then I refocused my attention on the dining room. I was looking for anyone who might pose a threat to the money, or to us. I knew that there always existed the possibility that Norman was setting us up for a rip-off. It certainly wouldn't be the first time that a drug dealer pulled that stunt. A hundred thousand dollars was a lot of money. I thought of a story I had read in the morning paper about a teenager who shot and killed another kid for his sneakers. You could buy a lot of sneakers for a hundred thousand dollars!

There were surveillance agents seated at tables nearby so that they could react quickly in the event of a heist. They were searching the dining room and watching the doorways for anything gone awry. Outside, agents watched the restaurant intently from cars on the street and a small surveillance plane high above. The tension rose as we got closer to our meeting time.

"I'm gonna take a leak," Danny announced as he crushed his cigarette butt into the ashtray, got up, and stretched.

"I'll be here," I replied.

When Danny walked away from the table I noticed the outline of his pistol in his waistband. He carried it on his right hip under his shirt, unnoticed by anyone but me. I wondered which one it was. I was carrying two pistols myself. My 45-caliber was tucked in the small of my back, concealed only by my tan leather vest, and my 38-caliber revolver was strapped to an ankle holster, concealed by my bell-bottom jeans. As I was thinking about the guns, Danny returned and sat down across the table from me.

"Danny, what are you carrying for a weapon?"

"My 38," he answered. I nodded, continuing to think about the guns.

"Which one?" I queried.

"My government issue."

"Now, who is going with the dopers, and who is gonna stay with the money?" I asked, knowing the answer already.

"I'm gonna go with 'em. You're gonna stay with the money," Dan answered, tired of discussing the details.

"What if they search you before you go to the lab?"

"Search me?" Dan asked.

"Yeah, remember they said that they did not want any guns? They said that they did not like guns."

"They ain't gonna search me."

"Danny, we have to think of everything."

"I'm not goin' nowhere without a gun."

"If they find your 38, then that's it, case closed. They won't do the deal. They'll know you are the man," I explained. Danny looked at me stubbornly at first, but then agreed.

"Hand me your 38 under the table," I instructed him. Danny fumbled awkwardly for his pistol, trying not to draw attention to himself. He pulled his chair closer to the table, and lowering his right shoulder, he reached below the tablecloth under the table and handed me his government-issue, 38-caliber blue pistol. I slipped it into the waistband of my jeans and covered it with my leather vest. I lifted my right foot up, and resting it on the bench, I unstrapped my small, 38-caliber, nickel-plated police special.

"You didn't think that I was going to let you go unarmed, did you?" I asked Dan, while I reached under the table again and handed the pistol in the ankle holster to him. Danny looked at me seriously as he took hold of it and surreptitiously strapped it onto his ankle. Then he smiled as he straightened up in his seat. No sooner had we finished, when Norman and Ralph walked into the restaurant.

"It's show time," I said quietly to Danny when I spotted our subjects standing next to the maitre d'.

"Good timing," Danny whispered under his breath, as he turned to look at them.

When I was sure that the surveillance agents saw them, I waved Norman and Ralph over to us. They walked up and slipped into the empty seats on either side of the table. Both of them were nervous, and they smiled, tight-lipped, at us without saying anything.

"You guys ready?" I asked. Norman and Ralph both nodded and shrugged their shoulders.

"Here's the money," I said, matter-of-factly, opening the briefcase to display the neatly packed money. Norman looked down at the open briefcase resting on the seat beside me, and he stared, wide-eyed, at the bills. Ralph leaned over and stretched his neck to peek at the cash. They looked at each other and nodded their approval.

"Now, let's see the lab," Danny said to them.

"Who is going?" Norman asked.

"Me," Danny answered quickly and stood up with Norman and Ralph. My mind began to speed up as last-minute worries occurred to me.

"Danny," I said.

"What?" he prompted me. I leaned close and put my arm around his shoulder while I quickly whispered in his ear, "Take your jacket off when you come out of the lab if the drugs are there. That's the signal. If your jacket is off, we bust 'em, if not we wait." Danny nodded his head to let me know that he understood, while Norman and Ralph stood quietly waiting for him to join them. I smiled at them and gave Danny a last-minute love tap on the arm as he turned and walked out of the restaurant with them. I kept wondering if there was something we had forgotten to plan for, but in any case, it was too late now. Danny was on his way. Several of the surveillance agents followed them out, and I could see them standing on the outside deck watching Danny and the druggies as they walked past the agents on the way to the parking lot.

"Dom, Danny is out of the restaurant with the two subjects, and they are going to the lab," I reported from the pay phone in the foyer of the restaurant to Delario, who was conducting surveillance on the outside from his car, which was set up adjacent to the parking lot. I wanted to make sure that the surveillance agents did not lose Danny after he left the restaurant with Norman and Ralph.

"Where is the money?" Dom asked with concern.

"It's with me. I have it," I answered quickly.

"We have an eyeball on them. They are frisking Danny next to a black van at the far end of the parking lot," Dom reported. "There are two others with the original subjects. They are placing a blindfold on Danny right now and putting him into the side door of the van," Delario continued. My heart was pumping because I was concerned for Danny, and there was nothing more that I could do at this point.

"Go outside now, Paul. Someone will pick you up. They are moving. They are in the van, and the doors are closed. I repeat, they are moving! Let's go!" Delario spoke to me urgently, while simultaneously instructing the surveillance agents over the radio. The adrenaline began to flow when I realized that they had Danny blindfolded and were starting the trip to the lab. I clutched the briefcase containing the hundred thousand dollars, and I nervously fingered the weapons in my belt to reassure myself that they were still there as I hurried out of the restaurant. A tan-colored Chevy driven by a guy in his midtwenties wearing aviator-style sunglasses pulled up to the entrance of the restaurant, and I recognized immediately that it was Chuck Thompson. I opened the car door and climbed in as fast as I could. He smiled at me as I jumped into the front seat, and I knew by the way that his large hands clamped onto the steering wheel, with his shirtsleeves rolled up over his biceps, that he did not intend to lose Danny on this surveillance. It was comforting for me to know that one of the best agents in the country was behind the wheel. I could hear different voices shouting out locations of the van over the radio, as Thompson drove quickly up and down hills, through intersections, and past cable cars, alternately putting his foot to the brake and then hitting the accelerator pedal while steering through traffic to avoid crashing. My stomach felt like I was on a roller-coaster each time we crested another San Francisco hill. We listened to the radio transmissions and didn't say much to each other because we were concentrating on the surveillance. Every once in a while, Chuck would look over at me, and wink or smile, to let me know that we were hot on Danny's trail. Then my heart sank.

A DEA agent in a U.S. Customs' spotter plane was directing the entire surveillance operation from the air because it was impossible to follow the bad guys closely enough on the ground through the traffic- and tourist-clogged streets of San Francisco. We began to hear unintelligible sounds coming over the radio speaker, noises like sound effects. Suddenly, sounds turned into words that I would rather not have heard.

"I've lost 'em," the voice from the spotter plane announced dejectedly from the sky, high above the city. The announcement made me feel sick to my stomach. Visions of the bad guys murdering Danny flooded my head, and a feeling of rage swept over me. More unintelligible sounds came over the radio, then a different voice spoke.

"This is the pilot. Your spotter agent is a little airsick right now," the calm, almost cocky voice with a southern drawl announced. A series of those unintelligible sounds continued in the background as he spoke. We knew now that our surveillance agent in the plane was throwing up. It was a harrowing moment.

"Guys, I see the van!" the pilot announced triumphantly, and then he described the exact location.

"I am right there! I am paralleling the van, one street over," Supervisor Delario announced from his car. It reminded me of the classic scene in old movies, when the cavalry arrived dramatically at the last minute. You could feel the relief in the air when Delario spoke. A sense of power and strength flowed into my system again. We knew that we were still in control.

"You better get over there real fast and set up. The van is pulling alongside a building in a warehouse area and slowing," the pilot coached those of us in cars loudly in his southern drawl.

"We got 'em. I'm at the end of the street that the warehouse is on," Delario said.

"We're at the other end," another agent said.

"I have a good eyeball on the van," the pilot announced.

"Okay, everyone else stay out of the area until we move in for the bust," Delario announced.

"Pilot, keep us informed. Call out their every move. Don't lose the undercover man!" Delario transmitted over the radio. My thoughts drifted back to the recent rash of agent shootings. I kept picturing the shootings in my mind. I was worried about Danny.

"Will do," the pilot responded confidently in his cocky, southern voice.

There was a short period when the radios were silent, and it seemed like an eternity. Then the pilot began to speak in short, urgent sentences.

"They are out of the van. Four guys, and your guy. He still has the blindfold on."

"Pilot, when the undercover man comes out of the warehouse, tell us if his jacket is on or off. That is the signal. It is very important," I spoke quickly and clearly into the microphone, trying to be as brief as possible.

"10-4, will do," he responded calmly.

"That's very important, pilot," Delario added.

"They are entering a door at the south end of the warehouse. They are all inside the warehouse now. They are out of my view. The door is about five car lengths from where the van is parked," the pilot announced quickly before Delario finished his sentence.

"10-4," Delario answered, and the rest of us clicked our radios to acknowledge that we had also heard the pilot.

The wait was the longest ever. Knowing that my partner, Danny, my closest friend, was inside a huge warehouse with four druggies raised my anxiety level to the nth degree. I was so wrapped up in the magnitude of the situation that the world around me did not seem to exist. All of my attention was focused on the door that Danny had entered. Chuck Thompson was geared up also, focusing on the surveillance and listening for the pilot's voice. A series of crackling sounds sputtered out of the radio and drew our eyes to the dashboard of the car in fearful anticipation. Then the lyrics of a Beatles' song purportedly about LSD, "Lucy in the Sky with Diamonds," came out of the radio speaker. It brought nervous smiles to our faces, and the short appropriate tune served to break the tension.

"Knock it off," the voice of Supervisor Delario ordered over the airwaves. I smiled, and I knew by the tone of his voice that Delario enjoyed the levity himself. We had to keep the airwaves clear, though, so that we could hear the all-important words from the pilot. Suddenly, the radio began to crackle again, some more static, and then the pilot's voice.

"They are out of the building. The four that went in are out with the undercover, and two more are following. They are heading back toward the van," the pilot announced clearly. My energy surged and my heart pounded. I was ready to go as I hung onto every word and waited for Delario's command to move in for the arrest. Chuck Thompson and I looked at each other, anxiously waiting for the command.

"Is the jacket on or off?" I asked Chuck.

"I don't know. He didn't say," Chuck answered.

"They are approaching the van," the pilot said.

"Is the undercover's jacket on or off?" Delario demanded loudly and clearly.

The pilot answered, but his response was garbled.

"Is it on or off?" Delario yelled.

"It's off. The jacket is off!" the pilot announced anxiously.

"Move in! Let's go! Hit 'em!" Delario's voice screamed out the commands over the radio.

Thompson slammed our car into gear and jammed the gas pedal to the floor. My head snapped back as we accelerated up the hill toward the warehouse. I could hear the tires of the other surveillance vehicles screeching, and sirens wailing as they answered the same call to move in. Thompson yanked the steering wheel hard, and we made a right-hand turn so sharp and fast that I almost fell onto his lap. My right hand moved nervously between my pistol and the door handle, in anticipation of my next move. Thompson stomped the pedal to the floor again, and we barreled down the street toward the warehouse. I could see the dealers and Danny, still blindfolded, standing next to the van about two hundred feet in front of us. I felt like I was about to explode as Thompson jammed on the brakes and the wheels screeched again, stopping next to Danny and the bad guys. We jumped out with guns drawn and ran toward the subjects next to the van. Cars full of other surveillance agents raced to the scene, nearly crashing into us as they stopped suddenly and bailed out onto the street. There was so much noise and commotion that the subjects were paralyzed. The sirens blasting, horns blaring, tires screeching, footsteps pounding, and voices yelling stunned the drug dealers. They stood with looks of shock frozen on their faces, while the agents moved in quickly and arrested them before they could understand what was happening. Perfect order and execution in the midst of chaos.

Danny tore his blindfold off as I pointed my revolver at the drug dealers and placed them under arrest. I judiciously removed Danny's gun from my belt with my left hand and handed it to him while I recited the Miranda warnings to the drug dealers.

"You are under arrest for violation of the federal narcotic law. You have the right to remain silent," I advised them.

Ralph and Norman looked over at Danny with confusion in their eyes as they tried to comprehend the situation. Danny faced them, and I leaned over and put my left arm around his shoulder as we stood pointing our guns at the drug dealers.

"We did it, Dan," I said proudly.

"Amen, brother," Danny replied smiling.

Some of the surveillance agents handcuffed the six drug dealers and put them into the backseats of their cars, while others ran into the warehouse to seize the drugs and confiscate the laboratory equipment. Norman and Ralph stood quietly, saying nothing, when the arresting agents cuffed them. One of the other subjects, a tall, thin guy with long blonde hair that made him look wild, moved his head from side to side, observing the agents getting out of their cars and running in and out of the warehouse with guns drawn.

"Like, wow!" he said dreamily to no one in particular.

"Cool!" another defendant said as he looked at us and then looked at the guy with the wild blonde hair, as if he had just witnessed something amazing. I guess he did. He watched himself getting arrested. We later learned that these two guys were the chemists. Their work as LSD chemists was obviously connected with their odd reactions and bizarre behavior in the face of their arrests. They inadvertently inhaled the dust and fumes of these highly toxic chemicals when they cooked the LSD. That's why they acted like they were in another world. Their brains were cooked!

The case was a success. We arrested a total of eight people in California. We also seized hundreds of thousands of hits of acid and hundreds of pounds of precursor drugs, the ingredients necessary to complete the chemical process resulting in the finished product, LSD. Most importantly, we got the lab that seemed impossible to snag. The case proved that cooperation between agents and agencies and a combination of good undercover work and surveillance, under the direction of a talented and dedicated supervisor, could deliver a death blow to a highly successful and well-organized drug distribution system.

I could hear someone speaking over the radio, so I walked over to our car and picked up the microphone. "Repeat the last transmission," I said.

"This is the pilot. Mission accomplished?" he asked spiritedly in his southern drawl.

"Mission accomplished. Our undercover man is safe, and we got the lab. Thanks for everything, birdman," I answered proudly.

"Yaaaahooooo!" he answered jauntily.

"Look out!" Thompson yelled before being drowned out by the loud noise of an airplane engine. We all looked up to see the spotter plane diving in our direction at a ninety-degree angle! When we thought that he was just above our heads, he pulled the plane up and tilted to one side as he zoomed away.

"Yaaaahooooo!" the pilot screamed over the radio again as he departed. Raising my head to look at the plane, I picked up the microphone again, and I noticed the beautiful background of puffy white cumulus clouds in the clear California sky. It didn't get any better than this, I thought.

"Good job, flyboy!" I said, and I wondered if the airsick DEA agent in the airplane was feeling any better.

A LIGHT IN THE DARKNESS 6

I woke up suddenly, choking and gasping for breath. My heart was racing and my body was covered with sweat, my pillow and sheets were soaked. I was waking up like this with alarming frequency.

I thought about the horrible nightmare, the recurring dream; faceless men coming to kill me. My gun jams, they keep coming, closing in. I run desperately, examining the cylinder of the pistol for bullets, trying to unlock the mechanism so that I can shoot at them and defend myself. It's no use. I am cornered, with no place to go, so I turn to face my aggressors and fight. I punch out furiously with both fists, but my punches are powerless. It is useless. The terror of the men coming at me and my inability to stop them is frightening.

Overcome with emotion, embarrassed by the shame of succumbing to fear, I look at my wife sleeping beside me, hoping that I did not disturb her. She is still sleeping soundly, undisturbed by the terrifying attack. It was real. I know it was real. They were after me, but I was saved. I got away. I made it this time. I looked around the room, trying to focus my eyes.

As she sighed in her sleep, Pam interrupted my thoughts and drew my attention to her. I watched as she shrugged her shoulders unconsciously, drew her hands up to her chin, and rolled onto her side. We were as close to each other physically as two people could possibly be, and yet we were so far apart. We were in two completely different worlds. I was at war, and she was at peace.

I stole out of bed and went into the room where my two daughters slept. I stood silently and watched, absorbed in the tranquility surrounding the beautiful babies at rest. They were a heavenly sight. I leaned close, and kissed them both gently. The clean, freshly powdered baby smell and the sweet sound of their breathing in the quiet stillness of their room filled me with wonder and awe. The terrible anxiety brought on by the emotional turmoil of my fight-or-flight encounter evaporated like smoke in the wind. A feeling of inner harmony and serenity took over.

The next day, Danny and I attended the funeral of a dead Disciple. Lucky died with his motorcycle boots on, as they say: a heroin overdose. I was working in an undercover capacity, but I actually felt sad for Lucky's poor-looking and obviously unlucky widowed mother. I was not moved, however, when the Disciples crowded around the earthen rectangle and urinated on Lucky's freshly covered grave—his final farewell. After departing from the dearly departed, Danny and I bounced around with these motorcycle guys all day long. With so little sleep the night before, I was literally exhausted. We had dropped in and out of the motorcycle club, their girlfriends' apartments, and now we were headed for the Last Stop Lounge on Dorchester Avenue, a street that stretched from the gritty, working-class waterfront neighborhood and docks of Southie to the manicured green lawns of Milton, where the Irish on the upswing lived. Dot Ave., as it was called, teemed with thriving families and prosperous small businesses as the steady influx of hard-working Irish immigrants kept streaming in. Sometime in the 1960s, however, things began to change and the triple-deckers and businesses along the avenue fell into disrepair. Other immigrants from Puerto Rico, the Azores, and Vietnam crowded into the area and many white Irish families moved out. The whites sold their triple-deckers at low prices to these new immigrants or to speculators, who converted them to apartments. "White flight" spelled an uncertain future for the neighborhood, and it changed. The whites who could not afford to move out, could not sell their houses, or refused to were left behind to live with the darker-skinned immigrants speaking unfamiliar languages. The poverty of the people was reflected in the ever-increasing broken glass, boarded-up windows, and graffiti that marred the avenue.

Harley-Davidsons were lined up next to the trash-strewn sidewalk directly in front of the steel-grated, dilapidated brick building with faint neon beer signs barely visible through the two small windows, thick with dirt and soot, on either side of the heavy front door, which was laden with hardware and locks. There was no welcome mat. This was a hangout for an eclectic assortment of criminals and ne'er-do-wells from the rough-and-tumble Dorchester area of Boston, a hardscrabble section that had seen better days. The joint consisted of a large open area with a horseshoe-shaped bar in the middle of the floor and wooden booths along the side walls. Danny and I were seated in a booth across from two bikers. I was positioned so that I could see the front door. It was the first Friday of the month, which meant, in this neighborhood, that people were rich with welfare and benefit checks. In addition to the bikers, the bar was swollen to capacity with drug dealers, hustlers, and gamblers—the typical first-of-the-month crowd. We didn't plan it this way. It just happened.

I nursed my beer as I eyed the front door. According to the plan that we had rehearsed at the briefing the night before, Chris Regan would walk in the front door of the bar and identify himself as a federal agent. Danny and I would then identify ourselves, place the two bikers under arrest, and escort them carefully out of the bar. There were a number of undercover DEA (Drug Enforcement Agency) agents already in the place. Trish O'Malley, a young agent right out of the academy and a very attractive young lady at that, was positioned directly opposite me at the bar. Trish, tall and striking, with long black hair draped over her shoulders, cozied up to Agent Jack Fender and played with the collar of his shirt as she watched our every move over his shoulder. Tom Batten, the Wolfman, dressed in a well-worn black leather jacket, denims, and motorcycle boots, was seated alone in the booth adjacent to ours; he was in good position to assist us in the arrests if we needed his help. Wolfman looked as at home in this bar as any of the regulars.

As it so often happened in the realm of the lawless, the well-thought-out, prearranged arrest plan went awry. I saw Chris open the front door of the lounge and step inside. He planted himself like a statue and looked around the bar carefully to make sure that all of the agents were in place. He glanced over at me, and I nodded. Chris held up his gold DEA shield and, in a loud, clear voice, announced with authority, "Federal agent! Everyone freeze! Put your hands where we can see them!" Quickly, almost as an afterthought, Chris added dramatically, "Or bad things are going to happen!"

Needless to say, bad things did happen. Unimpressed by the announcement or the power of the United States government, the biker opposite me was about to reply to Chris with a bullet. He stood up, reached into his waistband, and with one sweeping motion, pulled out a Walther PPK semiautomatic pistol. Reacting immediately on reflex, I stood up and hit the biker with a right cross that knocked him backwards and caused him to drop the pistol to the floor. I grabbed him by the throat and leaned over him. Out of the corner of my eye, I could see our back-up team of agents running in through the back door of the bar. Jimmy Giambro, armed with a 44 magnum nickel-plated pistol, crashed through the back door and led the charge, vaulting onto the bar and shouting, "Federal agents! Don't anybody move!"

The clientele of this shady establishment paid absolutely no attention to Agent Giambro's order and appeared totally unfazed by the police presence. I quickly decided that the best thing for me to do was to stay low to the ground to avoid being hit by wild punches or stray bullets, so I dragged the biker that I had just knocked down across the barroom floor toward the front door. From my crouched position, I could see that an older Boston Police sergeant, probably on his routine walking beat, had entered through the front door of the bar and was surprised at the chaotic scene unfolding before him. He stood still, momentarily frozen at the sight of the violent frenzy, before he gathered himself together.

"Police!" the sergeant shouted. He may as well have been speaking a foreign language. After a few seconds, the sergeant realized that no one responded or cared who he was, so he casually walked outside of the bar. I followed behind him, out through the opened door, crouched down like an Indian, dragging the struggling biker. The sergeant looked down at me and shook his head. I continued dragging the biker, kicking and punching, out into the street, and the sergeant raised his hand to stop oncoming traffic while he called for assistance on the police radio. Danny and Jimmy Giambro were muscling a couple of uncooperative bikers out of the bar, and they came tumbling out behind me onto the street. It was like a three-ring circus. I put my knee on my guy's back and handcuffed him in the middle of the street, in the headlights' glare of a huge tractor trailer.

As I was pulling the biker to an upright position, I heard a loud bang. I never mistake the sound of a pistol shot. It was so loud and so close that I thought I was dead. Simultaneously, I heard a scream for help. As I looked toward the sidewalk, I could see that Jimmy Giambro was struggling frantically with a biker, and there was blood all over both of them. My ears were ringing as I ran toward them, and I could see that the biker had a solid grip on the barrel of Jimmy's gun. I grabbed the biker's wrist with my left hand and pressed him up against a car, my face against his head as I choked him in a stranglehold with my right forearm. Danny pounced on the biker, and pried his fingers backward until he was able to take the gun away from him. The biker slid down the side of the car to the pavement, and I fell on top of him with my forearm locked around his neck. His head hit the sidewalk and made a noise like a coconut hitting the pavement. Blood spurted out from his head. I pulled his hands behind his back while someone else handcuffed him. As I stood up, I saw Danny slap Giambro hard across the face. They stood toe to toe.

"Snap out of it, Jimmy!" Danny yelled.

Giambro stood frozen still, staring straight ahead and obviously in shock. In the course of the struggle for the weapon, the biker managed to squeeze the trigger of Giambro's 44 magnum pistol and shot one of Giambro's fingers off. A couple of the agents threw Jimmy into the back of their car and sped him off to the emergency room at Boston City Hospital.

Dick O'Meara, our supervisor, observing that the defendants were arrested and in custody, ordered the group of agents to leave the bar to avoid any further danger and to return to the federal building. He told Danny and me to transport the shooter across the city to the Boston Police station in Charlestown because it was the only place with cell space for prisoners that night.

As we drove cross town, through the dark city streets, the biker threatened us and told us that he was going to bring charges against us for violating his civil rights, how he would make enough money to buy a new Harley, and on and on. He boasted that we would never have been able to take him if the rest of the Disciples were there. And then he told us that we were "marked men" when word got out on the street that we had arrested him. I was trying to control my anger the entire ride as I thought about what a punk this guy really was. I wondered which one of his pals shot that girlfriend of the heroin addict who squealed on Danny and me in the head on the Jamaicaway and killed her. I suddenly exploded as Danny turned onto the Charlestown Bridge.

"Pull over, Danny," I said.

"What?" Danny asked.

"Pull over, and stop," I ordered.

"Where do you want me to stop? I can't stop here. We're on the bridge."

"Just pull the car over, I know where we are!" I shouted.

Danny swerved to the right and slammed on the brakes. We stopped at the curb in the middle of the narrow bridge. The cars behind us, surprised by our sudden stop, blew their horns as they swerved to avoid crashing into us. Danny grabbed me before I could get out of the car. I somehow returned to my senses. I closed my eyes.

I got out of the car quickly and opened the rear door, then I pulled the biker out of the backseat and threw him on the sidewalk between the car and the iron bridge railing.

"What are you gonna do now, big man, give me a beating with my hands cuffed behind my back?" the biker taunted me.

I stared coldly at him as I took the handcuffs off. He got up off the sidewalk slowly, looking almost quizzically at me.

"What are you gonna do now, man, shoot me?" the biker taunted cautiously. He couldn't figure me out, so he didn't want to push his luck.

"No, I am going to give you a chance to go free. You and I are going to go at it right here on the bridge, and if you win, you go free," I explained, calmly.

"You're crazy, man!" the biker shouted, looking at Danny for help or an explanation.

"Why am I crazy? I want to give you a chance. Is that crazy?" I asked.

"You're gonna do something, I don't know what it is, but you're gonna do something!" he yelled, hoping that someone would intervene.

A look of fright came over the biker's face when I reached in my waistband and pulled out my 38-caliber Smith and Wesson. I held the pistol in my hand for a moment to let him suffer, then I handed it to Danny. I stepped close to the biker, and I told him to throw the first punch. He turned his head to the side and watched me uneasily with a cowardly look in his eyes. As soon as he wound up with his right hand and telegraphed a haymaker, I hit him with a straight right-hand punch and opened a cut over his left eye, and I followed it up with a left hook that caught him flush on the nose as he tried to turn away. His knees buckled. He landed several weak punches on my face as he went down, but I knew that he wanted to quit. He tried to grab my hands. He made me angry because he fought like a sissy. I grabbed him by his collar under his chin with my left hand and I grabbed him by the crotch with my right hand and I picked him up and hung him over the iron railing, high above the dark water of Boston's inner harbor. He was screaming and hollering. The sickening smell of sweat, blood, and leather made me gag. Danny leaned over the railing next to me and grabbed onto the biker.

"Paul, let's go. He's a piece of shit. Let's drop him off at the police station and go home," Danny reasoned with me.

I thought for a while, and then I pulled the biker back over the railing and fell on top of him on the sidewalk. He looked desperately out of the corner of his eye at me with silent suspicion. I was gasping for breath and my stomach felt sick. We lay there together in the middle of the Charlestown Bridge, but in my mind we were a million miles away from the rest of the world. I put the cuffs back on his wrists and placed him in the backseat again. I fumed. I wished that he had put up a fight so that I could have killed him. I hated everything he stood for.

The car stopped. I opened my eyes. We were in front of the police station. To my shock I realized the scene on the bridge had never happened. I was shaken to the core and perspiring profusely. I wondered if I was losing it.

The crusty old desk sergeant, obviously in the twilight of his career, was used to seeing sights that would shock most people, but even he was unprepared for this situation. The three of us stumbled up to the booking desk in the ancient police station. The handcuffed biker was sandwiched between Danny and me, and I could see by the sergeant's expression that he was perplexed by our appearance. The other cops in the station were quiet as they stopped what they were doing to witness the scene. The biker's face was smashed up. He was bleeding profusely from his nose and a cut over his left eye, and his long hair and beard were caked with dried blood. I had blood from the biker and Agent Giambro all over my bruised face and hands. My clothing was torn and splattered with blood from the fight. Danny looked like a North End wise guy. I slid my badge out of my back pocket and showed it to the desk sergeant.

"This guy is under arrest for violation of the federal narcotic laws. We want him locked up until his court appearance in the morning," I instructed.

It was almost two o'clock in the morning when the police doctor arrived. An old man, perhaps seventy, in a rumpled suit and scuffed shoes, the doctor walked in through the front door of the station carrying a leather bag and went directly to the desk sergeant. After a brief conference, the doctor turned around and walked toward us. I noticed that he wore black-rimmed eyeglasses with very thick lenses. As he came closer, I reached my hand out to greet him. Ignoring my gesture, he stopped too close to my face and stood with two hands grasping his leather bag in front of him. The doctor's eyes, magnified by the thick lenses, moved back and forth blurrily from Danny to me.

"Which one's the prisoner?" the expressionless doctor asked.

I almost started to laugh, then I caught myself. Maybe he was joking, but maybe he wasn't. The old doc's deadpan face gave no clue. I looked at Danny and saw immediately that he was as confused as I was.

"The prisoner is over here," I said, leading the way through the doorway to the holding block. A uniformed clerk opened the cell with a large iron key and led the doctor inside, while Danny and I exchanged questioning glances on the outside. We were both wondering the same thing as the doctor looked over the prisoner carefully with his eyes almost pressed against the prisoner's skin, putting his finger on the various cuts and abrasions.

The methodical examination, coupled with the doctor's mutterings under his breath, would have been comical, if it were not being conducted in the wee hours of the morning. The macabre absurdity of the scene made me smile involuntarily.

"I wonder if the doc is going to examine him for athlete's foot," I whispered to Danny in tired frustration. Danny was too tired to respond.

"Why don't they just let this innocent biker out of the cell and lock us up for police brutality," I added, sarcastically. It occurred to me at that moment that we really could be charged with brutality, and it all depended on this crazy-looking doctor, who was now stuffing his stethoscope and blood pressure gauge into his leather bag. The exam was over. Abruptly, the doctor turned away from the prisoner and walked out of the cell, still muttering to no one in particular.

"Bruises received consistent with force necessary to arrest." The doctor's finding was music to my ears. The prisoner did not feel the same way.

"You pig! You're gonna' die!" the biker yelled from the cell. The doctor, unruffled by the prisoner's threats, walked like Mr. Magoo through the holding cell door as I held it open for him.

"Thanks," I said. He walked out of the station and into the night, without acknowledging me.

I dropped Danny in Medford, and declined his invitation to go in for a beer. The sun would be coming up in a few hours, and I wanted to get home and get some sleep. Sometimes the drive is longer than others, but this night it seemed an eternity. My eyelids were heavy and more than once I found myself weaving in and out of the traffic lanes. Finally, I came to my exit and drove three-quarters of the way around the rotary and made a right turn onto Canton Street. In the wooded area behind the guardrail, I glimpsed the face of someone whom I had arrested. It didn't make sense to me. The guy was in federal prison in another state. I made the next right at the break in the guardrail, heading toward my home. Ironically, this is the spot where a drug dealer pulled his car over a couple of years ago and killed his partner, then shot it out with two Westwood policemen, killing one and wounding the other, before he was captured himself. As I drove down this road, I saw faces looking out at me from the dark shadows. They were hidden in the brush, leering at me just below the tree branches. They moved like ghosts and taunted me grotesquely as I drove slowly past. I felt extremely calm, but sweat broke out all over my body and I could feel the heat escaping from my head. It was like an adrenaline rush. I convinced myself that I had to go after them. I could not run away. It didn't make sense, but they were all there. I was not going to lead them to my home. I decided to drive around the block and confront them. I would walk right up to the dead guys, then I would shoot the others. I drove past my street, took a right, came onto the rotary again, and started my approach. Peering into the trees, I could not find the disembodied ambushers. There was no one there, just the motion of the branches and the tall grass waving back and forth. I pulled over with my high beams on, got out of the car cautiously, and walked into the woods. They were gone. How could it be?

I arrived home completely exhausted and collapsed on the bed with all my clothes on. I struggled to force the ghostly faces out of my thoughts and eventually fell asleep. The unpleasant ring of the telephone woke me up.

"It's eight o'clock," Pam announced brightly. She had a way of speaking that made even the time sound good.

"Thanks," I managed.

"I love you!" Pam added. I hung up. The image of Pam in her white hospital uniform lingered in my thoughts. I was still tired, and it was difficult to drag myself out of bed. I remained on my back with the pillow over my head, picturing Pam's beautiful smiling face, and I wondered what she saw in me. Finally, I crawled out of bed and made it to the office.

The strange faces on the side of the road kept invading my thoughts as I struggled to concentrate on the exact details of the previous night's arrests. I was startled by the ringer of my private line. As soon as I answered, I heard my name spoken softly, almost pathetically. The faint voice on the other end of the line began tentatively at first, crying quietly as she described her son's death almost in a whisper, her only son; how he drove her car into the city early this morning to buy drugs, how he crashed into an oncoming truck and died instantly. The hypodermic needle was hanging out of his arm and glassine bags empty of heroin were found lying next to him on the seat. It would be on the television news. She told me I could see it on the news later because the news crews were there at the accident scene. Her son was my informant, a sad case who lived with his single mother, a nurse. I had spent a couple of hours with her last week, trying to get him into a heroin detox center, and he was supposed to start today, the earliest opening we could arrange. What a nice way to start the day. That's two deaths in a row. The saying "three on a match" came immediately to mind when I hung up the phone. I wondered who would be next.

Seated at my desk with my chin resting on my hands, I began thinking about another experience I had had the week before. I pictured the body in the hallway. It seemed so unreal to me; a prolonged pose, as if he had taken his final bow after a curtain call. The first death had occurred over the weekend. I was sitting in the back of a Boston Police cruiser with two uniformed police officers from District Two. It was late at night, and we were combing the streets of Roxbury looking for a federal fugitive. The police dispatcher announced over the radio in a scratchy voice, almost drowned out by static and undecipherable to the untrained ear, of a shooting in progress. Automatically, both officers repeated the address of the shooting out loud. The screeching of rubber and the wailing sound of the siren filled my ears.

"Shots fired!" That's how the call suddenly burst over the radio. The dispatcher followed immediately with the address. Tossed around in the backseat and thrown from side to side, my head bumped against the roof of the cruiser as the officer spun the vehicle around and raced to the scene of the shooting. I braced myself with my arms extended out straight, elbows locked, my hands tightly gripping the backrest of the front seat. The driver stomped the brake pedal to the floor, the siren died, and the tires skidded as the cruiser slid to a halt in front of a wooden triple-decker. The three of us bailed out at the same time with guns drawn, slamming the cruiser doors behind us. One officer went around to the back of the house, while I ran up the wooden stairs and in through the open door at the front entrance, following directly behind his partner. An old black woman was standing in the hall as if she expected us. Her wide eyes, her most notable feature visible from under a bandana wrapped around her head, looked up the stairway. I followed the officer, running as fast as I could, with my eyes darting from side to side searching for the gunman. The officer, his gun in his hand, straightened up when he reached the top of the stairs. He spoke to a matronly-looking middle-aged brown-skinned woman in a faded cotton dress.

"Where'd he go?"

"He gone."

"You sure?"

"Yeah."

I could tell by the officer's conversation with the woman that the victim of the shooting was a marijuana dealer. Marijuana almost seemed benign in comparison with the heroin and cocaine that devastated this neighborhood.

The officer holstered his pistol and relaxed his stance. My eyes were drawn to a solitary drooping figure in front of a half-opened door. I was transfixed by the sight of the still-life scene. The victim was seated on the floor. His back was straight, but his head had dropped down on his chest. The long slender arms spread out gracefully to either side, and with pointed fingers touched the wooden floor on which the body sat. Its left leg extended straight to the front, and the right leg extended fully to the rear in a perfect split, with the toe of the front shoe pointing up toward the ceiling. It would have been a beautiful statue in a museum, but it was stark reality; it was a dead body. The second officer came up the back stairs cautiously at first, then joined his partner in conversation with the old female witness. The two officers and the woman were talking about the figure like he wasn't there.

"You play, you pay. Mmm . . . ," the old woman said rather indignantly, while shaking her head from side to side.

"Was there a lot of traffic in and out of his apartment?" one of the officers asked her indifferently.

"Mmm hmm!" she replied, pursing her lips tightly and flaring her nostrils.

I continued moving slowly up the stairs and carefully crept closer to the statuelike man. I stared at the figure, which remained completely still, unaffected by the activity around him. There were no apparent marks on his body; no gaping bullet holes or stab wounds. There was, however, a dark red puddle expanding slowly, in almost a perfect circle, on the wooden floor directly underneath the figure. I touched the young man's warm, coffee-colored cheek with the back of my fingers, then I touched the artery in his neck to confirm there was no pulse. I remained on my knees next to the dead man, thinking to myself that only moments before, he was alive. Police officers began streaming into the building and walking in and out of the apartment behind the young man. I could not move away from the body. For some strange reason, I felt as though I should not leave him alone. The voice of a homicide detective caught my attention. I turned and looked at him, then I stood up and backed away from the corpse. I thought to myself, it's a matter of minutes. I'm alive and he's dead.

The sound of my name coming over the intercom in the federal building brought me out of my reverie. The receptionist announced that Danny was at Charlestown lockup waiting for me to meet him and transport the biker to federal court. I looked at the clock, scooped my keys off of the desk, and flew out of the office to meet Danny.

He was standing in front of the police station, waiting with a cup of coffee for me. We discussed the previous night's events, including the arrest of the biker, finished our coffee, and went into the station to take custody of our prisoner. He looked worse than he had the night before. The biker's unattractive features, hidden by the darkness of the night, were there for all to see in the light of the sun: his dirty hair, greasy fingernails, blackheads, and sallow jailhouse complexion. The beady-eyed stare was still there, but now his eyes looked smaller and closer together, like they were trying to hide from the sun. Evil uncovered.

We made it to the federal courthouse at Post Office Square, where the biker was arraigned with several other arrestees. The U.S. magistrate refused to set bail and remanded our arrestees to the custody of the U.S. marshals. With the bikers behind bars, Danny and I went to the Boston City Hospital to visit Jimmy Giambro, whose right hand was wrapped up in a ball of gauze that was the size of a football. Giambro was in good spirits in spite of losing part of his middle finger.

"You can't flip 'em the bird any more," Danny joked.

"Right here!" Giambro answered loudly with an exaggerated smile, while he flashed the bird to Danny with his left hand.

For the rest of the day, Danny and I sat at our desks and wrote up our reports. I went straight to the gym after the long, boring hours and then I went home. Pam cooked the most delicious pasta and veal parmesan, and we ate together with babies Stacey and Christy. I had almost forgotten how much fun it was to share a meal with them. By the time we were finished eating, the girls had red spaghetti sauce all over their faces, and when I laughed at the sight of them, they laughed too. They were miniature mimics. It was hilarious. I had a cup of coffee while Pam cleaned up the kitchen and excused herself and the girls from the table. When I was finished with my coffee, Pam returned with Stacey and Christy, smiling widely to show me that they had brushed their teeth. Dressed in their pajamas, fresh out of the bathtub, they asked me to put them to bed. Pure innocence. How good does it get? I watched them as we said our prayers together. Stacey enunci-ated each word perfectly as she peeked through eyes that were closed tightly into an exaggerated squint. Christy, with an expression known only to chil-dren who communicate directly with God, held her hands clapped tightly together with her fingers pointing up to Heaven. Our time together was beautiful and I wished that it would never end.

In the morning we had breakfast together. Pam and I took spoonfuls of oatmeal for ourselves between spoonfuls that we put into the girls' mouths. When I left for work, I wondered if people with normal jobs got to live like this all the time. It was a wonderful way to live.

As soon as I arrived at the office, the telephone began to ring, and it was back to reality and life on the street.

"Hello, Paul?"

"Yeah, what's up?"

"This is Joey, Paul."

"Yeah, I know," I laughed. Joey Reardon had a very distinctive voice. The gravelly hoarseness, the nasal tone, and the thick Boston accent were unmistakable. It was humorous to think that Joey felt he had to introduce himself. "What's up, Joey?"

"I'm in Florida, Paul, and I need a favah. Can ya help me?" Joey pleaded.

"I'll try," I answered honestly.

"Paul, I never asked you for nothin' before, but I need some help now."

I could tell by the tone of his voice that something very serious was going on. I got a strange feeling deep in my stomach as I asked, "What is it, Joey?"

"I'm gonna level with ya, Paul. I fucked up. This asshole came to me a few days ago and asked me to get him some Dilaudid, a drug that is six times more potent than morphine. He gave me three hundred and told me he wanted a thou."

Joey normally talked fast, but he was talking very fast now as he de-scribed the complicated incident to me over the phone. I could hardly un-derstand him.

I cut him off. "Joey, slow down. Who is this guy?"

"His name is Degnan, Billy Degnan, a Disciple."

"A Devil's Disciple?"

"Yeah."

"And he wanted a thousand Dilaudid?"

"No, no, he wanted me to get him three hundred Dilaudid, and he said he would make a thou on it."

"You mean he wanted to make a thousand dollars selling the shit?"

"Yeah."

"Okay, go ahead, Joey."

"So, he gives me the cake, the money, and says he'll see me tomorrah. Tomorrah comes and I can't get the shit, so I just gives him the money. He won't take it. Wants to know where the rest of it is."

"The rest of what?"

"The rest of the money! He says, you either get me the DLs [Dilaudid], or you give me a thou. So, I says 'Fuck you, get lost.' I forget about it and now I'm in Florida. Last night, he calls up my muthah, goes over to the house in Brighton, scares the shit out of her, threatens her, tells my muthah he's gonna throw acid in my sistah's face, says I owe him a grand, and they gotta pay!"

"Okay, Joey, relax. Slow down. This guy sounds like a beauty. Do you think he'll do it?"

"I dunno, Paul, but try to do somethin' for me, will ya?" he pleaded.

"Okay, let me check things out, and I'll get back to you."

"Thanks, Paul, I really appreciate it. Here's my numbah, it's a hotel lobby. I'll be there after eleven every mornin'. See what ya can do."

"Take it easy, we'll do our best," I said as I ended the conversation. I hung up the phone, wondering how I could help. I looked into my supervisor's office, hoping to ask for direction, and saw him laboring over a report. It's futile to ask his advice, I realized, so I began checking Degnan's name out in the DEA files. Bingo, he was there! I studied his rap sheet while I made a copy of his mug shot. He was definitely a violent guy. I noticed that Special Agent John Fender was listed as the arresting officer in one of the cases, so I walked around the office till I found Fender.

"What's up, Big Jack?"

"Hey, Paulie, nothin' much, my man, nothin' much," Jack said as he looked up from his desk and smiled.

"You arrested Billy Degnan?" I asked.

"Yeah," Jack laughed as he continued, "he's a cuckoo, Devil's Disciple, crazy as a bedbug."

"Is he dangerous?"

"Yeah, I'd watch out for him. He's capable of anything. Why, you got something on him?"

"No, not yet, just wondering," I answered.

"Paul, if you need anything else, just give me a holler. Don't arrest him by yourself," Jack cautioned.

"Thanks, Jack, I appreciate the help," I answered. I walked back to my desk still wondering what I should do. Jack was an experienced street agent. If he thought that Degnan was dangerous, then he probably was. I called the Boston Police, the Massachusetts State Police, and the ATF (Bureau of Alcohol, Tobacco, and Firearms) for record checks. Every agency had Degnan in their files and their intelligence corroborated Fender's evaluation unanimously. They confirmed my initial fear that Degnan was for real. He was a longtime member of the Devil's Disciples motorcycle gang and a pervert who liked to fool around with little girls and boys. He went speeding for weeks at a time on crystal methamphetamine, and he was unpredictably violent. In addition to this, he loved guns. I was still mulling it all over in my mind when my new partner walked in. Danny Santarpio, my usual partner, was assigned to a wiretap for the next sixty days.

"Sergio, what should I do?" I said as I ran the details by him for the first time.

Sergio Santini puffed on his stogie and stared at me, as he listened. When I finished, he shrugged his shoulders and said, "I dunno, what can we do?"

I telephoned the Boston Police again and explained the situation, without mentioning names. The desk sergeant said, "Well, if the guy threatens them again, have them come in and swear out a complaint, and we'll go arrest him. It's a misdemeanor. He'll be right back out on the street. Otherwise, wait till the guy does something, assaults them or something." The sergeant's tone of voice indicated that he realized how foolish his instructions sounded, but that's the law. He's only doing his job, I thought.

"Thanks, sarge, thanks a lot," I answered as I hung up the phone. I could sense the impotence in his voice. I sympathized with him, because he probably gets calls like this all the time from potential victims, and he can never help anyone. He has to respond with a silly answer, like wait till the guy does something. When someone is threatening to kill you, it's not an easy thing to wait till the guy does something, because then you may be dead.

The law does not protect the public in cases like this. It actually protects the offender. I was puzzled as to how I could help the Reardons. How could I protect Joey's innocent mother and sister from this nutcase? If someone threatened my family like this, I know what I would do. I would have to kill him. Suddenly, I felt like ice ran up my spine. The horrible recurring dream came to mind. I sensed Sergio looking at me.

"Sergio, I feel a responsibility to this kid. I like him. His mother and sister never hurt anybody. Why should they be maimed or disfigured?"

Joey was a street kid from Brighton. He was a friend of my brother, Hank, when we all lived in the Faneuil Housing Project. Hank never got a chance to grow up because he was killed in Vietnam. I remembered Joey when he was a boy. He was one of the younger kids when I was growing up, and he always made everyone laugh. Somehow, Joey took a few wrong turns, and now he was a junkie. Heroin has its way of destroying people.

It was odd the way that Joey and I became reacquainted. One night I arrested a guy, the owner of one of those overpriced hair salons on fashionable Newbury Street, who catered to Boston's upper crust. Unfortunately for the salon owner, we executed a search warrant and arrested him as he was hosting a party attended by the Back Bay's high society. After we handcuffed the host and sat him down in the middle of the floor, I took over as doorman and buzzed the partygoers inside as they came into view of the video camera in the lobby. When the guests got off the elevator, another agent opened the door and greeted them. They entered the apartment and stood dumbfounded while we frisked them, confiscated their drugs, and arrested them. Joey was one of the guests. When the door opened, a surprised Joey hugged me like the long-lost friend that I was. We hadn't seen each other since our days growing up in the project, save for my brother's funeral when his body was shipped back from Vietnam. At first Joey laughed when I told him I was a DEA agent. He continued to laugh until I showed him my badge, and he looked around the apartment nervously at all the other agents and all the people in handcuffs. It was a bizarre reunion for both of us. Joey handed me a bag of heroin, and I arrested him. I was doing my job, and he knew it. It was one of those strange moments in life that happen without warning. After Joey was convicted and sent to prison, I visited him. We had some heartfelt talks through the glass in the "no contact" visiting room at Walpole State Prison. I always say to myself, "There, but for the grace of God, go I."

Several years later I was working undercover with some mob guys who were planning to rob and kill me. I never had a clue as to their intentions. I thought that everything was going fine, until I got a call from Joey.

"I'm no rat, Paul," Joey said apologetically after tipping me off. "I just don't want you to get hurt."

Thanks to Joey, I took the offensive and with a small army of agents to back me up, I arrested the bad guys without incident. It's a good thing too, because they were armed to the teeth. They really planned to kill me. How could I forget a favor like that? Joey knew where I was at, and I knew where Joey was at, and when anyone does me a favor, I never forget. That is why I was so concerned about the current threat situation. My partner sensed my commitment.

"Sergio, I'm gonna grab this guy tonight and shake him up, see if I can make him back off."

Sergio puffed on his stogie as he dialed the phone and said coldly, in a flat voice, "Hello, Degnan." Sergio hung up, then looked at me with a deadpan expression.

"He's there, let's go."

We both got up silently, left the office, and drove toward Degnan's house near Brighton Center without speaking. We were thinking of what we had to do, and how we were going to do it.

"I'm gonna walk right into his house and slap him around. You stand there for protection in case he pulls a gun," I said.

"No, the house is no good. It's too easy to get set up ourselves," Sergio reasoned.

"Then let's draw him outside somehow," I figured.

We considered several possible plans, depending on the circumstances we might encounter when we arrived at Degnan's house. As I turned the corner and drove down his street, I slowed down to get a better look. A biker type was working under the hood of a car that was parked in the driveway of Degnan's house, but I could see that it was not Degnan. The biker looked up and "made" us right away. He went into the house immediately, and I drove right by.

"Sergio, that's not him. I'm gonna turn around and stop directly in front of his house this time. You ask for Billy."

We still didn't know how we were going to present ourselves or what we were going to do as we came to the end of Degnan's dead-end street and turned around. Pulling up slowly to Degnan's house, and then stopping, I could see two or three blurred figures on the other side of a screen door. It was impossible to determine which one was Degnan.

"Billy, hey, Billy!" Sergio called loudly.

"Yeah," a voice answered belligerently, challenging us from behind the screen.

With my arm out the window up to my elbow, I pointed my gun toward the door. The streetlight was reflected by my shiny, nickel-plated revolver as I pulled back the hammer.

"Die, Degnan!" I hollered out the window.

"No, no, that's not him!" Sergio shouted.

"That's him, man, he's dead!" I yelled as I deliberately fired five bullets into the door frame. I figured that he would think I missed him accidentally and take it as a warning.

The figures behind the screen door crouched down and scrambled in all directions. Through the ringing of the gunshots, I could hear a dog barking and loud crashing sounds as the bikers scattered, bumping into furniture. I watched the door as I pulled my smoking pistol back into the car and screeched away from the curb. The smell of gunpowder filled my nostrils, and rubber was still burning from the tires when I wheeled onto the main drag, speeding away from Degnan's. I switched the headlights on when we were a safe distance away.

"I think we scared him," Sergio said, facetiously.

"If he ain't scared, no one is," I laughed. "Now, let's put down another call."

I pulled over to the curb next to a gas station. With me standing beside him, Sergio dialed Degnan's number from a pay phone. I watched Sergio as he spoke into the receiver. "Listen, Billy boy, you fuckin' jerk, you got lucky tonight. The next time you won't be so lucky. Shut up! You got lucky. We got hired to do a job, and we're gonna do it, but we're not gonna shoot the wrong guy, we're gonna shoot you, unless you back off! You understand? Back off!"

Sergio hung up the phone and we got back into the car. I watched Sergio, anxiously waiting for him to tell me about the phone call. He stared straight ahead, puffing on his stogie. After a few moments, he looked at me out of the corner of his eye.

"He said, 'Just for that, you owe me two thousand,'" Sergio mumbled in disbelief.

"What?" I responded incredulously.

"He said, 'You owe me two thousand now.' Just like that. Paulie, the guy's a nut."

There was complete silence in the car as I drove all the way to Sergio's house in Hyde Park, thinking, What next? What now, I wondered? When I stopped the car in the driveway, Sergio looked over at me with a puzzled expression, and we both went inside without speaking.

"Sergio, I'm gonna call Bobby Breed. He used to be a bikie, and he knows a lot of these guys personally. Let's see what he thinks. Maybe he can reach Degnan," I said, as I dialed the Boston Police Drug Control Unit and asked for Bobby Breed. He was actually president of a motorcycle gang before he decided to become a cop.

"Bobby!"

"Hey, brother," he greeted me enthusiastically. "What can I do for you?"

"Listen, Bobby, I need a favor," I began. "Do you know a guy named Billy Degnan?"

"The bikie?"

"Yeah, the bikie."

"Sure, I know him good," Breed replied. "He's crazy. What's the matter, you got a ticket for him?"

"No, it's not that. He's ah, he's," I began, then hesitated. "He's been threatening some people, threatening to blow them up, throw acid in their face," I answered.

"He'll do it, Paul, he's nuts!" Bobby assured me. "I know him good!"

"Well, what should I do? These are nice people, innocent types," I added.

"I don't know, Paul. I really don't know."

"I was thinking that you could call him up, one old biker to another, you know, like you are a cop, but your allegiance is still to the bikies. Tell him that you are calling him up as a favor, to tip him off. Tell him that you got the word that some underworld guy was going to 'off' him, and you just wanted to let him know, for old times' sake. Tell him that the cops are also aware of his threats, and they are waiting to arrest him as soon as he makes a move. Suggest that he lay back a little, so that he don't get arrested or killed. What do you think? Can you do that? I'm trying to buy time. I'm trying to protect this family for a couple of days," I explained.

"I'll do it, man, I'll call him," Bobby replied. "He's crazy, though, it's hard to predict what he'll do."

"I'm in a bind, Bobby. I don't know what else to do. I don't want to make matters worse. I just want him to lay off, stop the threats," I explained.

"I can dig it. I'll call him right now. He knows I'm a cop, though, and I don't mess around anymore. I locked up Deacon, the president of the Disciples, and they were all pissed for a while. They know I got balls, though. I'll call him right now. Where are you?"

"I'm at Sergio's," I answered. "Call me right back."

"Alright, man, hang on," Bobby said as he hung up the phone.

Men of Irish descent from working-class families traditionally have made up the overwhelming majority of the Boston Police Department. As time goes on, this phenomenon is changing. Women, blacks, Hispanics, and other ethnic minorities are joining the police force in large numbers. The department increasingly reflects the heterogeneous nature of the communities that they serve, enabling the police to gather intelligence about groups they could not infiltrate in the past. Breed's unique background as a member and past president of a motorcycle gang provided the Boston Police with the opportunity to gather intelligence that they were never before able to access.

Breed had become disenchanted with his motorcycle gang when they shed their free-spirited rebel image and became outlaw drug smugglers and dope pushers. He burned his "colors" (worn by bikers), cut his long hair and beard, and then joined the Boston Police Department. Prior to his assignment to the Drug Control Unit, he was partnered, in uniform, with Jack Parker, a handsome young cop from West Roxbury and a former paratrooper. Breed and Parker were the busiest cops in District Five. They were not only the sharpest-looking cops in uniform, but they also had the highest arrest statistics in the district. They also developed the deepest pool of informants. People began calling them supercops. Wherever a crime occurred, it seemed that Bobby Breed and Jack Parker responded. Their outstanding record led to a transfer to the Boston Police Drug Control Unit.

Rrrrinng! Rrrrinng!

"Hello? Bobby?"

"Paul," Bobby laughed, "you're not gonna reach this guy. He's nuts! I mean, he was nuts before, but he is G-O-N-E now. Too much angel dust! His brain's fried. You know what he said to me? I finished my spiel, and he says, 'Tell them guys they owe me two grand now, Bobby. That's it. If they want to kill me, I'll be home.' Paulie, he is crazy! Degnan says, just before I hung up, 'Hey, Bobby, you're doin' a pissa job. Keep lockin' up those junkies. You're alright.' Then he laughed and hung up the phone."

"Bobby, what do you do with a guy like this?"

"How close are you to the people he's threatening?" Breed asked.

"They're pretty close, Bobby. They did me a favor once, and I owe them."

"There is only one thing to do with a guy like this. You know what I mean," Breed said.

"Yeah, I know. That's what I thought. Thanks, Bobby." I hung up.

"Sergio, this guy's dangerous," I said as I dialed the number for the Boston Police District Fourteen in Brighton.

"District Fourteen," a sergeant answered loudly, but I didn't catch his name.

"Hello, sergeant, this is Paul Sullivan from fed narcotics, I . . ."

"Hey, Paul, how you doin'?" the loud voice asked, before I could finish my sentence.

"Good, who is this?" I replied.

"Red Clancy."

Red was an old friend of mine from the drug control unit. He recently made sergeant, and was transferred to uniform and assigned to District Fourteen. Red was a good cop, a guy whom I felt comfortable with.

"Red, I never got the chance to congratulate you on making sergeant. Congratulations!"

"Thanks, Paul," Red answered modestly. "What can I do for you?"

"Joey Reardon had some trouble with some bikies in your district, and they've been threatening his mother and sister." I described the situation.

"Joey's been doin' drugs around here pretty heavy, Paul," Red explained.

"Yeah, I know, Red, but I owe him a favor, and besides, his mother and sister are straight," I reasoned.

"Alright, what's the scoop?" Red asked.

"This guy, Billy Degnan," I began.

"We had him the other night, a pervert. He was fooling around with a thirteen-year-old boy from the projects. When we went to his house to arrest him, we spotted an Uzi in plain view, so we got a warrant for the house. We confiscated shotguns, pistols, rifles, everything. He had his own arsenal. He's out on bail. Go figure."

"That's him! Well, to make a long story short, Degnan's been making threats to Joey's mother and sister, and he says he's gonna do something soon."

"He's a maggot, a dangerous maggot," Red confirmed with disdain in his voice.

"Yeah, I know. That's why I'm calling. I was wondering if you could brief the troops and alert them to the situation, so that they will respond immediately in case a call comes in. Let them know that it is a serious matter if they hear an emergency call from Reardon's mother's house."

"Consider it done, Paul. I'll put a car on the Reardon house to keep an eye on the mother and sister," Red volunteered efficiently.

"Thank you, Red," I said as I hung up.

"That was Red Clancy, a good man. I used to work with him when he was in drugs. Good people," I said to Sergio, as I dialed again with the phone up to my ear.

"Hello?" a throaty female voice answered.

"Mrs. Reardon?" I asked carefully, not wanting to frighten her.

"Yes, who is this?" she inquired timidly in a soft, uncertain voice.

"It's Paul Sullivan, Mrs. Reardon, a friend of Joey's. Has that nut called again?"

"Oh, Paul, I'm so glad it's you. He just called. He said," she began talking fast, then hesitated, and sniffled, "he said that he was going to throw acid in Laura's face." Mrs. Reardon then broke down and began crying hysterically.

"Calm down, relax," I implored gently.

"Hello?" another female voice, throaty but more composed, spoke into the phone.

"Hello, this is Paul Sullivan," I said again.

"Paul, this is Laura."

"Laura, I realize that you and your mother are very upset, but try to relax a little. This guy is more talk than anything else, so don't worry yourself to death," I lied. "The police are watching your house, and they're gonna scoop him if he shows up."

"Thank you, Paul. My mother and I both appreciate it."

"Hey, don't mention it. Keep your doors locked, though, and don't go out if you don't have to," I instructed her matter-of-factly, to keep from alarming them further.

"We're scared to death. We're not going anywhere," Laura assured me.

"Just stay in, and try to get some sleep," I added.

"Thank you, Paul," Laura answered, and we hung up. She sounded tough to me, but she was scared.

The following day was a blur to me. I got dressed with my eyes closed, then drove in a daze to Hyde Park and picked up Sergio. We did not talk on the drive to the John F. Kennedy building until I pulled the car into a spot in the underground garage. Sergio, expressionless, with an unlit stogie hanging from his lips, looked at me for a moment, then said facetiously, "Another day fighting for truth, justice, and the American way."

I watched Sergio get out of the car, wondering to myself what really went on inside his head. I rode the elevator with him up to the ground floor, got off alone, and walked through the building. Then I crossed Tremont Street and hurried up the cement stairs leading to Pemberton Square. I walked into an old granite building and stood, rubbing my tired, bloodshot eyes, as I waited for the elevator under the high ceiling murals in the ornate lobby of the Boston Municipal Court. Red Clancy approached with a sly smile on his face, and I already knew why. I had made a telephone call to Degnan late the night before, and he sounded surprisingly sane. I agreed to meet him, alone, at his house. It was a mistake.

"Paul, you're gonna love this story," Red said, as we shook hands and walked away from the elevator together. "We got a call about three a.m., disturbance down at Degnan's house."

I watched Red's eyes to see what he knew as he continued.

"Some guy broke Degnan's living room window. When he comes barrelling downstairs to see what was the matter, the guy with a ski mask is waiting for him. He beats the shit out of him! When we got there to answer the call, he was lying in the hallway, his head split open, his eyes closed, blood everywhere. The guy must have beat him with a club, and then stabbed him with his own bowie knife. He did a beautiful job on him, whoever the guy was!"

The guy was not wearing a ski mask; I had a stocking cap pulled down over my ears. As soon as I stepped into his house, I knew that I had made a bad mistake. I picked up a wooden bar stool instinctively and broke it over Degnan's head as soon as I saw the bowie knife that he had drawn from a sheath on his belt. I didn't beat him with a club; I beat him with my fists as I fought to survive. I stopped when Degnan was flat on his face. I picked the bowie knife up from the floor and left. How could I ever have walked into such a trap? I was really losing it. I smiled nervously, watching Red's eyes as he continued to describe the call that he had responded to.

"He could hardly move. We thought he was dead at first, but he looks up, and guess what he says? He says, 'Who called you? I don't want no fuckin' pigs in my house!' I turned around and told the ambulance driver everything was fine, no further assistance needed. Then I walked over and stepped on his fingers and said, 'Die maggot.' It was a beautiful job, though," Red concluded. We continued looking into each other's eyes like we were trying to analyze the other's response, then Red ended the encounter with a tap on my shoulder.

"Gotta run, Paulie, I got a case in superior court. See you later," he said, hurrying off to his courtroom.

As Red walked away, I thought to myself, how lucky I was to be alive. There are some bad people in this world. This guy is going to need more than a beating to change his way of thinking. This guy is more than crazy. He's a sadomasochistic psychopath. What do you do with a guy like this? The only thing he likes more than hurting people is having someone hurt him. I decided that the best thing to do was to talk with Joey's father, Roscoe. Roscoe was wise guy lingo for the pistol he always carried with him. That's where the nickname came from. Roscoe had not been living with Joey's mother for years, but I figured he should know that she and his daughter were in danger. Roscoe, a colorful Runyonesque character, was an old-fashioned crook with ties to Boston mobsters that went back to the thirties. Roscoe was cracking safes and hijacking trucks before I was born. A guy like Roscoe ought to know what to do. And besides, it's his wife and daughter.

I drove through the open gate into the construction yard surrounded by a chain-link fence, and parked under the yellow billboard with the words Reardon Construction spelled out in large black letters over the silhouette of a dump truck. A stocky, solidly built man about fifty-plus years old stepped out from between the row of backhoes and trucks and walked directly over to meet me. His thin black hair was combed straight back and receded in such a way that it exaggerated his big broad forehead.

"Hullo!"

"Roscoe, I'm Paul Sullivan, Joey's friend."

"Paul, I know all about ya," Roscoe beamed as we shook hands. "Dat fuckin' kid of mine don't know how ta treat friends, Paul. I preciate everything you done for my son. It's dat goddam dope."

"Roscoe, the reason that I am here is to make sure that you know what's going on. Do you know this guy, Degnan, who's threatening your wife and daughter?" I asked confidentially. I could tell by the blank expression on his face that he had no idea how serious the threat was, so I filled him in.

"I'm a cop, Roscoe, and I shouldn't even be here, but Joey was a friend of my brother and he's a friend of mine, and I have two daughters myself."

"Sorry bout your brother. He was a good kid," Roscoe said, referring to my brother's death in Vietnam. I could tell by his voice that he really was sorry.

"Thanks. I know," I replied.

A thoughtful expression came over Roscoe's face. The cat-and-mouse game that guys like Roscoe played instinctively when talking with cops suddenly ended. I knew then that he trusted me, and realized I was there to help him. I saw the change in his eyes.

"Paul, I could have this arsehole knocked off, but I don't know," Roscoe wondered out loud. "I heard that he threatened Laura. I checked him out, he's got no one in his cornah. The bikers don't even like him. He's not connected, he's a nobody, but I wanted ta give 'em a chance. You think he's capable?"

"Roscoe, let me put it this way. The guy has a history of violence, his record is long. He's a diddler, too. He likes to play with little boys and girls. He's a pervert. He called Laura up and threatened to throw acid in her face. Does that answer your question?"

"He did?" Roscoe asked, while the look in his eyes became more intent.

"Yeah, early last night," I confirmed.

"Jeezuz Chrise, I din know dat. I been livin' away from da wife, you know," Roscoe explained.

"Maybe dats da problum wid Joey. I shoulda been home more. Laura called da office and said dat nut called again dis mornin' and said dey owed him two tousand foddy or sumptin'." Roscoe laughed. "Sumptin' bout a broken window last night."

I thought about the broken window and the beating. This guy was crazier than I ever imagined.

"Paul, tanks a millian for comin' ovah. I mean dis. You evah need anytin', it's yaws. You need a driveway or anytin'?"

"Roscoe, I came here out of friendship. I don't want any favors. But thanks, anyway," I said.

"Paul, I mean it. You evah wanna build a house or anytin', I'll be glad to," Roscoe persisted.

"Forget about it, Roscoe."

"Take care, Paul," Roscoe said finally. "Dat fuckin' Joey, he don know how lucky he is to have friends like you!"

The first thing the next morning, just as I put the key into the drawer to open my desk, I heard the receptionist announce my name over the intercom.

"Paul Sullivan, 7-0, Paul Sullivan, 7-0."

"Hello, Paul Sullivan speaking."

"Hello, Paul, this is Bronco Fitzgerald. Do you know where Joey Reardon is?" a familiar whiskey voice asked.

"Hello, Bronco," I answered cautiously, knowing that our government telephone lines were recorded. "He's in Florida."

"Well, that's good," Bronco laughed, "because we got a guy with his leg blown off. Those shotguns do a nasty job. The guy says Joey and his father did it. That's a long shot from Florida to Brighton! Can you get in touch with Joey, wherever the fuck he is, and have him call me?"

"You got it, Bronco," I answered, as Bronco laughed at his own joke. Then I inquired, "Who's the wounded one?"

"Some dirtball. A no-good bastard named Billy Degnan. About two a.m. officers responded to . . . ," Bronco began reading parts of the police report: "individual, found bleeding profusely from right leg, in semiconscious condition." Bronco laughed. I could hear his congested lungs over the phone. "The cops said he was covered with stab wounds and bruises. I guess someone kicked the shit out of him the night before. They said there was blood everywhere. We picked up Joey's father this morning down at the yard. Said he didn't know nothing about it. He was still drunk from the night before!" Bronco laughed harder.

"What was the bail?" I asked.

"I got him out on personal, Paul, he's old school, always been stand-up. He ain't goin' nowhere," Bronco answered.

"Okay, Bronco, I'll try to call Joey and have him get in touch with you," I promised.

"Okeydokey, Paul, cuz we have to do an investigation. If he can prove he is in Florida, it will clear him."

"Will do," I said, and hung up. Why didn't they kill him? I wondered. There is no sense calling that telephone number that Joey gave me now, I thought, it's a pay phone. He's not there, anyway. I dialed the telephone number for Roscoe at the yard.

The telephone rang for a while. Finally, someone answered. It was Roscoe.

"Hello, Roscoe?"

"Yeah, who's dis?" Roscoe, no doubt bolstered by some alcohol intake, answered in good humor.

"It's Paul Sullivan, Roscoe."

"Oh, yeah, Paul, hullo, Um sorry, I taut it was someone else," Roscoe apologized for no reason.

"Listen, Roscoe, it's important that I get in touch with Joey right away. Have him call me at the undercover phone as soon as you can, alright?"

"Okay, Paul, right. I'll make a few calls and have him call you asap. Thanks, Paul," Roscoe answered, and we hung up simultaneously. I paused to contemplate the situation. I was reflecting on the events of the night before, when the undercover phone rang in the hallway. I rushed out and picked up the receiver.

"Hello, Paul, it's Joey."

"Yeah, Joey, I know, uh, don't say anything over the phone. Uh, you know what I mean. Talk to me when I see you. You know what I'm talking about, so just listen," I awkwardly advised.

"I hear ya, Paul, I hear ya," Joey laughed, nervously.

"The police got a call last night for a shooting down at Degnan's place. Someone shot his leg off with a sawed-off shotgun. Now Degnan, who we know is crazy, told the cops that you and your father were the shooters. I know better, though, because you were never involved in crimes of violence and have no reputation for violent behavior. You know what I mean? The cop that arrested your father knows better, just like me, and he's a personal friend of mine, and a stand-up guy. So, be that as it may, my man, call me tomorrow morning. You know, as soon as you get back from Florida. You know what I mean. That way, I can walk you into District Fourteen, and you can surrender yourself, so that you can defend yourself against these false charges. Okay?"

"I hear ya, Paul. I'll call ya first thing in the mornin'," Joey replied with appreciation in his voice. "And thanks, Paul. I mean it."

"Lay low, Joey," I cautioned. "Get popped in Boston tonight and you're a goner." I knew that Joey was probably somewhere in Brighton as we spoke.

"Paul, I'm hibernatin'," Joey assured me.

The next day Joey called, as predicted, and Sergio and I met him at his father's construction yard. As we drove toward the police station, Joey gave me the old "I wanna level with you, but not in front of this guy" look. It was amusing to me because I read Joey perfectly, while Sergio had no idea.

"Degnan's really messed up," Sergio tried.

"Yeah, whoever did it did a messy job, I heard," Joey answered, laughing nervously.

I told Sergio to pull over at Twin Donuts so I could get some coffees to bring down to the police station. As soon as the car stopped, I jumped out and Joey followed me into the donut shop.

"They really messed up Degnan, huh?" Joey laughed again.

"They? They really messed up Degnan?" I mimicked Joey. "Don't break my aggies, Joey. Who do you think you're talkin' to, one of those assholes you hang around with? I'm the man, Joey! The man!"

Joey laughed nervously again. "I know, Paul, I'm only kiddin'. No offense or nothin', but I don't know this guy Sergio like I know you. Ya know what I mean?"

"Joey, I can't believe that you shot his leg off! How stupid is that? Did you get mixed up? Don't move, Degnan, or I'll blow your head off, I mean your leg? What the hell is that? Now you really made him mad! Are you alright?" I teased.

"I know, I know," Joey apologized. "I thought we were gonna give him a beatin', and that's that. My old man and I went in there about two a.m. We were both feelin' pretty good. Paul, I beat the fuck out of him. I mean, I broke everything in the house over his head. You wouldn't believe it.

There was nothin' but broken tables, and chairs, and lamps layin' every-where. He was hangin' onto my leg, his arm wrapped around my ankle, and he says, 'Joey, I'm sorry. I had enough.' His head was split open, and he was bleedin' everywhere. I looked at my father, like 'let's go,' you know, we served our purpose. The old man says to me, 'Get the gun.' I couldn't believe it. I just looked at him. He gives me the keys to the car, and says, 'Get the gun outta da trunk.' So I go to the trunk and there's a sawed-off shotgun. Holy shit! I get the gun and run back inside. My old man's givin' Degnan a bunch of shit, like 'My son's got your life in his hands. He makes the decision whether you live or die. It's up ta him.' I thought he was con-nin' the guy, you know, scarin' him. Then the old man turns to me and says, 'Shoot 'em, Joey.' Like he was saying, good afternoon. He says, 'Shoot 'em, Joey.' So I aimed the shotgun at Degnan. I didn't even know if it was loaded. I aimed low. I didn't want to kill the guy," Joey explained.

"You should have listened to your father, Joey, he's been around a long time."

"Yeah, I know," Joey agreed penitently. "You should have seen him, though. When we got there, he was all beat up. Someone beat him up the night before and cut him to ribbons with a razor or a knife. What a job, Paul, he looked like they put him through a meat grinder! And we had nothin' to do with it, believe me, Paul. It had to be a strong-arm guy, though, to beat him like that. He thought the guy was a friend of mine!" Joey laughed again.

I stared at Joey as scenes from the night before ran through my mind, and I said, "Maybe they were friends of yours, Joey. Sometimes people don't realize who their friends are." Joey knew then what I was talking about. Joey and Roscoe pleaded innocent to attempted murder in Brighton District Court and were released on bail.

That same day, I returned to the DEA office in the JFK building and sat down at my desk to catch up on my reports. The administrative part of my job was always a burden to me. The criminals did not go to jail, however, unless the meetings and drug buys were documented. It was as necessary as the actual undercover work, but I found it difficult to actually sit down and put the facts on paper. This particular day I was unbearably bored from sitting, while my mind kept wandering back to my undercover life. I needed a break.

I got up from my desk, put on my jacket, and went out for a walk. When I got out onto the street, I thought about everything that had happened dur-ing the last couple of months. As I walked down Tremont Street, I looked at the people passing by and wondered what the possibility was that I would meet someone I was dealing with. The air was damp and cold on my face, but my body was warm from the exercise as I briskly crossed the

Charles Street footbridge and continued through the brown grass and fallen leaves along the muddy banks of the Charles River. Danny and I had so many investigations going at the same time that we didn't really have a minute to ourselves. Time alone like this was a luxury.

Our lives were the job. We changed our personas chameleon-like, from one case to another. Danny and I had infiltrated both the Boston and New York City organized crime scenes. Traveling back and forth regularly from Boston to New York City was beginning to put a strain on our already overworked minds and bodies. We were buying heroin, cocaine, and hallucinogenic drugs simultaneously from Irish, Italians, Blacks, Hispanics, Chinese, and motorcycle gangs. It was difficult to keep up with so many bad guys, and it was becoming increasingly dangerous.

The Italian and Irish mob wars in Boston had been going on since the sixties, and there was no slowdown in sight. The New York mob was in turmoil and the violence was on the increase; mobsters were gunned down in the street on a regular basis. It seemed that Danny and I were in the middle of it all. When would our time come? It was as if we were in a protective bubble. I thought about the deal we did the previous week in Umberto's Clam Shack in Little Italy, the same place where Crazy Joe Gallo was gunned down in plain view of all the customers. Investigating detectives were unable to locate a single witness to the cold-blooded killing. People feared the mob more than the police.

The blurred images of New York City raced through my mind: Greenwich Village, Washington Square, the hippies, the beards, the drugs, the music. Signs and posters were plastered everywhere: to urge Stop the War, for the *Village Voice,* for concerts by Bob Dylan, Pete Seeger, and Joan Baez. Danny and I, dressed in tight silk open-necked shirts and bell-bottomed pants that covered up our pistols holstered on our ankles, maneuvered through the streets of the Village, Bleecker, Carmine, and MacDougal.

Frank Sinatra's music was in the background accompanying us on our sojourns in and out of the small cafés, bars, and gambling clubs on and around Mott, Hester, and Canal Streets in Little Italy. Images of arrogant Italian faces with hard lines, expensive silk suits, Rolex watches, and pinky rings filled my mind. The cash we encountered in the drug business, sometimes hundreds of thousands of dollars, seemed like nothing anymore, like Monopoly money. Death, dire newspaper headlines, corruption, bodies in the East River, shootings in the street . . . the title of the Broadway play *Stop the World, I Want to Get Off* played over and over in my mind.

By the time I returned to the office, almost everyone in my group had gone home. I went to my desk and found a note from Danny telling me that he was going to the Bell in Hand for a few beers with some state troopers and he would meet me there. I crumpled up the note and threw it into the wastebasket. I didn't want to meet anyone; I just wanted to be alone. I picked up where I had left off when I went for my walk. The lack of distraction was good. My head was clear now. I had finished most of my outstanding case reports and prepared myself to testify in a case that we worked jointly with the Boston Police. It was around seven o'clock when I decided to wrap it up and go home.

I pulled my undercover Cadillac over to the curb in front of a CVS on Tremont Street and went inside to get some chewing gum. When I came out, I stopped momentarily under a streetlight to open the packet of gum, and I was distracted by a stranger trying to get my attention.

"Pssst. Hey!" an unfamiliar voice hailed. I looked to my right and there was a guy standing in the shadows in a black stocking cap, army jacket, and jeans looking back at me. I put a piece of gum in my mouth.

"You lookin' to score?" the guy asked. I looked around. I was the only one standing there. It was clear that he was talking to me. He had that evil Charles Manson look in his eyes.

"Huh?" I answered in disbelief.

"You, asshole, you wanna score?" he said. I could feel my blood begin to boil. I just wanted to be left alone, to go home, and this creep invades my privacy. The butterflies started to flutter around in my stomach. I struggled to remain calm.

"Whaddaya got?" I managed, falling immediately into my undercover role.

"What I always got!" he answered, belligerently. He must have me confused with someone else, I thought. I just nodded in the affirmative. The guy turned and walked into the alley next to the store, and I followed him. The adrenaline was pumping. I was planning my strategy. I would see the drugs, badge him, then walk him out into the street and call for a wagon from Boston Police District One.

"The money. Gimme the money!" the guy demanded.

"Man, you forgot to show me the stuff. You show me the stuff, I show you the money. That's the way it goes," I answered. The guy glared at me glassy-eyed, with his jaw set, then pulled something out of his jacket pocket.

"Pure heroin, man," he taunted, waving the bundle in front of my face. I nodded.

"The money, asshole!" he persisted. This guy was asking for it.

"The money, yeah," I repeated in an effort to delay him while I reached for my badge. My right hand felt the empty rear pocket of my jeans, and I suddenly realized that I did not have my badge. My badge, handcuffs, and gun were locked in my desk at the JFK building. The blood rushed to my head. I hesitated.

"What happens if I don't have any money?" I asked.

"Don't play with me, man. I don't play. You wanna mess around, ass-hole?" he challenged, as he snapped the blade of a buck knife out from his pocket and pointed it at me. That was the wrong thing to do. He invaded my privacy, he called me asshole, and now he was challenging me. I was in no mood for this.

I put my left hand up like I was afraid. An evil smirk appeared on his thin lips. As soon as he hesitated, I grabbed his right wrist and brought my right knee up hard into his crotch. I locked my right hand also around his left wrist. With both hands, I bent his wrist until I heard it break. The guy fell onto his back with a scream of pain, and the buck knife fell out of his hand. He rolled onto his left side and started to get up. As soon as he stood up, I punched him and as he was falling, I kicked him in the ass. He fell onto his side. I bent over and reached into his jacket pocket, pulled out the bundle of heroin, and tore it open. The fine white powder disappeared in the wind, and I threw the baggie on top of him. While he was sprawled out on the garbage-strewn alley, I stooped down and picked up the buck knife. Out of the corner of my eye, I saw him scrambling to his feet. Still cradling his broken wrist, he started to run. I stood up quickly and kicked him again in the seat of his pants. He groaned as the kick propelled him.

"Mess around?" I taunted loudly as I let him escape through the back of the alley. I listened as he scurried away like a rat, then I paused to catch my breath. I folded the blade of the buck knife and put it into my pocket, dusted myself off, and walked cautiously out of the alley, the same way I had entered it. I stepped out into the light of the street, then I leaned up against the wall, took another piece of gum out of the pack, and put it into my mouth.

I continued leaning against the building, looking around to see if anyone could have witnessed what had happened. Satisfied there was no one, I began to walk toward my car. Meanwhile, a noisy old automobile with a hole in the muffler pulled up to the curb. The driver said something to me, but I couldn't hear him. I walked closer. Next to the skinny, pimple-faced driver I could see a frail-looking teenage girl and a nervous-looking young guy in the backseat—junkies.

"Spike around? You seen Spike, man?" the sad-eyed junkie driver asked. I leaned over to get a better look at the girl, and I could see that she was only about seventeen years old. The dark circles under her eyes gave her a phantomlike appearance against the pasty white color of her skin. Her nose was running and she was shivering uncontrollably. She was dope sick, suffering from heroin withdrawal. I had seen this condition too many times.

"No, man, Spike's not around," I answered definitively.

"You holdin', man?" the driver asked, pathetically.

"No, man. No one's holdin'."

"Where's Spike?" he asked again, desperately.

"Spike's on vacation, man, he ain't comin' back. You better get her to the City [Boston City Hospital], man, she looks sick," I suggested in a brotherly tone.

The driver looked at me for a moment with that far-off stare, then he drove to Boylston Street and took a right turn, in the opposite direction of the hospital. As I got in my car and headed home, I thought about the drug dealer in the alley. Was I losing it? Was I becoming one of them? The thoughts started coming again like a freight train.

I drove straight on Tremont, past the Boston Common, and stopped when the light turned red at Stuart. I watched the couples heading for the theaters. Well-dressed men and women come into the city to the theater district to enjoy a play, musical, or concert. I knew the motorcycle cop who was directing traffic. He puts up his hand to stop the cars, and when it is safe to cross the street, he waves the people on. I wonder if the people even notice him and how important he is. When the shit hits the fan, he is the only thing between them and the criminals. The theater district is bordered by the Combat Zone. Predators like Spike lurk in its alleyways and back streets. Muggers and purse snatchers wait to pounce on their prey. The young motorcycle cop and the rest of the police presence on detail in the theater district keep the predators at bay. The area changes into an underworld when the plays and concerts are over and the theatergoers are gone. I take a left on Herald Street, a right, and then pull onto the expressway. I try not to think about anything.

A strange feeling suddenly comes over me. I feel as though I am flying. I know that I am in the car, but we are lifting up off the pavement. The steering wheel seems to be disconnected from the wheels. I am losing control, then I have no control. I look at the cars around me, worried that I will crash into them. Butterflies rush into my stomach. My heart is racing and I am sweating profusely. Somehow, I manage to regain control of the car without crashing into anyone. My heart slows down and I stop sweating. Wow! That was a close call. Is there something wrong with my steering? I wondered. But how could the car lift off the ground? I struggled to put the strange thoughts out of my mind and concentrated on driving home. I needed to get some sleep.

The following morning I hurried into the Mayflower Coffee Shop after testifying in Suffolk Superior Court, and I spotted Warren Tabor waving to me from the other side of the restaurant. He was sitting at a booth by the window. It was always good to see Warren. He slid closer to the window and I sat beside him in the booth. Warren's friend reached over the table that separated us and I shook his hand.

"This is my good friend, Joe Constantino," Warren said. Joe wore his neatly cut black hair combed straight back. Dressed in a stylish suit, starched white shirt, and conservative tie, Joe Constantino looked like the classic big-city detective. I had never seen him before.

"Nice to meet you, Joe. Drug unit?"

"Rubber gun squad," Warren joked. Joe's bright eyes lit up as he laughed.

"I run the Boston Police Stress Unit. I used to work in the district with Warren," Constantino said good-naturedly.

"He started Stress so guys would have a place to go to talk things out, without letting anybody else know," a more serious Warren explained.

"You know how it is," Joe elaborated, "nobody wants to open up when they have a problem or need a little help. If you say something to your boss, he sends you to a shrink and you get labeled. No one wants that. You get labeled and your career goes down the drain. I started this unit with the blessing of the commissioner, and we operate independently. We're there to help the guys and they know it. Everything is confidential and we help each other. Everyone is a cop. We're all street. No other departments have anything like this. We have a couple of state troopers and we even have a fed, an ATF agent," Joe went on. It seemed like an interesting concept, but I never gave it much thought after we finished our coffee and left the coffee shop.

When I first met Warren Tabor, he was a detective on the Boston Police Drug Control Unit. The chemistry was there and we liked each other immediately. Warren and I were brought up in the same Boston neighborhoods and we found out later that our mothers were friends when they were young girls. Warren seemed to have it all together. He was only a couple of years older than me, but he was a young sage. He used to remind me that I was not going to solve the drug problem single-handedly. He would tell me not to take things personally, not to make a case into a vendetta. If I don't get him today, I'd get him tomorrow. He used to say, "All we see is the dark side of life." He also reminded me not to take the job home with me and not to become callous. Most of all, he told me not to shut out the light and let the darkness overcome me. It was a propitious beginning.

In the early days, Warren took me along as his money man and introduced me to small-time drug dealers in joint investigations with the Boston Police. We bought drugs in the Combat Zone and the Back Bay. Dressed casually in blue jeans, T-shirt, and sneakers, Warren, with his slim, wiry build, disheveled curly brown hair, and pockmarked face, was never suspected of being a policeman. His looks and demeanor seemed to invite criminals to deal with him as an inferior, but in fact, none of the characters we encountered in the criminal world could hold a match to Warren's intelligence and wit. I never had as much fun as I did working the cases together with Warren. A quote from Cervantes comes to mind when I think of Warren: "The cleverest character in comedy is the clown for he who would make people take him for a fool, must not be one."

One of our first cases involved a Back Bay pharmacist. Warren introduced me to the pharmacist, who immediately said that he liked the leather coat that I was wearing. I thanked him for the compliment and told him promptly that Warren stole it for me. Warren's cover at that time was that of a high-level booster, someone who steals for a business. Without blinking, the pharmacist told Warren that he wanted the same coat. When Warren tried to dodge the request, the pharmacist told him smugly that he did not need him and that the only way he would continue dealing was for Warren to steal the coat for him. Warren swallowed and began again.

"But," Warren protested.

"Ah, ah, ah," the pharmacist interjected, arrogantly. "Forty-four long, black." Warren looked slyly at me.

"Okay," Warren replied.

I was able to obtain federal funds for Warren to buy the coat, and I was there when he presented it to the pharmacist. The pharmacist tried the coat on in the back room of the pharmacy and modeled it for us, then smiled haughtily.

"Now we can continue, Warren."

I took the case from there after Warren made the introduction. Six months later, after a series of buys, we got search and arrest warrants and went to the pharmacy. Warren was there to put the cuffs on him. The pharmacist, who had been particularly insulting to Warren, almost puked when he spotted Warren in shirt and tie, with the gold Boston Police detective shield prominently affixed to the breast pocket of his sport jacket.

"The coat," Warren said. The pharmacist, surprised by the comment, gave Warren a puzzled look. "The coat, it's evidence, now," Warren reminded him.

The pharmacist slipped the coat off reluctantly, and I took it from him. Warren placed the handcuffs on the pharmacist, then, holding him under his armpits, we walked outside into the sudden, unexpected snowstorm, sliding and skating over the ice-covered red brick sidewalk to the police cruiser. Warren sat on one side of the trembling pharmacist and I sat on the other. Wondering if he was shaking from the cold or fear of going to jail, I leaned forward and looked at Warren.

"Irving, we'll be there in a few minutes. It will be all right. Just tell them to give you what you want. Forty-four long," Warren said.

Every time I saw Warren after that I used to greet him with "Forty-four long." After our coffee together at the Mayflower that day, I never saw Warren Tabor again.

Months after that chance encounter, I found myself at Warren Tabor's parish church. I was lost in thought, staring straight ahead at the flag-draped casket. I felt someone leaning against my shoulder and I turned to look. It was Jerry O'Dea, impeccably dressed as ever, holding his open hand close to his body to shake my hand. His eyes smiled as he watched me come out of my momentary trance. I reached for his hand and held it tightly as I pushed closer to Al Forte and moved him further into the pew. I looked down the line at the men in the pew and I realized that we were all there, all except Warren. They were the same guys whom I worked with night after night, making undercover drug buys, chasing dope dealers, and crashing down doors. We survived high-speed automobile crashes, knife attacks, and shoot-outs. We were still standing. I wondered, why?

Warren died suddenly, the obituary read. The obits used kind words like "suddenly" or "by accident." In low-profile cases, the cops on the scene could soften the shock to the families in cases like these by labeling the death an accidental shooting while the man was cleaning his service revolver. The headlines in Warren's case were hard. One paper ran with "Cop Commits Suicide." The other paper read "Cop Kills Self." The stories inferred police corruption or wrongdoing, as they always did. There was no police corruption in this case, however. The only corruption was in the thought processes of Warren's mind, which succumbed to the demons that possessed him.

This was the third funeral of a police officer that I had attended in the last several years. Officer Martin Mulcahy died by accident, the obituary read. Not long before, Special Agent Frank Tumello was shot to death by drug dealers while agents listened through the walls of an adjoining hotel room in New York City. I could understand Frankie's death, but not Warren's or Marty's. None of these deaths should have occurred, but at least as far as the public was concerned, Frankie died in the line of duty, with honor, whatever that means. In reality, they all died in the line of duty. Only a cop could understand that, though.

At graveside, I was mesmerized by the burial rituals that had become almost routine for me by now, the plaintive, primordial sound of the bagpipes, the final words of the priest, the marine escort folding the American flag from the casket and presenting it to the grieving widow, the rhythmic beat of the drum, then the harsh, sudden rifle salute interrupting the calm, and the melancholy sound of the trumpeter playing taps as the casket is lowered into the grave.

I turned my head toward the sound of a sudden snap and rested my eyes on the flag blowing in the wind. I felt a tingle run down my spine. I looked around at the faces of the men surrounding the grave and returned my eyes to the flag. There was a ray of light beginning to shine through the overcast sky. I remembered the saying that the tiniest light will overcome the darkness. I had that light in my heart. It was there all along.

Each of us, in spite of our imperfections, plays an important part in this perilous journey through life. As Warren said, "You cannot judge a man by a moment in time." Except for one moment in time, Warren played his part well. We were all proud of him. I think I will stop in and spend a little time with Joe Constantino tomorrow. I wish I could see Warren one more time to thank him for the introduction.

EPILOGUE

Pam, my three daughters, and I mixed in with the stream of theatergoers emptying out of Boston's Wang Center, and found ourselves on Tremont Street. The freezing cold air stung our faces. Bundled up in winter clothing, everyone seemed to be smiling cheerfully, spellbound after a wonderful matinee performance of the *Nutcracker* ballet. It was only days before Christmas, and a magical spirit was in the air. It was around five o'clock—dinnertime. We held hands and started walking, stiffly, over the mounds of snow and across Kneeland Street toward Chinatown.

When we reached the restaurant, I opened the door and waved everyone inside. The girls followed Pam closely, like a line of ducks. A smiling young hostess led us to our table. Pam and I helped the girls out of their Sunday-best matching woolen coats, hats, and mittens. Then they scrambled into the booth. I could watch Pam and the girls forever. Red-cheeked from the cold, and wide-eyed with excitement, the girls blurted out their observations about the *Nutcracker*, each vying for her mother's attention. Pam listened lovingly with an unmistakable expression of interest on her face. It all made me smile.

Suddenly and inexplicably, I sensed that something was wrong. An uncomfortable feeling came over me; someone was watching me surreptitiously. When the waiter approached us for the second time, Pam sorted out our requests and gave our order. The waiter seemed unaccountably hostile. I fidgeted and looked around the room carefully. I began to feel as if I were in the sights of an enemy's gun. I wanted to fall to the floor and drag Pam and the girls with me, but I fought to keep the emotion to myself. My stomach tightened involuntarily, and I struggled to control my breathing.

Our waiter nodded brusquely and walked toward the kitchen with our order. He stopped suddenly and leaned over to whisper in the ear of an elderly Chinese man. When the waiter straightened, my eyes met the old man's stony, unforgiving stare.

I hustled Pam and our hungry and very unhappy daughters out of the booth, ignoring their startled protests. I pushed them crazily, hats awry and coats unbuttoned, out of the restaurant. Once outside, I told them to hold hands and to move as quickly as they possibly could. I dragged Pam and the girls down an alley, across Kneeland Street, and along Tremont again till we came to our parked car. I wouldn't explain my actions, because I did not want to alarm them. I pulled out of the parking space and drove away as quickly as I could.

The elderly man in the restaurant was the drug dealer, Kyung Fung.

CONCLUSION

Most would argue that we are losing the war on drugs. They are more plentiful and pure and less expensive than ever before. Yet, I remain cautiously hopeful. We live in a big world, and the United States of America is a superpower with great responsibilities. Even though our country has made many mistakes in past alliances that we cultivated, we must have international partners to combat drug traffickers. Partnerships with other countries are necessary to interdict drug shipments and arrest violators.

At times our partners have subverted our intentions. In the 1950s the U.S. and France forged alliances with warlords in Laos, Thailand, and Burma, an area known as the Golden Triangle, in an effort to contain the spread of Communism. The U.S. and France supplied the warlords with weapons, ammunition, and air transportation. Our well-intentioned plan backfired when a new problem arose. The warlords used the resources they were given to develop their opium business. The problem did not go away.

From 1965 to 1970, during the Vietnam War, there was a surge in heroin entering the U.S. Opium from the Golden Triangle was smuggled into Marseilles. It is believed that Corsican gangsters then shipped the refined heroin to the United States for distribution to the country's 750,000 addicts. The supply of heroin continued until the United States and France worked together on the famous French Connection case to put the heroin processing plants out of business.

In other parts of the world, we continue to struggle with allies who do not share our concerns about drugs. Afghanistan, for example, illustrates the point. The United States backed the Northern Alliance against the Taliban in the war on terror because the Taliban were closely tied to Al Qaeda operatives. Ironically, recent history indicates that when the Taliban were in power, their ban on opium production in the year 2000 was widely respected and adhered to. Unfortunately, members of the Northern Alliance, our allies, cultivate opium poppies. An interim authority was formed per our agreement on December 4, 2001, with Hamid Karzai acting as interim chairman. Since then, neither the Taliban nor the Northern Alliance has taken any real initiative to seize stored opium or precursors or to arrest and prosecute narcotic traffickers.

Domestically, the problem has been one of perception. It was not until the middle of the Reagan presidency that we stopped viewing the drug problem as a regional matter. Up until that time, if heroin use grew in New York City or Cocaine Cowboys got too violent in Miami, the government sent more agents or money to the affected geographical area to contain the problem. It was like putting out scattered brush fires while the forest fire blazed. Finally, the Reagan White House, after listening to suggestions by the DEA, realized that drug trafficking was a national security problem that necessitated an international plan of attack. As a result, the White House finally began to look at the drug problem globally and to implement a plan to identify and target major traffickers.

Unfortunately, the principal source of cocaine, heroin, and marijuana has moved dangerously close to our borders. Colombia, with its modern, sophisticated processing labs, is now the world's leading producer of cocaine, and supplies virtually all of the cocaine distributed in the United States. Almost 60 percent of the heroin distributed in the United States comes from opium poppy that is grown, harvested, and processed in Colombia. In addition to this, Mexican heroin, known as Mexican mud, flows freely over the border. These are some of the problems that continue to confront and frustrate drug agents today as we struggle with the drug problem in our country. It is time to put drug trafficking, along with terrorism, on the top of our country's agenda.

The recent DEA administrator, Asa Hutchinson, believes in a three-pronged approach of prevention, enforcement, and treatment to fight drug use in the United States. No single approach will work. Prevention, beginning with education at a young age, is crucial. There must be a concerted, concentrated program that introduces grammar school students to the danger of drugs. The program needs to grow with the students, matching their intellectual capabilities and curiosity. The program must deal with facts, not hysteria, with particular focus on health risks. Several studies indicate

216

that programs in our schools such as Drug Abuse Resistance Education, or DARE, although well intended, are not effective. It is not enough to "Just say no!"

In addition to prevention, enforcement is a must. Without it, the tide of drugs will overflow our borders and flood the streets and school yards of our cities. We must police our borders ever more vigilantly and use the latest technology to detect illicit drugs. Intelligence gatherers must keep up with drug smugglers' ever-changing tactics. Drugs must be traced to their sources, and we must follow the money.

We also must help those who have fallen victim to drug addiction by implementing programs to help them overcome their dependence. Drug abusers must be given the tools they need to recover from the curse of addiction.

Most importantly, every mother and father and sister and brother in America must make a commitment to themselves and to their families to resist the temptations and false promises of drugs. This, I believe, is crucial. Today we place too much emphasis on the importance of athletes and superstars as role models for our children, and the power of ordinary people is overlooked. Whenever I speak to a group of students about drug abuse, I always ask them what the single greatest deterrent was for them. Who or what influenced them not to take drugs? Inevitably, I find that the example or advice of an older brother, sister, cousin, friend, parent, aunt, or uncle was the reason.

Special agents risk their lives every day in every region of the world and match wits with well-equipped, nefarious criminals. I was fortunate to have served in the government with brave, committed people. I was in the company of heroes who dedicated themselves to protecting our freedom, decency, and democracy.

The American public must be shown that illicit drugs are undermining our civil society, weakening our moral fiber from within, and fueling attacks against us from terrorist organizations. Intelligence gathered from international drug investigations by the DEA indicates unequivocally that profits from the drug trade are used to fund terrorism. In the Middle East Al Qaeda, Hamas, and Hezbollah are fueled by drug dollars. In South America the FARC (Revolutionary Armed Forces of Colombia), the AUC (United Self-Defense Forces), and the ELN (National Liberation Army), as well as the Shining Path terrorist organization in Peru, are all linked to drug trafficking. Americans must commit themselves fully to the task of dealing with the nation's drug problem.

ACKNOWLEDGMENTS

I am forever grateful to Paddy and Gertrude Doyle for taking me into their stable when there was no room in the inn. They showed me what sacrifice was all about and taught me what I needed to survive. Paddy taught me to read and Gertrude taught me to dream. Beverly and Henry, I wish we knew what really happened; perhaps it's better that we don't. I am indebted to my first-grade teacher, Sister Mary Mercedes, of Our Lady of Perpetual Help Grammar School, in Roxbury, Massachusetts, for planting that seed of faith that has survived the storms. This story could not have been written without Pam, my rock, and our daughters, Stacey, Christy, Kerry, and Jamie, who inspired me to tell my story and then guided me painstakingly through the process. Thanks to Patrick and Matthew—better men, I do not know—and Patrick and Kerry, our grandchildren, for reminding us that life goes on and keeps on getting better.

Hoorah for Professor Terence P. Moran, who gave me the encouragement to persevere, and thanks to Frank McCourt, Malachy McCourt, Professor Eugene Secunda, Professor Charles DeFanti, and Patrick Mulligan for taking me into their fold and inspiring me to talk and write. Thanks to Michael Annunziata for listening so well. Many thanks to Dr. Charles Hatem, Dr. Neal Cannon, and Dr. Paul F. Mitchell for keeping me healthy. Thanks to Denis Heaphy for his big heart. Thanks to Jack McElroy for his courage. Also, thanks to Kenneth Amesbury for leading me to the great books. Many thanks to William Frohlich and his entire staff at Northeastern University Press, particularly Sarah Rowley, and to Pamela Smith, university counsel, Professor James Alan Fox, and Associate Dean Robert D. Croatti.

Here's to the fidelity and courage of Christopher E. Egan Jr. and Daniel Staffieri, special agents, who lived the story. Thanks to the other men and women of the DEA, past and present, who fought the good fight. They know who they are. I will never forget those who have died especially Enrique Camarena and Boston Police Detective Sherman Griffiths. I would also like to thank Peter Bensinger, the director of the DEA when these events took place, for his leadership in difficult times, and Jack Lawn, who also led the troops and never left our side. A special thanks to former special agents Robert Nieves, who shared his knowledge, his notes, and his experience unselfishly; William Alden, who steered me in the right direction; and Robert "Bobby" Canales, who understands more than anyone. More thanks to former special agents Jack Kelly, for his constant encouragement; Larry P. McManus, for his friendship; and Patrick Hunt, for his undying loyalty. Also, John Fallon, Louie Diaz, Louie Gonzalez, Benjamin Fitzgerald, Frank Iappolo, Marty Maguire, Frank Balazs, Chuck Carter, and Richard Johnson. To the men and women, my brothers and sisters, of AFFNA (Association of Former Federal Narcotic Agents), who have given their blood, sweat, and tears setting high standards that make the DEA what it is today. Thanks to the dedicated police officers and all the dedicated lawmen and -women I have worked with over the years; those of the Boston Police, New York City Police Department, and the Massachusetts State Police deserve much of the credit for the words on these pages. Also to Reverend John Coholan, Maryknoll missionary, who explained the great philosophers in detail and discussed the classics in such simple language that even I could begin to understand. For directing me through the labyrinth of life, I am indebted to Reverend Terry Attridge, Reverend David Delaney, Reverend Lawrence Pratt, Reverend Arthur J. DePietro, Reverend Frederick J. Murray, Reverend Robert A. Ward, Reverend John E. Kelley, Reverend Michael Steele, Reverend Joseph Blattner, Reverend Edwin D. Condon, Reverend Gregg Grovenburg, S.J., Reverend Paul Carrier, S.J., Reverend Charles Allen, S.J., and Reverend Dan Finn. Finally, thanks to Mother Teresa for holding my hand and leading the way through the darkness.